A Daybook for September

In Yellow Springs, Ohio

A Memoir in Nature

and a Handbook for the Month,
Being a Personal Narrative and Synthesis of
Common Events in Nature
between 1981 and 2023
in Southwestern Ohio, with Applications
for the Lower Midwest and Middle Atlantic
Region, Containing Weather Guidelines
and a Variety of Natural Calendars,
Reflections by the Author
and Seasonal Quotations
from Ancient and Modern Writers

By

Bill Felker

A Daybook for the Year in Yellow Springs, Ohio
Volume 9: September

Cover from a watercolor by Libby Rudolf

Copyright 2023 by Bill Felker

Published by The Green Thrush Press
P.O. Box 431, Yellow Springs, Ohio

Printed in the United States of America

USBN-13: 978-1721729630
USBN-10:1721729631

To Jeanie

Bill Felker

No one suspects the days to be gods.

Ralph Waldo Emerson

Bill Felker

Introduction

Here are no stories told you of what is to be seen at the other end of the world, but of things at home, in your own Native Countrey, at your own doors, easily examinable with little travel, less cost, and very little hazard. This book doth not shew you a Telescope, but a Mirror, it goes not about to put a delightful cheat upon you, with objects at a great distance, but shews you yourselves.
Joshua Childrey, 1660

The Daybook Format

The format of my notes in this daybook owes more than a little to the almanacs I wrote for the *Yellow Springs News* between 1984 and 2018. The quotations, daily statistics, the weather outlooks, the seasonal calendar, and the daybook journal were and still are part of my regular routine of collecting and organizing impressions about the place in which I live.

Setting: The principal habitat described here is that of Glen Helen, a preserve of woods and glades that lies on the eastern border of the village of Yellow Springs in southwestern Ohio. At its northern edge, the Glen joins with John Bryan State Park to form a corridor about ten miles long, and half a mile wide, along the Little Miami River. The north section of the Glen Helen /John Bryan complex is hilly and heavily wooded, and is the best location for spring wildflowers. The southern portion, "South Glen" as it is usually called, is a combination of open fields, wetlands, and wooded flatlands. Here I found many flowers and grasses of summer and fall. Together, the two Glens and John Bryan Park provide a remarkable cross section of the fauna and flora of the eastern United States.

Other habitats in the daybook journal include my yard with its several small gardens; the village of Yellow Springs itself, a town of 4,000 at the far eastern border of the Dayton suburbs; the Caesar Creek Reservoir, twenty miles south of Yellow Springs and created by the Corps of Engineers in 1976. My trips away from that environment were principally northeast to Chicago, Madison,

Wisconsin and northern Minnesota, east to Washington and New York, southeast to the Carolinas and Florida, southwest to Arkansas, Louisiana, and Texas, and occasionally through the Southwest to California and the Northwest, two excursions to Belize in Central America, several to Italy.

Quotations: The passages from ancient and modern writers (and sometimes from my alter egos) which accompany each day's notations are lessons from my readings, as well as from distant seminary and university training, here put to work in service of the reconstruction of my sense of time and space. They are a collection of reminders, hopes, and promises for me that I find implicit in the seasons. They have also become a kind of a cosmological scrapbook for me, as well as the philosophical underpinning of this narrative.

Astronomical Data: The *Daybook* includes approximate dates for astronomical events, such as star positions, meteor showers, solstice, equinox, perihelion (the Sun's position closest to earth), and aphelion (the Sun's position farthest from Earth).

I have included the sunrise and sunset for Yellow Springs as a general guide to the progression of the year in this location, but those statistics also reflect trends that are world wide, if more rapid in some places and slower in others. All times listed here are given in Eastern Standard Time.

Even though the day's length is almost never exactly the same from one town to the next, a minute gained or lost in Yellow Springs is often a minute lost or gained elsewhere, and the Yellow Springs numbers can be used as a simple way of watching the lengthening or shortening of the days, and, therefore, of watching the turn of the planet. For those who wish to keep track of the sun themselves in their own location, abundant sources are now available for this information in local and national media.

Average Temperatures: Average temperatures in Yellow Springs are also part of each day's entry. Since the rise and fall of temperatures in other parts of the North America, even though they may start from colder or warmer readings, keep pace with the temperatures here, the highs and lows in Yellow Springs are, like solar statistics, helpful indicators of the steady progress of the year throughout most of the states along the 40th Parallel (except in the mountains). The daybook journal entries can be cross-referenced with the list of monthly average temperatures between 1981 and 2017 in order to compare the daily inventories with the month's weather in a given year.

Weather: My daily, weekly and monthly weather summaries have been distilled from over thirty years of observations. They are descriptions of the local weather history I have kept in order to track the gradual change in temperatures, precipitation and cloud cover through the year I have also used them in order to try to identify particular characteristics of each day. They are not meant to be predictions.

Although my interest in the Yellow Springs microclimate at first seemed too narrow to be of use to those who lived outside the area, I began to modify it to meet the needs of a number of regional and national farm publications for which I started writing in the mid 1980s. And so, while the summaries are based on my records in southwestern Ohio, they can be and have been used, with interpretation and interpolation, throughout the Lower Midwest , the Middle Atlantic states and the East.

The Natural Calendar: In this section, I note the progress of foliage and floral changes, farm and garden practices, migration times for common birds, and peak periods of insect activity. Some of these notes are second hand; I'm a sky watcher, but not an astronomer, and I rely on the government's astronomical data and a few other references for much of my information about the stars and the sun. I am also a complete amateur at bird watching, and most of the migration dates used in the seasonal calendar come from published sources. And even though I keep close track of the farm year, the percentages listed for planting and harvesting are interpretations of averages supplied by the state's weekly crop reports.

At the beginning of each spring and summer month, I have included a floating calendar of blooming dates which lists approximate flowering times for many plants, shrubs and trees in an average Yellow Springs season. The floating chronology describes the relationship between events more than exact dates of these occurrences.

Although the flora of the eastern and central United States is hardly limited to the species mentioned here, the flowers listed are common enough to provide easily recognized landmarks for gauging the advance of the year. I found that a record of my drives south during April complemented the floating calendar and allowed me to see the approximate differences between Yellow Springs and other locations. I also learned that April in the Lower Midwest is more like March in the Southeast and more like May in the Upper Midwest. This daybook and its natural calendar summaries, then, are records of a moveable seasonal feast that shifts not only according to fixed geographical regions but also according to the weather in any particular year.

Daybook Entries: The journal entries in the daybook section provide the raw material from which I wrote the Natural Calendar digests. The daybook section is a collection of observations made from the window of my car and from my walks in Glen Helen, in parks and wildlife areas within a few miles of my home, and on occasional trips. It is a record that anyone with a few guidebooks could make, and it includes just a small number of the natural markers that anyone might discover.

When I began to take notes about the world around me, I found that there were few descriptions of actual events in nature available for southwestern Ohio. There was no roadmap for the course of the year. My daily observations, as narrow and incomplete as they were, were especially significant to me since I had found no other narrative of the days, no other depiction of what was actually occurring around me. In time, the world came into focus with each particle I named. I saw concretely that time and space were the sum of their parts.

As my notes for each day accumulated, I could see the

wide variation of events that occurred from year to year; at the same time, I saw a unity in this syncopation from which I could identify numerous sub-seasons and with which I could understand better the kind of habitat in which I was living and, consequently, myself. When I paged through the journal entries for each day, I was drawn back to the space in which they were made. I browsed and imagined, returned to the journey.

Journal Essays: At the end of many of the daybook entries, I have included brief essays from my almanac column in the *Yellow Springs News.*

Companions: Many friends, acquaintances and family members have contributed their observations to the daybook, and their participation has taught me that my private seasons are also community seasons, and that all of our experiences together help to lay the foundation for a rich, local consciousness of natural history.

The Month of September
September Averages: 1981 through 2022
Normal September Average Temperature: 65.4

Year	Average
1981	63.4
1982	63.9
1983	66.2
1984	62.5
1985	66.3
1986	68.8
1987	67.4
1988	65.4
1989	64.1
1990	65.1
1991	66.0
1992	64.3
1993	62.7
1994	64.9
1995	63.5
1996	64.5
1997	64.5
1998	70.6
1999.	66.8
2000	64.2
2001	62.9
2002	69.7
2003	63.1
2004	66.6
2005	68.9
2006	62.1
2007	68.8
2008	68.5
2009	65.1
2010	67.9
2011	63.6
2012	64.2
2013	67.6
2014	65.5
2015	69.6
2016	69.7
2017	66.4
2018	70.2
2019	73.8
2020	67.2
2021	68.9
2022	67.7
2023	68.6

September 1st
The 244th Day of the Year

First September touching
puffballs-in-the-grass
(like moons)
and fondling yellowed sassafras.

bf

Sunrise/set: 6:02/7:07
Day's Length: 13 hours 5 minutes
Average High/Low: 81/60
Average Temperature: 70
Record High: 97 – 1953
Record Low: 44 – 1967

The Daily Weather

Temperatures today are usually in the 80s (a 55 percent chance) or 70s (a 40 percent chance), with only a five percent chance of a hot day in the 90s. There is a 30 percent chance of a thundershower, 25 percent chance of completely overcast conditions, 50 percent chance of a pleasantly cool night below 60 degrees.

The Weather in the Week Ahead

The likelihood of rain remains at 35 percent though September 3rd, then diminishes to 25 percent on the 4th and 5th, finally dropping to ten percent on the 6th - the lowest of the entire month. The effects of the first September cold wave usually appear by the 2nd, which is the first day since June 4th that 90s become unlikely. Then on the 3rd, there is a 55 percent chance of highs only in the 70s, and the chances of frost suddenly become one in a hundred.

The long period during which there is at least a ten percent chance of highs below 70 degrees begins on September 4th. Warmer conditions typically return on the 5th and 6th, but the second high-pressure system of the month, which arrives between the 5th and 11th, pushes lows into the 30s one year in 20.

September 6th is the first day of the season on which there is about a five percent chance of light frost on the gardens of the Lower Midwest. Chances increase at the rate of about one percent per day through the 15th of the month. Between the 15th and the 20th, chances grow at the rate of two percent per day. Between the 20th and 30th, they grow at the rate of five percent per day.

The day's length shortens by 14 minutes this week, dropping below 13 hours for the first time since the first week of April, and down 120 minutes since solstice.

The Outlook for September

Throughout the month, normal highs drop eight degrees, falling to the lower 70s across the Lower Midwest. Average lows decline from the upper 50s to the upper 40s.

September's average precipitation usually drops below three inches (2.70 is the Dayton area average) for the first time since February. The days most likely to be dry are the 6th, 10th, 11th, 13th, 15th, 19th, 25th, 26th, and 28th, each having a 20 percent chance or less for rain (the 6th and the 28th have less than a ten percent chance).

The wettest September days, those with a 40 percent or better chance of precipitation: the 9th, 18th, 21st, 22nd. September's cloudiest days, those with better than a 40 percent chance of completely overcast conditions throughout the day are: the 12th, 18th, 21st, and 22nd.

The sunniest days, those with at least a 75 percent chance of sun, are the 5th, 6th, 7th, 8th, 9th, 10th, 11th, 19th, 20th, 24th, 25th, 26th, 27th, 28th and 29th, with the 6th, 7th, 8th, 10th, and 28th having a 90 percent chance of clear skies.

The warmest September days, those with a 50 percent chance of highs above 80 degrees, usually occur during the first 11 days of the month, the warmest days of all being September 1st, 2nd, 6th, 7th, 9th, 10th, 11th, and 30th.

The chilliest days of the month, those with better than a

30 percent chance of highs only in the 60s, are September 19th, 22nd, 23rd, 24th, 25th, and 26th.

Lows in the 30s occur as early as September 6th, but there is usually little danger of light frost until the end of the month's third week. The September mornings most likely to bring a light freeze are 24th and the 27th (20 percent chance). Each day after the 19th carries about a ten percent chance of lows in the low 30s.

Summercount and Autumncount

Between the last week of May and the first week of September, the 15 major cool fronts of summer cross the United States. The last of these weather systems arrives as September begins. Subsequent fronts belong to the 18 major weather systems of early, middle and late autumn.

September 2: This weather system is typically a gentle one, and Late Summer continues throughout the central and southern states for the next few days. Chances of precipitation are low both before and after this first September high. In spite of the mild nature of this front, it does reflect the gradual transition to fall, and brings one chance in a hundred for a light frost as far south as the Border States.

September 8: The likelihood of precipitation increases at this front's arrival, and once the system goes through, it almost always brings in Early Fall, a month-long period of Judas maples, late goldenrod, and the encroachment of chillier nights. Temperatures, which began to cool at the pivot time of August 10th, decline more noticeably.

September 12: A slightly stronger system often follows the September 8th high, making the 12th one of the two cloudiest and wettest days in September. The 12th also marks the beginning of a decline in percentage of daily sunshine, a downward shift that continues through December (the year's darkest month). Chances of a light freeze increase on the 13th and 14th as this third high-pressure system of the month shows its full power.

September 15: The fourth high of September is followed by one the greatest shifts so far in the season. As the sun moves to within a few degrees of equinox, Late Summer's grip grows measurably weaker. As this weather system moves along the 40th parallel, brisk afternoons in the 50s or 60s are four times as likely as during the first week of the month. The mornings are chilly, and the possibility of a light freeze grows steadily.

September 20: Although the day before the September 20th front is one of autumn's warmest, when the front actually arrives, the likelihood of days in the 90s disappears all across the northern half of the nation. Even 80s will be gone there in only three weeks. The odds for an afternoon in the 50s or 60s this week doubles over those odds last week. And the season of light frosts deepens all across the northern half of the country. The chances of a light freeze become a minimum of ten percent per night until the first week of October—when odds quickly increase. On the positive side, pollen season declines quickly after the passage of this weather system.

September 24: Chances of precipitation increase as this front approaches from the west, and after the September 24th high moves east, light frost occurs more often than at any other time up to this point in September.

September 29: Although the day before the September 29th front's arrival is usually dry and mild, this final high of September is the first to bring real danger of a hard frost to the North and slight risk of tomato damage across the mid-Atlantic region and the East. Average temperatures now start to fall at the rate of four degrees per week.

Key to the Nation's Weather

The typical September temperature at average elevations along the 40th Parallel, the average of the high of 77 and the low of 57, is 67 degrees. Using the following chart based on weather statistics from around the country, one can calculate approximate temperatures in other locations close to the cities listed.

For example, with the base of 67 you can estimate normal temperatures in Minneapolis by subtracting five degrees from the base average. Or add 7 degrees to find out the likely conditions in Atlanta during the month.

Fairbanks AK	-23
Cheyenne WY	-10
Seattle, WA	-7
Portland, ME	-7
Minneapolis MN	-5
Des Moines IA	-2
AVERAGE ALONG THE 40TH PARALLEL:	**67**
St. Louis MO	+4
New York NY	+2
Washington D.C.	+2
Atlanta GA	+6
New Orleans LA	+12
Miami FL	+14

Frostwatch

The following chart shows the chances that frost will have occurred at average elevations along the 40th Parallel by the date indicated. The data can be adjusted by adding five percent for each 100 miles north or south of the 40th parallel.

Date	*Chance of Light Frost*	*Chance of Killing Frost*
September 1:	5%	0%
September 10 :	10 %	1%
September 15:	15%	2%
September 20:	30%	3%
September 25	55%	5%
September 30:	80%	8%

A Floating Sequence
For the Blooming of Wildflowers and Perennials

August 1:	Mad-Dog Skullcap (*Scutellaria lateriflora*)
	Giant Yellow Hyssop (*Agastache nepetoides*)
August 2:	Prickly Mallow (*Sida spinosa*)
	Great Ragweed (*Ambrosia trifida*)
August 3:	Milk Purslane (*Euphorbia maculate*)
August 4:	Willow Herb (*Epilobium angustifolium*)
August 5:	Japanese Knotweed (*Fallopian japonica*)
August 7:	Love Vine (*Cassytha filiformis*)
August 8:	False Boneset (*Brickellia eupatoriodes*)
August 9:	Bur Cucumber (*Cucumis anguria*)
August 10:	Three-Seeded Mercury (*Acalypha rhomboidea*)
August 11:	Water Horehound (*Lycopus americanus*)
August 12:	Tall Goldenrod (*Solidago altissima*)
August 13:	Climbing False Buckwheat (*Fallopia scandens*)
August 14:	Great Blue Lobelia (*Lobelia siphilitica*)
August 15:	Shaggy Soldier (*Galinsoga quadriradiata*)
August 16:	Rose Pink (*Glandularia canadensis*)
August 18:	Carpetweed (*Mollugo verticillata*)
August 19:	Heart-leaved umbrellawort (*Mirabilis nyctaginea*)
August 23:	Hog Peanut (*Amphicarpaea bracteata*)
August 24:	Jerusalem Artichoke (*Helianthus tuberosus*)
August 29:	Beggarticks (*Bidens frondosa*)
August 30:	Bur Marigold (*Bidens tripartite*)
August 31:	Heath Aster (*Symphyotrichum ericoides*)
September 1:	New England Aster (*Symphyotrichum novae-angliae*)
September 3:	Small White Aster (*Symphyotrichum ericoides*)
September 4:	Heart-Leafed Aster (*Symphyotrichu cordifolium*)
September 6:	Nodding Bur Marigold (*Bidens cernua*)
September 8:	Zigzag Goldenrod (*Solidago flexicaulis*)
September 10 :	Panicled Aster (*Symphyotrichum lanceolatum*)

Estimated Pollen Count
(On a scale of 0 - 700 grains per cubic meter)
September 1:   300
September 5:   240
September 10 : 160
September 15:   60
September 20:   10
September 30:   10

Estimated Mold Count
(On a scale of 0 - 7,000 grains per cubic meter)
September 1:   5500
September 5:   4800
September 10 : 4300
September 15: 2600
September 20: 3600
September 25: 1500
September 30: 1300

When-Then Phenology
When asters bloom in the waysides and bur marigolds flower in the swamps, then farmers start cutting corn for silage.

When zigzag goldenrod blossoms in the woods, then the rose of Sharon shrub drops most of its flowers and the great decline of summer wildflowers begins in the fields.

When fallen leaves start to accumulate in the backwaters and farm ponds, then the grapes should be getting ripe, and over half of the tomatoes and potatoes should be ready for harvest.

When the first black walnut trees are almost bare, then the third cut of alfalfa is typically complete and farmers are preparing the soil for planting canola, grasses and small grains.

When bright patches of scarlet sumac and Virginia creeper mark the fencerows and streaks of gold have appeared on the silver olive bushes, then kingbirds, finches, ruddy ducks, cedar waxwings, herring gulls and yellow-bellied sapsuckers move south. Bobolinks and woodcocks follow. The last young grackles and hummingbirds leave their nests.

When katydids refuse to chant and cricket songs are slow, then frost could threaten near dawn.

When squirrels scatter buckeye hulls along the trails and locust pods fall beside them, then the first soybeans will be ready to harvest.

When farmers plant wheat in northern fields, then throughout the South, cotton growers defoliate their cotton plants, a process that increases fiber quality.

When doves stop calling in the mornings, then Fletcher scale attacks the arborvitae. Locust borers assault the locusts. Pine root collar weevils move to the pine trees.

When cobwebs are all over in the woods and butterflies multiply in the garden, that's the time to plant the last lettuce and radishes of the year, complete the harvest of summer apples and start to pick fall apples.

When red berries appear on the silver olives, orange berries on the American mountain ash and purple berries on the pokeweed, then violet autumn crocuses blossom in town, and sandhill cranes have started their migration to the Gulf Coast.

When the autumn leafturn has begun along the 40th Parallel, the deciduous trees are bare in northern Canada. In New England and in the Rocky Mountains, foliage colors are approaching their best.

When the huge pink mallows of the wetlands have died back, then the juniper tip midge appears on junipers, and gall adelgids attack the spruce threes.

When milkweed pods open, then late hosta bloom comes to a close in town. In the woods, Middle Spring's sedum is growing stronger. Henbit, mint and catchweed revive as the canopy thins. Waterleaf has fresh shoots. Snow-on-the-mountain has recovered from its mid-summer slump and can be as thick and as beautiful as in Early Spring.

When most of the black walnuts have fallen and wood nettle seeds are black and brittle, then gardeners begin autumn bulb planting and the transplanting of perennials in the garden.

When the ash trees turn red and gold, then the season of killing frosts has arrived.

When the day's length falls below 12 hours, then the sugar beet, pear, cabbage and cauliflower harvests commence in the Great Lakes region. In Wisconsin, Massachusetts, New Jersey, Oregon and Washington State, the cranberry harvest begins as berries darken in the cooler weather.

When goldenrod flowers are tufted and gray, then daddy longlegs disappear from the undergrowth and bird migrations reach their peak.

Natural Calendar

In the last week of Late Summer, the final tier of wildflowers starts to open. White and violet asters, orange beggarticks, burr marigolds, tall goldenrod, zigzag goldenrod and Japanese knotweed bloom, blending with the brightest of the purple ironweed, yellow sundrops, blue chicory, golden touch-me-nots, showy coneflowers and great blue lobelia. In gardens, September hostas, virgin's bower and late heliopsis keep their color.

On the farm, pickle season is usually over, and peaches can be done for the year. Grapes are about to come in, and elderberries are deep purple and sweet for picking. Nearly half of the tobacco has been cut, half the commercial tomatoes have been picked, about a fourth of the potatoes dug.

Hickory nutting season opens as sweet-corn time winds down. Burrs from tick trefoil stick to pants legs and stockings. Lizard's tail drops its leaves into the creeks and sloughs. Beside the deer paths of the forests, the undergrowth is tattered and cluttered with the remnants of the year.

Firefly larvae flicker in the grass, the adult fireflies gone. Red-headed woodpeckers, red-winged blackbirds, house wrens, scarlet tanagers, indigo buntings, Eastern bluebirds and black ducks migrate. Sometimes great swarms of dragonflies migrate through the Lower Midwest.

Daybook

1983: Geese fly over to Ellis Pond, 6:30 p.m.

1985: Jacoby East: First small white asters are blooming. July's avens is yellowing. Cobwebs everywhere. Watercress growing back. Joe Pye still strong. Squirrels have been opening the buckeyes. Flurries of leaves falling through the trees. Some jumpseeds completely done jumping. Waterleaf growing back. Two huge puffball mushrooms found. Brown acorns on the path. Two smaller puffballs seen growing in the shade across the creek, like moons in the dark grass. Some wingstem bowing to set its seeds. Some ironweed done. Agrimony gone. Cicadas loud, insistent. Touch-me-nots still full. One rose pink found in full bloom at Upper Prairie.

1987: Cardinal songs, intermittent.

1988: Stopped between the Covered Bridge and Corry Street: Waterleaf has grown a whole new layer of foliage. Most agrimony gone to seed, burs on their stems. Cardinal sings 5:30 a.m., heard off and on before 7:00, then again late afternoon. Yellow elm leaves falling.

1991: Purple loosestrife gone now.

1992: Our cherry tree has lost almost all its foliage. Maple leaves falling in front of the house. Mornings heavy with dew, cool in the 50s, smell of autumn, of vegetation past its prime, settling into the earth, bearing fruit. Raspberries continue to come in. I pick them remembering Marshfield, when I filled pans with raspberries, exulting in my picking skills and my mother's admiration.

1993: All the purple loosestrife in the yard has finished blooming, but in the countryside, some plants are still open. What appears to be the final balloon flower opened today. Doves still called before sunrise. More patches of yellow on the poplars and black walnut trees. On the way to Wilberforce, dozens of monarchs seen, most of them flying across the road south. I ran into two or three, many more killed on the highway. All the Japanese beetles have disappeared in the rose garden.

1997: Japanese beetles still present in the yard. Tonight just one firefly, and he was blinking in the grass. Deterioration of the showy coneflowers is underway today.

1998: Sparrows in the pear trees on Xenia Avenue: 5:50 a.m., crows: 5:37, cardinal 5:40. A few dozen yellow coneflowers left in the garden, five golden mums open. The pond is clear in the cool morning. Two water lilies blooming. Hops still flowering along the north hedge. Pokeweed growing back and in bloom.

1999: Doves were calling this morning at 7:00. At 8:30, the sun was well up into the southeast, and cirrus clouds north of it glittered with a rainbow sundog, sign of fall. The last arrowhead flowers wilted by sundown.

2000: With Buttercup at the Cascades: Robins clucking, asters budding, jumpseeds jumping (had been loose in front of the house three days ago), red Virginia creeper leaves on the path, touch-me-nots popping, zigzag goldenrod just opening, white snakeroot early. Sprouts of garlic mustard up in a runoff area of one hillside, responding to the increase in moisture there. Along the highway, more and more Judas maples. Soybeans have started to turn. Catalpas and cottonwoods aging to ocher. In town, stonecrop sedum approaching full bloom.

2001: Cardinal at 6:45 a.m., doves, crows and a jay a minute or so later. A brief flurry of song, then quiet again. Fishing all day with John at Caesar Creek. Not even a nibble in eight hours on the water. Many cormorants or darters in the water and roosting in dead trees at sundown. Great blue herons common. Arrowhead: last day of blooming season, the same as in the pond at home. No other flowers seen except some patches of goldenrod along the highway.

2003: Virgin's bower is in full bloom in the back yard and everywhere in town.

2004: New England aster buds are turning purple by the north trellis. Virgin's bower is only maybe a fifth in bloom there. Goldenrod has emerged fully here, and a great ragweed plant in the garden is still bright with pollen. One yellow swallowtail in the zinnias this afternoon, no monarchs. Showers of black walnut leaves off and on through the day.

2005: Casey called this morning from the golf course at the edge of town. "Blackbirds are movin'," he said. "Can you hear them?" And I heard a faint clucking over the phone. He added that a friend had seen a female turkey with seven chicks in a tree near G. Stanley Hall at the edge of town. Some virgin's bower is in full bloom around town, but ours is still not flowering. The very first goldenrod, however, is coming in along the north garden. Most of the peaches fell from their branches yesterday, only a handful left.

2007: The tall coneflowers in the alley have ended their season now. A few yards away, the thin-leafed coneflowers are still in full bloom. One giant swallowtail visited the zinnias and butterfly bush this morning. A large flock of geese flew over the center of town about 6:00 this morning.

2008: The skunk was in the back yard when I got up this morning around 6:00, and it stayed until broad daylight at 6:35. One painted lady (Cynthia) in the butterfly bush this noon. Jeanie found a three-inch praying mantis in the hosta and fern bed. A starling came to the suet feeder this morning, the first time I've seen one here through Late Summer. Large yellow garden spider (black-and-yellow *argiope*) in the front garden.

2010: Only a few intermittent crow and cardinal calls off and on after 5:30 this morning, no robins heard. Dry, hot weather continues. A few monarchs, tiger swallowtails, spicebush butterflies today, skippers numerous. In the alley, Mateo's black walnut is almost bare, and the tall yellow coneflowers are more than half gone. Scattered tall goldenrod seen in full bloom around the village. A few New England asters are open at the store. A great flock of blackbirds filled the back trees at noon, then moved on. No robin vespers heard this evening.

2011: Rain near sunrise quieted the tree crickets. Crows at 5:45, cardinal chipping call at 6:00, and hummingbirds, too. Squirrels started exactly at 7:00. One spicebush swallowtail seen this morning before I left for work at the center. Mateo's black walnut still has most of its leaves. High in the middle 90s today, and the most oppressive evening of the year when I walked Bella at 7:00. One firefly seen at the triangle park. So hot, the tree crickets were silent until we went to bed at 7:00. Marianne called tonight to say that a giant swarm of dragonflies was circling above her house. Cynthia McDonald also saw swarms in Cedarville.

2012: Soft rain, the remnants of Hurricane Isaac, this morning. Humid and hot throughout the afternoon. Many skippers, whites, admirals, fritillaries and checkerspots today. All the peaches fell by evening, almost all the phlox were gone, and the heliopsis were tattered. Wingstem and ironweed still in full bloom throughout the area. More webworms in our redbuds. A catbird seen in the quince, a young pair of cardinals at the feeder.

2014: A smaller, more colorful orb-weaver has set up its web in the back yard between branches of Jeanie's redbud.

2015: In the middle of a heat wave, monarchs and swallowtails continue to come to the zinnias and tithonias. The first beggarticks have opened by the back porch, and the first New England asters in the north garden are showing purple.

2016: A long flock of blackbirds passed over the highway as I drove south to Xenia. Soybean fields still solid green. Hurricane Hermine, the first hurricane to strike the United States this year, comes ashore on the Gulf Coast of Florida. In the east apple tree garden, the autumn hostas are in bloom: the large white-flowered ones and the narrow-leafed violet-flowered ones.

2017: Hurricane Harvey approaches from the south, brings two days of rain and cold temperatures in the 60s. One painted lady (*Cynthia*) came to the garden in the cold and drizzle.

2019: Hurricane Dorian, the strongest storm ever recorded in the Caribbean, devastates the Bahamas, stalls and spins just east of Miami. Here at Keuka Lake, acorns continue to accumulate, crunch as we walk.

2020: It seems the butterflies are fewer the past few days, this afternoon only one tiger swallowtail and a monarch, along with a silver-spotted skipper and a cabbage white. Tropical Storm Nana drives west into Honduras. No fireflies along Union Street tonight, the first time.

2021: The heat wave finally breaks as Hurricane Ida moves to the east, flooding parts of New England, dozens killed. Here, I noticed a hackberry butterfly at the hummingbird feeder and, for the first time this summer, yellowjackets there, too. This afternoon, several cabbage whites, three hackberry butterflies, one silver-spotted skipper and even a monarch. The rising barometer and cool wave seem to have motivated their emergence. Cardinal in the morning, and a dove, blue jays in the afternoon. Peggy's tall goldenrod is in full flower.

2022: Carolina wren still sings. Hummingbirds still seek the canna lilies, all the birds still ravenous at the feeders.

2023: Return from Keuka Lake in New York: The landscape throughout seems unchanged, the soybean foliage maybe even a darker green than it was last week. No butterflies of any kind noticed during the stay at the lake or on the drives. At home, I found an orb weaver web (spider missing), the first red honeysuckle berries, hops clusters pale and soft, major decline in phlox. the canna lily planting is reduced to 26 blossoms now, and the August Moon hostas, still in flower, are in decline. Now the

Autumn Joy sedum is opening along the back porch. False buckwheat has filled the New England aster banks, and the first beggarticks have blossomed. The Maximillian sunflowers are pretty much gone, dried up, and the cup plants have lost their peak exuberance. Although goldenrod was prominent in New York and Ohio, my goldenrod plants here have not started yet. Doves still calling. A green hummingbird visited the cannas while I counted.

Early September was a luxurious time. The air was warm and moist but not hot and sticky quiet but not stifling. The tangles of poison ivy and wild grape had thinned somewhat, and few biting insects were active. Early-turning leaves echoed the brilliance of late-blooming flowers, and the air was rich with pleasant smells — ripe apples, aromatic herbs, fallen leaves.

David Rains Wallace

September 2nd
The 245th Day of the Year

The squills and daffodils
Will give place to pillared roses,
And to asters, and to snow.

Amy Lowell

Sunrise/set: 6:03/7:05
Day's Length: 13 hours 2 minutes
Average High/Low: 81/60
Average Temperature: 70
Record High: 99 – 1953
Record Low: 40 – 1909

The Daily Weather

For the first time since June 4th, the chances of an afternoon in the 90s fall below five percent. Highs are in the 80s about 65 percent of the time, in the 70s twenty-five percent, and in the 60s ten percent. Morning lows fall below 60 a third of the years. Skies are partly cloudy ten years out of a dozen; but rain occurs one third of all September 2nds, often in the wake of Gulf hurricanes that move north into the Midwest.

Natural Calendar

Early Autumn brings on the flowering of Aster Season, Beggartick Season, Burr Marigold Season, Tall Goldenrod and Zigzag Goldenrod Seasons, Jerusalem Artichoke Season and Japanese Knotweed Season. Autumn Crocus Season arrives beside Virgin's Bower Season and Red Rosehip Season. In the roadsides, it is Elderberry and Wild Grape Picking Season. In the orchards of the Lower Midwest, early September marks the close of Summer Apple Season and the entry of Fall Apple Season.

The Stars

Several hours after dark, Perseus rises out of the northeast, and the Great Square fills the eastern sky, Cygnus the Swan is overhead, Hercules and the Corona Borealis in the west, and the Big Dipper low in the northwest. Taurus and the Pleiades are up by midnight, and they stay in the dark sky until middle spring when their disappearance coincides with the birds' return. At dawn, Orion is almost due south, the Great Square is setting, and Regulus, the planting star of April, is climbing in front of the Sun in Leo's sickle.

Daybook

1984: Beggarticks bloomed on schedule.

1986: Maples are turning more quickly now in town. Flocks of sparrows noticed along Wilberforce-Clifton. No beggarticks or asters seen in flower yet.

1987: Crows loud this morning, starlings gathering at Wilberforce.

1988: Crows and blue jays wake me up at dawn. A cardinal sings at 8:30, then is silent.

1990: Late Summer holds, warm. August-like damp, morning after morning with dew. Cardinals singing, sometimes still like July, doves calling: the days so full of sound, cicadas and katydids and crickets. Color, ripe color, deepening so completely, the complexity of the accumulation, the magnitude of the end of the summer so obvious now.

1991: Phlox still holding on. Yellow coneflowers die back at the south wall. First aster (*Novii belgii*) blooms there, too. Mums allowed to come in. Peas have been blooming three or four days. Along the railroad tracks, patches of brown and yellow in the redbuds.

1992: Cardinal sings at 5:55 a.m. Raspberries began their decline this morning, had been getting smaller and fewer, the corner turned when I picked a bowl just after dawn. Strong musky smell of autumn, sky overcast, high humidity, a hint of wood smoke coming through the flower garden. At Wilberforce, my ash tree is three-fourths bare. At South Glen, the wood nettle has all gone to seed, some of its leaves covered with white fungus. Tall bell flowers finally at the end. River high but slow, perfect for fishing. Leaves falling all along the path. Hickory nuts down. Squirrels eating black walnuts. Bright red Jack-in-the-pulpit berry cluster stark in the fading undergrowth. Deep blue cohosh berries not far away. Jumpseed full bloom, still not jumping. Touch-me-nots not jumping. Asters budding. Strong steady song of the crickets.

1997: Some pussy willow leaves have fallen. One ash tree north toward Springfield is half gold. The old maple in front of the house has huge blots of orange.

1998: Today has brought me where I've been before: just past the edge of summer, maybe just a handful of days past, but the subtle decays of early September have accumulated until the change seems sudden to me now. The rapid onset of color, the vague smoky tint of last week has quickly become clear and bright, streaking the maples.

Yesterday, I saw another long flock of grackles when I was on my way north of town. Every day on my drives, more birds. In the garden, swallowtails and monarchs have disappeared. Asters are still at their peak, but the first beggarticks are brown now near the river: white snakeroot is finally breaking down in the woods.

When I look back at my notes for this particular day from previous years, I feel like I am returning, after a long absence, to a comfortable, familiar place. If I remain in that feeling, I can be suspended in this one location and time, outside of the turning of the Earth, outside of the sequence which ages me with one season after another, and which pulls me out of the here and now and this one day.

So I bask in this stasis and suspension of knowledge. I

will die, after all, in the procession of days that follow one after another, along the straight road of some near or distant year. But if I stop now and step to the side, I hide the truth in the deception of my present.

1999: The ash in front of the house quickly turning pale, and the maple fringed with orange. Most of the phlox have gone, and their leaves are yellowing. All arrowhead in the pond has finished blooming.

2000: Today and yesterday, I found two small toads about an inch and a half long hopping in the grass. On the way to the Glen, three squirrels at different points in the half-mile trip ran in front of the truck. Light yellow caterpillar with a long brown tail and long ears at the hosta fence in the west garden. Birds filling the wires at Dorothy Lane. Showers of apple leaves, locust leaves, black walnut leaves in the sultry 90-degree afternoon.

2001: I've been thinking about how there haven't seen robins around for weeks and weeks, and I haven't heard robin calls, migration clucking, or summer's-end valediction songs. When did they disappear, and why? On the Springfield reservoir with John today: found a few catfish, watched monarchs fly across the lake. One yellow swallowtail came by the boat.

2002: Virgin's bower full bloom around town, still budding at home. Knotweed full, stonecrop just starting. Still a few sundrops, spiderwort, heliopsis. Russian sage and catmint still full. Some cottonwoods, locusts, ashes fringed with yellow.

2003: The last chigger bites fade around my ankles. The last chiggers complete their season with the last fireflies.

2005: At South Glen with Mike and the dogs: Goldenrod finally starting to turn, but not flowering yet. Bright yellow wingstem is in full bloom and fills the fields and woods. Some purple ironweed is beginning to go to seed but still complements dominant wingstem. Some ragweed with pollen found. Fruits of the wild cherry have turned. Monarchs seen off and on through an hour's walk. Crows and geese calling along the way. At home, the first virgin's bower bud has opened, and half of the stonecrop is in bloom. Overnight, a large camelback cricket got stuck in the bathtub.

2008: No birdsong this warm morning. The first of Mateo's goldenrod is in bloom, most only blushing. One monarch seen at the sand and gravel place in Enon. The box elder in the park is turning rust and gold. The ash at the southeast corner of the house continues its rapid transformation, almost like my early ash at Wilberforce used to do. This evening is muggy and hot, one of the most summery evenings of the summer. High very near 90 today. The woodshed spider, an arabesque orb-weaver (*Neoscona arabesca*), has once again put a web across the door, and I walked into it – just like I have for the last two years. An orb-weaver may have been making webs on the back porch earlier.

2009: Jeanie and I were sitting at the beach at Saugatuck along Lake Michigan, three hundred miles northwest of Yellow Springs. The wind was cool and the sun was hot, and we dozed and read and dozed and stared out at the clear blue, blue sky and water. In the distance, sailboats moved across the horizon, and seagulls bobbed in the waves.

Things were all in order. Lovers walked hand in hand along the shore in front of us. Children built sand castles. Fathers raced with their sons, and mothers huddled and chatted with their daughters.

Once in a while, a horsefly landed on one of us but then flew off without biting. Sometimes when a cloud covered the sun and the wind grew colder, three or four common black flies would take refuge on my jeans. In the course of the afternoon, butterflies came by, swallowtails and viceroys, their explorations light-hearted and playful.

In the middle of the afternoon, a ladybug landed on the novel I was reading. Not wanting to accidentally crush the insect, I gently pushed it off. Ten minutes later, it – or one like it – was back on the pages of my book as though trying to tell me something. I brushed it off again, but it returned again a little later, apparently in trouble, the fine beach sand sticking to its fragile wings. I got up and brought it to the dune behind me and set it on a blade of grass. It fell upside down to the ground beneath, and then I noticed that there were ladybugs everywhere.

Some of them were regular lady beetles with two or nine spots; others had no spots at all. But most were the pale brown Asian variety, the kind that appears throughout Yellow Springs in Late Summer and Early Fall.

Unlike all the other creatures at the beach, all of the lady beetles were clearly having problems. They were the most numerous creatures along the waterfront, but they were the least prepared to deal with that environment. And it also seemed they had no purpose for being there.

Landing or falling on the wet sand, they hobbled awkwardly toward the lake. When small, gentle waves spun them around and set them up higher on the beach, sometimes the ladybugs would turn around and head right back at the water. Sometimes, they tried to escape toward land, racing in the direction of a low mound only to be swept up and turned upside down by the pursuing tide. They seemed stupid and brave, helpless and blind, determined and dogged, unready, clueless.

Were they really playing like the butterflies and the children? Were they migrating? Had they crossed vast Lake Michigan on some high wind only to be dropped here on the sticky sand? What did the great architect of the universe have in mind for them here and now?

The activities of the gulls and the horseflies I could explain and anthropomorphize in order to pretend to recognize their function. I could see their activity on the beach as purposeful and focused. I could see the play and courtship and relaxation as making sense.

But then the absurd fate of the ladybeetles, the futility of their struggles, and my lack of understanding began to color the way I saw the rest of us at the beach. Instead of the false sense of comprehension, the hollow peace of finding each thing meaningful and in its place, joined by proximity on the great canvas of the lake and sky, I began to see our overwhelming lack of connection. Horseflies and children and lovers and I were all arbitrary and random objects, brought here together by motives so deeply discrete and distinct – the heart of the sailor out a mile from shore so distant from my own heart, the boats and the beetles all solitary and separate.

As the sun cooled and the wind grew stronger, I moved from the morning's sense to nonsense, taking things at face value, resigning myself to their influence, which was, after all, the very purpose of a day at the beach: pattern, design, control, explanation, context all unraveling as I let go of my spiritual reins.

2010: Another small spider in the bathtub this morning, three in as many days. Cardinals at 5:45 off and on. The female cardinal was again the earliest bird to visit the feeders before 6:00. Blue jays were calling this morning just after the cardinals began, and they have been calling, mostly bell calls, in the mornings this past week. In the butterfly bush and stonecrop garden, skippers still abundant. One tiger swallowtail came by early.

Dianne asked me to send her some notes about the hot summer. My message: "Things were early from the get-go. Once the snow melted, temperatures stayed above average - from March all the way through today. Spring wildflowers had a shorter-than-average season; flowering trees came in early and shed their petals early. Locusts were three weeks ahead of their blooming time of the 1980s. Clovers blossomed three weeks ahead of a few years ago. Fireflies came out in May, a week or two before they usually do. Corn was knee-high by the fourth of June, some fields over my head by the end of the month. Even though many summer wildflowers kept their Dog Day schedules, the midseason garden hostas and lilies blossomed and decayed way ahead of time. The butterflies were abundant this year - maybe partially because of the wet winter, and then the heat. The robins and cardinals sang later into the summer, inspired or tricked by continuing temperatures in the 90s. And then the cottonwoods started yellowing early. Maybe it will be an early fall."

2011: A very quiet morning: Crows at 5:50 but then silence. Chipping calls of two females and one male cardinal as they arrived to feed at 6:00. Starlings heard faintly at 8:00 for the first time since Early Summer, and a few seen on the high trees. Japanese knotweed in lush full bloom in the alley, phlox still holding in the garden. More peaches falling from Neysa's tree now; soon those that remain will be ready to eat. On the way to Fairborn, soybeans are turning quickly. A week ago, the fields were forest green all the way to West Virginia. Cicadas not heard on my early evening walk, the cricket songs changing, too.

2013: To the airport before dawn, new crescent moon rising high, fog across the hollows along Dayton-Yellow Springs Road, then home to thrips and a few field cricket chirps. Crows and doves at 5:45, one cardinal far off about five minute later. The giant orb-weaver is back on this date, putting a web across the upper part of the shed door, just like in 2008. Butterfly numbers still thinning out, but about 3:00 this afternoon I saw a male and female tiger swallowtail, several cabbage whites in randori, and a hummingbird moth.

2014: Keeping notes about events in nature over a number of years has shown me what I already knew: if something happens once, it will usually happen again.

When I see a particular insect or flower for the first time in the year, I check my daybook to find when I saw it in other years. Sometimes things are early, sometimes late, but they are almost always in the right sequence, the variations dependent on the quality of the season.

Often, however, I assume too much and go too far. When I see the same things happening every September, I develop expectations, and when those expectations are fulfilled, I take the expectations a little further, and then a little further still. I pretend to find rules and systems.

Finally, I start imagining that not only is each day's

journal a record of its own events, but a history of what has always occurred and what will occur again and again. I no longer wait for repetition in order to formulate patterns or predictions. One day's narrative becomes enough to defuse the need for replication.

Instead of the effect sought so diligently in the 19th century by the creator of the kinematoscope, in which still pictures were rotated or manipulated to create the illusion of motion, I find a reverse effect in multiple images and in repetition, an inverse kinematoscope that stills the disruption of passage.

Once I reach that point, everything makes sense. I settle in to the solid landscape of here and now. One event reaches back and forth through multiple seasons, is knit tightly with parallel events that are divided only by time, time that, in spite of appearance, and no matter how fast it seems to fly, makes the present only more fixed and indelible. Nothing is separate. One event is all there is.

2015: Tiger swallowtail, male and two monarch sightings in the garden. The first small white asters have just come into bloom.

2016: Many skippers today, and one spicebush swallowtail. In the woods, the asters have still not begun to flower. In spite of all the heat and rain, the wildflowers are late and most of the trees are remaining green.

2017: Another chilly and wet day, but a hummingbird visited the zinnias early. One cold scorpion fly in the zinnias, indifferent to my approach. From the rain and wind, many black walnuts and a few Osage fruits on the sidewalk near my house.

2018: To Yellow Springs from Lily Dale in New York: it seems that the soybean fields and corn fields have aged in just the two days we were gone. More shading has appeared in the tree line. At home, several monarchs and a great spangled fritillary in the afternoon garden, a cardinals vespers at 6:45 this evening, the female's "chits" accompanying the male's song. Cicadas called into the twilight, merging with the tree crickets' buzzing and the chirping of the field crickets and the high intermittent whistles of the tree frogs, then the katydids at 7:25 and then geese honking overhead in the full dark at 7:40.

2019: The small northern juncos chirp in the box elder tree down at the lake landing. They work the landing area for seeds or insects as we sit there in the late afternoon looking out at the rough water and let the wind soothe us.

2020: Two tiger swallowtails, one monarch, one hackberry butterfly, one checkerspot, a few cabbage whites on a mostly cloudy, mild day. This evening, a few katydids started calling at 7:09, then were silent until 7:25 when all the neighborhood katydids began to call. Tree crickets, field crickets, whistling crickets steady, comforting in the dark. Windfall apples on the sidewalk near Peggy's old property.

2021: Barometer continuing to rise, sunny and cool: more butterflies today, one black swallowtail, at least three hackberry butterflies, many cabbage whites, one small checkerspot. Outside the tavern downtown, Jill glimpsed a monarch.

2023: First jumpseed jumps. Time count: 26 canna blossoms. The castor beans have come into their own now, creating a tropical counterbalance to the autumnal mood of the knotweed, the aging phlos, the hops and the false buckwheat.

After all, anybody is as their land and air is. Anybody is as the sky is low or high, the air heavy or clear and anybody is as there is wind or no wind there. It is that which makes them and the arts they make and the work they do and the way they eat and the way they drink and the way they learn and everything.

Gertrude Stein

September 3rd
The 246th Day of the Year

Season of mists and mellow fruitfulness!
Close bosom-friend of the maturing sun;
Conspiring with him how to load and bless
With fruit the vines that round the thatch-eaves run.

John Keats

Sunrise/set: 6:04/7:04
Day's Length: 13 hours
Average High/Low: 81/59
Average Temperature: 70
Record High: 97 – 1913 and 2011
Record Low: 42 – 1908

The Daily Weather

Between today and the 6th there is an increased chance of an afternoon in the 90s (about a 15 percent chance). On the other hand, 40 percent of the afternoons are in the 80s, 40 percent are in the 70s, and five percent are in the 60s. Skies are clear to partly cloudy 80 percent of the time. Chances of rain: 30 percent. Lows in the 50s come a fourth of the early mornings, with 40s occurring about once in a decade.

The Natural Calendar

In warm years, tall goldenrod and New England asters come in, along with the heath aster, *Aster lateriflorus*, Short's aster, and the *Aster cordofolius*. Waysides show giant, golden Jerusalem artichokes. Beggarticks, white snakeroot, wingstem, ironweed, yellow hyssop, goosefoot, horseweed, clearweed, great blue lobelia and smartweed are still in full bloom in fields and woodlots. The violet September crocus have opened in the garden, now that the pale resurrection lilies have died back.

Enumeration

September 3, 1982 – 2020 : Early small white asters, New England asters, tall goldenrod, Japanese knotweed, first beggarticks, autumn crocuses, Jerusalem artichokes, virgin's bower, starlings in the trees, the last of the summer raspberries, windfall apples, patchwork landscapes, yellowing tulip trees and locusts and buckeyes, red and orange Judas maples, acorn fall, Diana and the Hickory Horned Devil, bittersweet autumn smell, crows and blue jays, screech owl, only few cardinals or doves or robins, dropping peaches, peak peach season, monarchs, swallowtails, hummingbirds, orb weavers, frogs at the pond, bittersweet berries turning pale orange, jumpseed time closing, zinnias and tithonias holding strong. Katydids, tree crickets, whistling crickets, field crickets.

Daybook

1982: The fall raspberry crop in the back yard has declined to about two pints a week.

1983: Starlings gathering in the locust trees behind the house. Thoreau remarks in his journal (September 30, 1858) that they arrive in the fall from their northern breeding areas.

1984: Joe Pye weed brown at Wilberforce. Field thistles still full bloom. Geese fly over the house 3:14 p.m.

1986: One goose flies over the yard at 2:30 p.m. Beggarticks still not blooming. Cardinals not singing. Goldfinch at the feeder, still gold. Raspberries declining quickly. First small white asters bloom in the back yard.

1987: Sycamore hole: One carp brought in at 4:45 p.m., after an hour with few bites but bait continually stolen. Strange fishing the last few times out, as if a major change was taking place in the habitat, the fish moving to an autumn location.

1989: Strong cool front dominates the morning. Silent geese going south, high. Bees, cold, clumsy in the zinnias.

1990: One goose heard in the distance, 7:00 p.m.

1991: At the Charleston Falls Preserve: first small white asters seen, some ironweed done, tulip trees with patches of gold, cottonwoods fading, many of their leaves on the path, soybeans throughout the county turned, brightening the patchwork landscape. Woods very dry, creeks very low.

1992: White cosmos, seven feet tall, facing south, bright against the predawn clouds. No cardinals this morning. Blue jay at 7:25, then crows passing through. Rose of Sharon continues strong, raspberries failing, a few everbearing strawberries still ripen. Bittersweet autumn smell of the days grows stronger. The ash outside my Wilberforce window is three-fourths gone, falling quickly.

1993: First beggarticks opened today in the yard.

1998: First New England aster in the south garden opened today, and the small white asters are just unraveling. End of the red cannas in town.

2001: Doves still calling in the morning, jays and crows too. One cardinal heard yesterday, none today. No fish caught at the reservoir today, although white bass were biting in the morning (one person at the dock told me). Wind came up strong in the afternoon, and the sky sent mixed signals, storm clouds then sun.

2003: Japanese knotweed, full bloom by the street for the past week or so, is starting to decline. More jumpseeds jumping by the sidewalk. The morning is wet and quiet, no birds heard. No monarch seen yesterday, the sky gray, rain intermittent, but this afternoon when I went out to the garden, there were two monarchs in the zinnias. And Diana called from the Children's center at about 3:00 p.m. She and the children had found several "Hickory

Horned Devil" caterpillars (caterpillar of the Royal Walnut Moth, *Citheronia regalis*). I went over to see; the caterpillar that had survived the children was fat and huge, maybe six or seven inches long, shiny green, horned, magnificent. Diana and Melody let it crawl on their bare hands while the children screamed with fear and delight.

2004: To Columbus: The tree line shows orange and yellow and red patches throughout the countryside, the leafturn continuing its early pace.

2005: Along the roads, false boneset is prominent, goldenrod brightening. When we got home from shopping this afternoon, we found three monarchs in the pink sedum. In the park across from church, the black walnut trees are almost bare. The peach tree along the north border continues to drop its sweet peaches.

2006: Screech owl at 5:00 a.m. and then again at about 7:30 this evening. In the yard, the Japanese knotweed is in full bloom, and the very first buds of our virgin's bower are opening. The peaches have been dropping for several days, just before they really become ripe enough to eat.

2008: No screech owls heard at all this summer. No skunk today. One monarch seen on the way back from Fairborn. The peaches are holding to their branches, the new tree apparently hardier and producing hardier fruit. I ate a reddish peach this afternoon, sweet and firm.

2009: Peaches coming in strong throughout central Michigan, and the last of the blueberries. The end of August seems to be the end of the U-pick season, too. Driving south toward Yellow Springs, we noticed more pale yellow in the trees, sections along the roadside where blanching was very strong.

2010: Only a few cardinal calls and crows near 5:45. Some robin peeping through the day. The last peaches continue to drop from the peach tree. One tiger and one spicebush swallowtail seen, skippers continuing thick.

2011: One male cardinal song at 6:10, two females giving their sharp call notes for an hour or so - they were the first birds at the feeder this morning in the twilight. Hummingbirds, males and females still feeding heavily, swooping back and forth around the feeder. Chickadees and the nuthatch fill in for the sparrows, which have stopped their summer rush for our seed. More heat in the 90s today. Peaches continuing to fall, and the first one eaten for breakfast today. Raspberries holding on at a handful a day. Joe Pye weed is done blooming, as is the very last orange day lily. Heliopsis and knockout roses, ironweed, spiderwort, and catmint complement the dominant clumps of zinnias along the fence. One monarch at 8:00, another later in the day. One great spangled fritillary, two Eastern blacks. Cicadas not heard today, and tree crickets less prominent. The katydid in Gerard's tree was quiet when I walked by; a few days ago, he was so loud he hurt my ears. Field crickets prominent in the early evening, then screaming tree crickets take over.

2012: The green frog sat at the same place on the edge of the pond up near the waterfall for at least eight hours today. Large orb-weaver with a web on the entry to the porch. No bird vespers tonight, distant katydids.

2013: The orb-weaver made another web across the shed door overnight, but it ran when he saw me coming – unlike yesterday when he lay still while I accidently broke the web going in the door. Along the north garden, the zinnias have started to decline, so many more decaying, even though they should continue for another six weeks. Peaches holding, maybe two-thirds down. The first flowers on Don's goldenrod have opened, and more are coming in along the way south to Wilmington. Still, the roadside bloom is pretty much unchanged from a week ago: sundrops, Jerusalem artichokes, wingstem, ironweed, early goldenrod. At the Ellis Pond arboretum, a little yellowing along the veins of the sweet gum tree, but the trees are still stable in Late Summer.

2014: A large orb-weaver (with striped legs) has put its web on the stop sign on High and Limestone Streets, and an unusually large long-jawed orb-weaver has created a fine web across the pond. Again, lots of cabbage whites and silver-spotted skippers and folded-wing skippers today. One great spangled fritillary, one Eastern black, and two monarchs seen in the zinnias. Across from the Covered Bridge, boneset is still dominant in the wetland there. At John Bryan Park, full-blooming white snakeroot lines the roadway. At the prairie location, most flowers of the Queen Anne's lace have curled and darkened. Patches of gold have appeared on the silver olive bushes. And the tall sunflower-like plant (seven feet, round thick stem, rough, narrow and very slightly toothed leaves, with one flower bud in each bract) has just opened.

2015: Light leafturn on birches, crab apples, maples, mostly in patches now. The yellowwood tree is a little ahead of the others, its dried seedpods adding to its autumn color.

2016: A spicebush swallowtail in the zinnias this afternoon. The new frog, maybe two or three inches long, jumped to the water when I came to feed the koi today. He has stayed over a week now.

2017: The viburnum on the north side of the house is quickly turning rusty red. The Limelight hydrangea in Peggy's yard is finally starting to rust. Euonymus flowers are all berries. The bittersweet berries on the vine above my trellis are turning pale orange. In the bright sun, temperature in the low 70s: a hummingbird, some cabbage whites, three monarchs, two bright yellow sulphurs. The hummingbird briskly pushed one of the monarchs off of a red zinnia blossom. At the mill habitat, great blue lobelias were tall and vibrant. The first violet flower was open on an *Aster sagittifolius*. Many patches of orange jewelweed. A father and son noticed netting crawdads among the shallow, rocky river bottom; the man said they had also come upon several orange sucker-like fish about the size of small bait minnows. Maybe koi someone had put in the river.

2018: All of the jumpseeds are gone now, their stems hard and gray. The virgin's bower from years ago has made a reappearance, climbing through the honeysuckles below Janet's redbud. Above the gray Joe Pye weed, bright ironweed brings cabbage white butterflies throughout the day, and monarchs – sometimes at least four at a time – sail through the zinnias and tithonias.

2020: Jumpseeds are still in full bloom, none jumping. Much of the landscape evades the developments recorded for this day. It is still summer today this year. In the garden, one monarch, many cabbage whites, a few silver-spotted skippers seen throughout several visits, fewer butterflies than a week or so ago, it seems. Not a single large orb-weaver seen this summer. At Ellis Pond, great blue lobelia and boneset in full flower near the drainage brook. Jerusalem artichokes are bright and strong behind the Danielsons' house. Yesterday, I saw another long flock of grackles when I was on my way north of town. Every day on my drives, more birds.

2021: No orb weavers seen this year, no painted lady butterflies. Blue jay calls off and on.

2022: First beggartick flower unfolds, New England asters budding, no spiders, one black swallowtail seen, blue jays silent. Jumpseed flowers are still moist, not ready to jump. *Heliopsis* has ended its flowering time by the gray Joe Pye. Honeysuckle berries turning.

2023: Time count: 25 canna blossoms. One sulphur or maybe small tiger swallowtail glimpsed near the house. Virgin's bower gathering momentum under Janet's redbud, in full flower among Peggy's fruit trees near the sidewalk.

First Spring, then Summer that away doth chase,
And must it self give place
To Apple-bearing Autumne....

Horace (Fanshawe)

September 4th
The 247th Day of the Year

My vicinity affords many good walks; and though for so many years I have walked every day, and sometimes for several days together, I have not yet exhausted them. An absolutely new prospect is a great happiness, and I can still get this any afternoon. Two or three hours' walking will carry me to as strange a country as I expect ever to see. There is in fact a sort of harmony discoverable between the capabilities of the landscape within a circle of ten miles' radius, or the limits of an afternoon walk, and the threescore years and ten of human life. It will never become quite familiar to you.

Henry David Thoreau

Sunrise/set: 6:05/7:02
Day's Length: 12 hours 57 minutes
Average High/Low: 80/59
Average Temperature: 70
Record High: 96 – 1897
Record Low: 45 – 1974

The Daily Weather

Today carries a 25 percent chance of highs in the 90s, thirty percent for 80s, forty percent for 70s, five percent for 60s. Skies are clear to partly cloudy nine days in a dozen; rain falls one year in four. Cool nights in the 50s occur four nights in ten. Once every few years, the low dips into the 40s.

Natural Calendar

Squirrels shred Osage fruits in the woods. Orb-weavers still weave their huge webs. But the rose of Sharon, which was bright from here to the ocean a few weeks ago, loses most of its flowers. Japanese knotweed petals darken and fall. False boneset becomes gray along the freeways. Ironweed deteriorates quickly, and wingstem is in its last week. Fawns born in the spring are now weaned and have usually lost their spots.

Daybook

1984: Knotweed along Corry Street is past its prime. Raspberries begin their decline.

1985: First new garlic mustard (which will bloom 18 months from now) sprouted today on the Covered Bridge hillside. My ash tree at Wilberforce is turning now.

1986: My ash tree a third yellow, leaves holding.

1987: Hummingbird in the zinnias.

1988: Woolly bear caterpillars were out today, three seen. Late honeysuckle berries just turning red. Japanese beetles still mating by the river. Blue vervain at the end of its stalks. Lobelia and monkey flowers, white snakeroot, jewelweed, boneset, horehound still full. Ragweed gone to seed, burdock brown. About a third of the wild cherries left. A few mulberries still purple. Three-seeded mercury flushed pink now. weed, *Mollugo verticillata*, and heart-leaved umbrellawort, *Mirabilis nyctaginea*, identified at the Jacoby tracks.

1990: Blue jays and crows at 6:00 a.m., no cardinals until 6:15. One robin heard, making migration clucking sounds.

1992: A cardinal sings out at 6:00 a.m., then is silent. At South Glen, the first white asters are open. Up into Near Prairie: Wingstem is full bloom in the shade, but losing petals in the open sun; ironweed at its height or just turning to seed. The first few zigzag goldenrod plants are coming in, patches of Judas color here and there, bees, and butterflies. Along Grinnell, more yellow sulphur butterflies than usual. Some monarchs, too. Field goldenrod not completely open throughout. Still not much decay on the coneflowers near Far Hole, but at the South Garden, I cut away the first cones, scattered them to set seed. I compare the exhilaration of this time with the anticipation in March and April, the piercing glory of May, full tide of the year in June, golden July, humid, frantic August, sear, crisp winter. Which time is sweeter? Which colors are more extravagant, which events move me more in this kaleidoscopic cycle?

1993: No katydids heard last night. Doves calling at 5:45 a.m. No cardinals. Three goldfinches came to the feeder today.

1999: Sitting in the greenhouse before dawn: Orion and the moon moving in from the east, Jupiter over my head, the lunar and the planetary. I could stay here and watch and watch the cycles wash over me. This afternoon I found the very first small white asters and the first New England aster in the South Garden. Then I saw the green frog sitting on the bench near the pond. Later, near suppertime, I almost stepped on a medium-sized leopard frog along the south wall.

2000: Thunderstorm at 3:00 this morning, heavy rain brought down yellow locust, black walnut, and box elder leaves: the first autumn rain. Half the rudbeckia gone.

2001: The yellow jackets are finally here. They came first to the catfish carcasses on the 2nd, then to the apples this afternoon. Lots of brown Asian ladybugs on the lake today. A skunk dug up the back yard last night looking for grubs. Rose of Sharon down to a small fraction of its late July bloom. Silvia brought a large puffball mushroom over last night, stolen, she said, from her neighbor's porch.

2003: Fog this morning after the passage of a cool front. No birds heard in the dark, just a whistling cricket; then one wren chattered at 6:00, no cardinals or doves. Late afternoon: three monarchs seen in the zinnias when I went out for a few minutes.

2005: Bumblebees sleeping in the stonecrop. Serviceberry leaves yellowing and falling along Dayton Street.

2007: This morning, a shower of black walnut leaves brought me a sequence of impressions that occupied my mind for the rest of the day. The images included the elm trees outside the window of my boyhood room, my father working in the yard, my mother in the kitchen, the smell of bread baking, the forced air heat on my bare feet before breakfast, walks to school in the cold, time alone hunting squirrels, feelings of comfort and regret, nostalgia, sadness, contentment.

This week the asters have bloomed in the garden, the small-flowered white ones and the purple New England asters Only a few flowers in the woods: some tall goldenrods, great blue lobelias, orange touch-me-nots, white snakeroot. Throughout town, late hostas hold their flowers, white and violet. When I walked through the park, I saw cabbage butterflies, one dark swallowtail, one painted lady. A groundhog was about to cross the way, saw me and retreated.

The pieces of past and present autumns continue to fit into place. Each fragment is an increment on the gauge of the year, measuring the relationship of the earth to the sun, and my relationship to the place in which I live. None of the notes or observations or memories seems irrelevant; each moment of awareness, like each physical particle observed, is a seasonal cell, similar to a holographic segment of September, containing the psychic and cosmic whole.

2008: All sorts of bees continue to swarm on the stonecrop. Along the Cedarville bike path, ironweed, goldenrod, orange touch-me-nots, huge field thistles, some butter-and-eggs, chicory, old Joe Pye weed and showy coneflowers, and strong, tall sunflowers with multiple heads, reddish stems, rough, thin-tapered leaves, leaves mostly alternate but some appearing opposite, with small leaves in the axils. Throughout the countryside, soybean fields are starting to yellow. One cardinal song at about 8:30 this morning. In the Atlantic, three hurricanes are lined up to approach the East Coast.

At the triangle park, the box elder is shedding. Here at home, our ash is losing leaves.

2009: The white autumn crocus has started to bloom at the northwest corner of the back porch.

2010: No robins, a smattering of cardinal and crow vocalizations before dawn. Judy, back from her trip to France, wrote: "In addition to all the oleanders, hydrangeas, jasmine, rose of Sharon, and other cultivated plants, there was Queen Anne's Lace in two varieties growing on the side of the roads, as well as those leggy dandelion-like plants that grow about two feet tall. Of course there's wild chicory, known as bluets, but those are farther north."

2011: High trill of tree crickets before sunrise. Crows at 5:50 this morning, the only bird calls except for the chipping of cardinals near the feeder. Squirrel chattered at 6:45, sparrows around 7:00. Storm last night and light rain through much of the day, the record heat wave breaking. Tonight, no katydids heard - the second night in a row they have been absent. And no cicadas during the day, the insects presaging the change in season as well as the more immediate shift in the weather.

2012: Light rain through most of the morning, no bird song heard. The first purple shows on the New England asters. The false boneset is opening in the yard (has been open along the freeway for quite a while). Peggy's virgin's bower is all in bloom now after several hot, wet days and nights. The orb-weaver is back tonight, weaving a large web on the front porch. Walking Bella at 6:30 this evening, only field crickets heard.

2013: The cool wave settles in, low in the upper 40s this morning for the first time since Early Summer. In the shed door, the orb-weaver holds its own, the web getting tattered. Winterberry berries fully emerged now, no more petals left. Crows were calling around 6:00 this morning. Walking Bella at 6:00, only a few field crickets heard, no sparrows or doves. Only the occasional "chit" of cardinals in the honeysuckles. Squirrel chattering in the back locusts at 6:30.

2014: The orb-weaver was still in its web by the stop sign at Limestone and High Streets. And I found a new orb-weaver between apple tree branches in the east garden. Many silver-spotted skippers, folded-wing skippers, several sulphurs, two monarchs, a great spangled fritillary and a painted lady (*Cynthia*) seen in my occasional looks outside.

2015: The latest hostas, the red-stemmed October bloomers, have just opened.

2016: Crows at 6:03 this morning. A few minutes later sharp repeated calls of a hawk. Half a dozen silver-spotted skippers in the zinnias today, a few cabbage whites, one blue, no swallowtails or monarchs.

2017: To Fort Hill in southwestern Ohio: partly sunny, temperature in the low 80s, steady south wind, the land deep green throughout the drive into the Appalachian foothills, most soybean fields solid deep forest green, corn rich gold and green. One monarch and one small black swallowtail seen. Many road kills.. At Jill's the first small white asters have opened.

2018: Hurricane Gordon comes ashore in Alabama, predicted to curve north and reach Ohio in a few days.

2019: After destroying many areas of the Bahamas, Hurricane Dorian heads toward the Carolinas. Here at Keuka Lake: Purple loosestrife, Queen Anne's lace, jewelweed, boneset, chicory and black-eyed Susans in flower, blushing burning bush, locusts speckled with gold, small juncos feeding and chirping at the lake shore, doves heard.

2020: A sharp cool front arrived in the night, the sky clear, the air brisk in the low 50s. Leaf drop so far this year has been tentative:

only black walnut, cherry and white mulberry leaves here and there. But the first milkweed pod came undone in the night, and the first tall bidens flowered at Ellis. No geese heard yet this summer. Two fireflies noticed after the katydids began to call.

2021: Blue jay calls off and on in the morning. To Pearl's Fen in the early afternoon, clouds moving in, humidity rising: The wetlands at their peak, the swamp area solid with flowers: full bloom of several varieties of goldenrods, Joe Pye weeds, and bonesets, giant sunflowers, cup plants, white snakeroot, jewelweed, pale touch-me-nots, purple ironweed, black-eyed Susans, sneezeweeds, small woodland sunflowers, Jerusalem artichokes, great blue lobelia, field thistle, tall blue vervain, a few asters, and several other flowers I didn't recognize. Numerous monarch butterflies seen, one checkerspot, one sulphur. At home, one monarch, one black swallowtail before a light rain began.

2022: Pearl's Fen like last year, except only three monarchs. First soybean fields seen with yellow patches in the foliage. The very first New England aster flower opened in a patch I hadn't cut back in the north garden. One black swallowtail glimpsed late in the day. Hurricane Danielle hovers in the Caribbean.

2023: Gibbous, waning moon high overhead at 5:00 this morning. Tree crickets, field crickets, tree frogs. Venus in the east above Stafford Street, Suddenly the neighbor's air condition went off at 5:25, and just as suddenly the tree frogs went silent. Blue jays at 5:38, crows at 5:43, "chee-up, chee-up" of cardinals at 5:48, no doves heard. Birds became active at the feeder, too dark still for me to see which birds, at 5:55. This evening, walking home in the dark from the movie with Jill, we were surrounded by an overwhelming chorus of katydids, field crickets, tree crickets, ground crickets and the "whistling" crickets, ground crickets and, as I once realized as I tried to identify other night sounds, there were so many other creatures I could not detect or name singing, too. There was no spaces between sounds, instead: a solid meditation of the sound field that left no space for the cars on the street or even our voices. A feeling of being held, massaged, covered, protected, supported by thousands and thousands of individuals that were creating the world as we walked, a force indifferent to the fate of the Earth, political or climatological. This was the cosmos. This is what space and time were like. Then, indoors again everything was quiet, consciousness stilled, and we were again alone in the universe.

There are promises of new life to be found in the seeding and dying of summer flowers and in the cocoons and galls that decorate the stems of weeds and the underside of leaves. Summer's insects have planted the seeds of life beneath the bark of trees and deep in the earth; cicadas and snowy tree crickets and katydids have laid plans for the future.

Cathy Johnson

September 5th
The 248th Day of the Year

One could give his life to watching the weather, and sky, stars, wind, just what can be seen by our eyes.

Harlan Hubbard

Sunrise/set: 6:07/7:01
Day's Length: 12 hours 54 minutes
Average High/Low: 80/59
Average Temperature: 70
Record High: 102 – 1899
Record Low: 41 – 1902

The Daily Weather

The second cool front of the month has often passed through by now, and Sun ordinarily dominates the days through the 11th. Today, highs in the 90s come only 20 percent of the time, 80 degrees 40 percent, 70 degrees 30 percent, 60 degrees ten percent. Lows are in the 50s forty percent of the mornings, in the 40s ten percent, and a dip to the 30s is possible (a five percent chance of that). A shower passes through just one day in four.

Natural Calendar

Sycamores, tulip trees, poplars, black walnuts, locusts, elms, box elders, buckeyes, dogwoods, chinquapin oaks, lindens, and redbuds begin to show their autumn colors. Leaves gather in the backwaters and on sidewalks and paths. Bright patches of scarlet sumac and Virginia creeper mark the fencerows. Streaks of gold have appeared on the silver olives. In some years, ash, black walnuts and cottonwoods are almost bare.

Daybook

1983: Washington, D.C. to Yellow Springs: Vetch, asters, wingstem, ironweed, sunflowers, horseweed, green amaranth, Queen Anne's lace, varieties of goldenrod, sundrops, chicory, sow thistles all in bloom. Brown dead teasel prominent throughout the drive. Joe Pye losing its violet blush. The dogwood which was in full flower at the rest stop in West Virginia the third week of August has some green berries, some white berries.

1986: No cardinals singing. Blackbirds cluck in the Wilberforce trees. Orange beggarticks just opening, locusts yellowing, zigzag goldenrod budding, a few small white asters now. Cicadas quiet.

1987: First small white asters bloomed in the yard today. At Far Hole, no bites, fishing at sunset. Sycamore leaves drifting down the low river. Tree line weathering. Zigzag goldenrod is budding along the upper trails. Cicadas quieter than a week ago. Wind seems to be picking up as Early Fall comes closer.

1989: South Glen: mist heavy over the open fields tonight. Amber wingstem half gone. Most ironweed has faded. Dogbane yellowing. Goldenrod is just showing color. The very first asters are open.

1992: First small white asters bloom against the south wall. Mums coming in now slowly. Tall blanket flowers are in, started from seed. Zinnias, cosmos holding well. Ranunculus surging, taking over the mallow bed, stronger the last few weeks than even in the spring. Dry south wind today, temperature rising toward the 80s, the garden glowing with the change of season, deepening, darker gold, a more intense and more final green.

1993: The September 8th cool front comes through early, lows in the 50s this morning, clear, with fog in the field along King Street. Mother cardinal feeding her baby at the gazebo feeder before dawn. Rudbeckia is three-fourths gone, the south garden tangled by Friday's rain. Geese flew over the west end of town at 8:15 this morning. A hummingbird came to the zinnias at noon.

Then to South Glen with Buttercup: Most ironweed and wingstem gone. Bur cucumbers have fully developed fruits. Rudbeckia still late full here, and sunflowers, white snakeroot, oxeye/helianthus. A few touch-me-nots. Jumpseeds jumping now. Scattered old mint still in bloom. Trees still solid except the tulip poplars, which are patchy with gold.

1998: Peak of Jerusalem artichokes, goldenrod, wingstem, false boneset. Last purple loosestrife and ironweed. Still chicory. Queen Anne's lace aging, most gone. Through southwestern Ohio, landscape still forest green. A few asters seen. Sycamores and tulip trees turning and falling. Countryside dry but holding. Greene County corn all brown and brittle.

1999: The green frog was sitting on the bench again today. Neysa sat down beside it, and they sat together for a while.

2001: Cottonwoods and sycamores turning more, an ochre color, worn. More yellow jackets on the apples. Another skunk struck on the road again last night. Chicory and Queen Anne's lace still strong. Goldenrod coming in more. More soybeans turning, corn withering.

2002: Butterflies today: one monarch, one spicebush swallowtail, several cabbage butterflies, spotted skippers and blues.

2003: South Glen: The river high again after inches of rain from Hurricane Grace. Under the canopy, tattered bellflowers, wood nettle leaves breaking down, more jumpseed seeds gone, white snakeroot early. Out in the field, goldenrod is just starting to come in as the purple ironweed decays quickly. Wingstem holds at full. Small white aster (very close to *Aster vimineus*) common. Wood thrush heard and seen. Lots of monarchs in the garden and crossing roads today.

2004: One monarch and a yellow swallowtail in the zinnias today. The first New England asters opened in the north garden. Stonecrop remains at full bloom, pink and red.

2005: Late peaches still coming in along the north garden.

2007: Monarchs and painted ladies in the stonecrop throughout the day, cabbage butterflies swarming. Moderate activity at the bird feeders. The first virgin's bower opened overnight, the New England asters showing some purple in their buds. Jerusalem artichokes still not budding. Along the freeway, cottonwoods are getting paler.

2008: Finally rain for the garden. In the alley, more apples are coming down. Pigweed is in bloom, along with the great ragweed, chicory, new goldenrod and bindweed. At home, the first New England aster buds show a little purple, and the Jerusalem artichokes have started to bud. Peaches ripening steadily. Finches and sparrows crowd the feeders. Loud chorus of crickets and katydids tonight.

2009: Cardinal at 5:45 this morning, then silence. No doves calling. Mateo's Virginia creeper is a deep maroon, tumbling through the honeysuckle. Don's serviceberry trees are speckled with orange and gold. Small white asters coming in along Limestone Street. Only a handful of tall coneflowers in bloom. First jumpseeds are jumping. First New England asters open in the yard. Buds have formed on the tallest Jerusalem artichokes. Seeds gone from many great ragweed plants. The viburnum next to the house is turning a rich red. Two hummingbirds seen today, no monarchs or swallowtails. The last tall hibiscus is blooming. Italian honeybees thick on the stonecrop flowers.

2010: No robinsong. A jay called at 5:45, then a few crows, then a cardinal, then quiet. A cold morning, but skippers work the flowers, one yellow tiger swallowtail seen early. Scent of fallen leaves now. No katydids after dark tonight!

2011: Cool today, 30 degrees cooler than three days ago! Tree crickets still strong at 8:00 a.m., and some field crickets. No birds singing near dawn except the crows. Mateo's black walnut tree holds at maybe three-fourths of its leaves, strong this year. A few serviceberry leaves yellowing along Dayton Street. In the Gulf, tropical storm Leah floods New Orleans and heads north. Hurricane Katia threatens the East Coast. Tonight, crickets still sang, the raspy high tree crickets, intermittent tree crickets and field crickets. Not as much volume, it seems, not as many singers as a week ago.

2012: No birds heard this morning. Frog still croaks before dawn. Orb-weaver missing when I went out to the porch. Heavy fog at sunrise, dew-covered gossamer webs in the lawn with passageways to the ground. A giant swallowtail seen when I went outside about 9:30, and then when the sun came out this afternoon, sulphurs and whites and checkerspots and fritillaries everywhere. At the northwest corner of the back porch, the white crocus has just bloomed. In the pond, the fish have been shy today, maybe had been attacked by a raccoon last night. Maybe reacting to the absence of Jeanie, who always called to them when she approached.

2013: Crows late at 6:15 a.m. To Wilmington: More goldenrod in bloom, stable primroses, artichokes, wingstem. The cottonwoods are paling, ochre in the tree line, more cornfields golden and brown. In the alley, small-flowered coneflowers are drooping (but the alley has been so transformed from a year or two ago, all the past gardens overgrown, paved over). At Limestone and West South College streets, the prairie dock is half to seed. In the yard, scattered fallen hackberry and white mulberry leaves, peaches maybe three-fourths fallen.

Late afternoon at the circle garden: male (yellow) tiger swallowtails, black swallowtails with prominent blue markings, cabbage whites, hummingbirds, hummingbird moths. The sun was making the trees glow, the zinnias shine. No sign of the white autumn crocus near the porch this year, but the virgin's bower that disappeared from the garden trellis several years ago is back, climbing over the tangles of wisteria. At Ellis Pond this evening, arrowhead bloom was over, orange jewelweed, swamp beggar ticks (*Bidens connata*) and common beggar ticks (*Bidens frondosa*) in full bloom all along the water's edge. The arboretum trees were still solid green except for a few yellow leaves of the tulip tree. Occasional cardinal calls in the late afternoon and evening.

2014: A monarch in the zinnias when I came back from walking Bella this morning. Another large orb-weaver in the yard, this one by the south hibiscus. In the Phillips Street alley, the first Heath's aster was open. Like last year at Ellis, the swamp and common beggarticks are in full flower there.

2015: A giant swallowtail in the garden today, but only cabbage whites through most of the day. Across from the Covered Bridge, the boneset has suddenly ended its flowering season, the flower heads so white two days ago now brown. And then I noticed that the six rudbeckia plants that had flowered all August have gone dark, too.

2016: Arriving home from a day trip to Ripley, along the Ohio River, we saw an Eastern black swallowtail in the zinnias. At 7:29 this morning, a substantial flock of honking geese flew over in the dark. Throughout south-central Ohio, a few changes from a week ago. Goldenrod was gaining prominence, more soybean fields were turning and Jerusalem artichokes were in full flower. In farmyards, the white folds of virgin's bower common. The woods were still deep green, with the exception of a handful of Judas trees. At home, golden centers on the beggartick buds, knotweed lush, rudbeckia in decline. At 7:29 this evening, another large, honking flock of Canadian geese flew over the house.

2017: After a storm last night, a chilly, humid day. Hurricane Irma spins toward Puerto Rico. A brief walk in the yard in the middle of the afternoon sun: two monarchs and two cabbage whites playing in the zinnias. Jumpseeds finally quite brittle.

2018: Another hot day of intense sun: I sat in the greenhouse and watched the hackberry leaves flutter down, guided a little with the south breeze, syncopated single then double then a handful of leaves, then none. A hatch of silver-spotted skippers: they were all over the circle garden. I walked in the north garden between the eight-foot castor beans and Mexican sunflowers, and cabbage white butterflies played in the shriveling knotweed flowers, and monarchs, maybe half a dozen, sailed from one zinnia and dahlia to another like leaves in a fickle wind.

2019: Keuka Lake, New York, south to Yellow Springs: Sun and mild throughout the drive. Many sumac bushes were reddening, and Judas maples appeared more often. The most remarkable aspect of the trip was the long fields of goldenrod all across the western highway of the state. And we saw five murmurations of starlings this trip, instead of just one on the way north. Along the freeway in Ohio: some large patches of false boneset. At home, acres and acres of tall, full-blooming sunflowers have attracted hundreds of sightseers.

2020: A perfect day for butterflies, sun and mild, but no monarchs or swallowtails today, and only a few skippers and cabbage whites. Then in the late afternoon, one monarch touched down in the zinnias and was gone. The first jumpseed seeds started to jump today. At Ellis Pond, the swallows still circle and weave across the water. Two fireflies seen this evening along Whiteman Street.

2022: Black swallowtail and a hummingbird passed by today. Leaves collecting in the backyard. A flock of robins seen in the Koogler Reserve. Jewelweed common in full bloom.

2023: Time count: 23 canna lily blossoms. One monarch, two tiger swallowtails, one cabbage white. Knotweed, virgin's bower, false buckwheat, stonecrop, giant castor bean plants and cup plants, hops florets. Leah reports multiple tiger swallowtails, painted ladies, red admirals and monarchs spending two weeks recently at her butterfly bushes.

Journal
And geography blended
With time equals destiny.

Joseph Brodsky

Summer was an entire life of landscape, lush and complete like the body and soul of a person grown to sweet and successful maturity. Now I see it coming all undone, see how perfection can unravel so swiftly and deliberately.

In the year's symmetry and counterpoint, however, nothing really falls out of place: descent is as impeccable as ascent, renewal as clear as decay. Everything proceeds with such exact measure, easing resurgence into decline, changes demonstrating the whole nature of each thing, a nature which is only progression, which never has to do with only this or only that at any given moment, and in which objects never lie in stasis as in a photograph.

The unfolding of fall, buds tucked inside of tragedy, reveals the truth of matter and time, simultaneous movement away and toward, tidal rotation, a perfect loop that denies cosmology of everlasting expansion, a circle which denies that everything is traveling toward some particular end, denies that our acts and our lives are expanding forever outward like the universe, exploding from a tiny seed and egg, their eventual end unknowable or tracked by Jesus for doomsday judgment.

Sometimes, of course, it doesn't help to try to understand how everything fits together, how bad is balanced out by good, how loss is soothed by gain, how everything must have a purpose, how life has meaning, how all my actions are watched and weighed. And when I try too hard to understand rebirth in dying, the truth of symmetry and counterpoint blurs all the edges of my autumn confusion. Looking ever more closely, I find the borders of my thoughts and emotions are lost from view. Questions of ultimate concern become cloudy and irrelevant in my escape to September myopia.

I concentrate just on what is here in front of me now, understanding less of what I see the closer I move until I reduce geography to my unfocused inner eye; there everything is present and porous and connected. Then I lose control of transcendence and destiny. Blinded by the world so close, I foil the receding glow of the Big Bang and linear time. I curl up and ride dizzy and undone on the foggy, spinning radii of seasons.

It has taken me half a lifetime of searching to realize that the likeliest path to the ultimate ground leads through my local ground. I mean the land itself, with its creeks and rivers, its weather, seasons, stone outcroppings, and all the plants and animals that share it. I cannot have a spiritual center without having a geographical one: I cannot live a grounded life without being grounded in a certain place.

Scott Russell Sanders

September 6th
The 249th Day of the Year

Our seasons have no fixed returns,
Without our will they come and go;
At noon our sudden summer burns,
Ere sunset all is snow.

James Russell Lowell

Sunrise/set: 6:07/6:59
Day's Length: 12 hours 52 min
Average High/Low: 80/59
Average Temperature: 69
Record High: 101 – 1954
Record Low: 41 – 1962

The Daily Weather

Statistically, this is one of the three driest days of September, with only a 15 percent chance of rain (the tenth and the 28th are the other two days). Highs are in the 90s on 15 percent of the afternoons, in the 80s on 45 percent, 70s twenty-five percent, 60s 15 percent. Today is the first day of the season on which there is a five percent chance of light frost. And, for the first time since June 11th, the likelihood of early morning temperatures below 60 degrees rises above 55 percent.

Natural Calendar

Bees are awkward and stiff in the cool mornings. Sometimes on sunny days, woolly bear caterpillars wander the warm blacktop back roads in search of winter habitat. Kingbirds, finches, woodcocks, bobolinks, cedar waxwings, ruddy ducks, snow geese, herring gulls, and yellow-bellied sapsuckers migrate. Great flocks of Canadian geese sometimes gather to feed in pastures. Smaller flocks sometimes fly over the village, honking. The last young grackles and hummingbirds leave their nests.

Daybook

1984: To the Vale: Goldenrod early full, some still not blooming. Great blue lobelia full, full white snakeroot. Some spotted touch-me-nots are fading. Purple-leafed willow herb discovered, heal-all gone to seed. A few fleabane noticed, a few last wild lettuce. Thin-leafed coneflower holds, and a few soapwort. First white asters are in bloom, *Aster pilosus*. Tall bellflower falling apart. Field thistle declining. Boneset hanging on. Giant yellow hyssop done. Bees awkward and slow this cool morning.

1987: Two carp caught, one at 8:30 this morning, another 15 minutes later. Through the village, tree colors shifting steadily. The ash by my Wilberforce window suddenly has a large patch of yellow. Three pale orange woolly bear caterpillars were crawling across Grinnell Road when I drove through at 10:30 a.m. Only one katydid heard last night.

1989: Woolly bears suddenly become come common. Most of them are quite dark this year. Low purple aster, *Novi-belgii,* blooms in the garden.

1990: Heavy fog, then a high in the 90s. Seems like the hottest day of the summer. No woolly bears so far this year.

1992: Clear decline in the coreopsis now, and a quick decay in the rudbeckia along the south wall. The purple coneflowers are already way past their prime. Cicadas louder than I've heard them for a while, and the crickets and katydids after dark are shrill.

1993: One more balloon flower blooms. Stonecrop past its prime. Only Evadine, with her tall Jerusalem artichokes, has much of a September garden in town now.

1995: At the triangle park, the box elder leaves have rusted steadily for a few weeks. Now the summer's breakdown is more obvious than just a few days ago. Every few feet of foliage has a small patch of brown. Today, the biggest change, the first couple of red maple leaves turned overnight.

1997: In the south garden, a third of the showy coneflowers withered. Ruby Nicholson called, told me that a nest of hummingbirds had two babies in it, ready to fly away.

1999: Showy coneflowers are almost gone, the last holding on with the tattered white phlox and a few petunias and heliopsis. Crows at 5:50 a.m.

2000: The prairie dock at the corner of High and South College streets has only a few flowers left. First daddy longlegs in the bathroom, even though the weather has been summer-like.

2002: Doves and jays at 6:30 this morning, cardinals at 6:45 – sleeping late as is their fall custom. Spicebush swallowtails, sulphurs, monarchs in the zinnias today.

2003: Cardinal, wren and robin this morning a little after 6:00. Blue jay calling while we were eating breakfast about 7:30.

2004: Crows at 5:50 this morning, doves about a half hour later. No other birds heard. Warm and clear all day, the sky extraordinarily blue. One monarch came to the yard off and on throughout the afternoon, ignored the zinnias, chose the dahlias. Two bright chartreuse Osage fruits fell by the shed last night. Squirrels continue to chatter throughout the day, a common sound of Late Summer and Early Fall.

2007: A cardinal sang at 5:51 a.m. and continued for several minutes. No other early birdsong. Pollen remains on the goldenrod in the alley. One black walnut tree near the church is almost completely bare. Acorns are down all around one red oak tree. Mateo's Jerusalem artichokes have small buds, buds on mine too. One New England aster opening along the north garden wall.

2008: One New England aster opened this afternoon, and gold

centers noticed on the beggarticks. One monarch seen, one bright yellow, large sulphur butterfly, one tiger swallowtail, one painted lady (*Cynthia*).

2009: Crow at 5:46 a.m., cardinal at 5:50, moon half an hour from setting, yard half dark. Moya's gallardias have faded.

2010: Cool and light overcast this mornings. Crows were the first to call today, 6:47. One cardinal five minutes later. And that was it for birdsong. Hummingbirds were feeding at 7:20. and the first yellow tiger swallowtail came to the butterfly bushes at 7:40. At 8:00, we found a large hawkmoth, a female *Celerio lineata* on the front door screen. A small bowl of raspberries picked and a few peaches gathered for breakfast, both fruits in their last week. About 10:00, we went out to the porch to watch the dozens of skippers (silver-spotted and small golden and brown ones), a monarch, two male tiger swallowtails, a brown, a common sulphur and cabbage butterflies. The hummingbirds came by every few minutes, the cardinals and sparrows feeding, too. The female hummingbird is coming by and forth so often, we think she probably has a nest (like in 1997). New England asters are budded now, one scraggly red hibiscus flower hanging on. Along the highways, the false boneset is in full bloom, still mostly budded in the yard, and the sunflower field north of town is in full bloom. Patty called this evening, about the same time as last year, asking about what could be blooming and causing her allergies to suddenly come in. I told her maybe goldenrod.

2011: Very cool and cloudy this morning, tree crickets trilling steadily. Three chipping cardinals came to the feeder at 6:00, two females and a male. Crows called at the edge of town at 6:02. A few "churr" sounds from a wren and one melodious cardinal song at about 6:30. The cool front having come through, the sparrows are feeding heavily. Full crickets tonight, in spite of fog and cool temperatures, and - after being absent for several nights - Gerard's katydid was singing in the dark.

2012: Bob from the *News* reports a perfect "V" of white geese flying to the northeast at about 7:30 this morning. Could have been snow geese at the edge of their migration area. In the sun of the afternoon, the zinnias are full of butterflies again, a giant and a yellow tiger, a great spangled fritillary and many, many painted ladies and checkerspots and admirals and whites. The frog continues to meditate by the edge of the pond throughout the day. At 8:00 in the evening, katydids, field crickets, tree frogs, and pulsing, whistling crickets, steady tree crickets.

2013: Crows at 6:00 this morning, perfect September schedule. A number of orange-gold leaves on the maples along High Street. Bittersweet berries not turning yet in the alley.

2014: Ruminations today: Since the past experience of natural history tells the present, it is easy to confuse the years or simply combine them, making all Septembers the same, one September. That blend of days and events is a kind of quantum travel which defies linear as well as circular boundaries, allows one to go backwards or forwards in time, suspended on the color of a leaf or the blooming of a flower.

And with such a radial experience that transcends leaves and petals, it is not so very difficult to see past individuality and local time and place, see through them with people as well as with seasons. Repetition blurs the ego's hold on experience. It enhances and augments affection and personal history, compounds the unique and unrepeatable until opposites combine and make sense and smooth the abrupt chasms between one love and life and another. And I look ahead: if I would be alive in 2040, age 100, would all these days seem even more the same, or would they be marked too deeply by anniversaries, climate change or war or sickness, by deaths in the family. Would life's winter alter my sense of all the seasons and events, erasing or magnifying differences in perception? Here, I hold tight to the security I have: leaves, flowers, birds, butterflies.

2015: Heat wave continues. Monarchs here through the day, more than I've seen here any day this summer, and an Eastern Black swallowtail, silver-spotted skippers, cabbage whites in randori, a golden sulphur. In the north garden, the thick bloom of knotweed suddenly wilts.

2016: Just a little time in the garden: One painted lady, one great spangled fritillary, numerous silver-spotted skippers.

2017: One monarch seen, when I was in the garden for just a few minutes.

2018: Hurricane Gordon comes ashore in Alabama, heads north. In Yellow Springs, Jerusalem artichokes and yellow coneflowers are still in full bloom, but the small-flowered coneflowers that dominated the late August gardens have mostly disappeared.

2019: Hurricane Dorian pummels the Outer Banks. A red-shouldered hawk called from the back locust trees after the sun came up. No monarchs, skippers or swallowtails today. The first buds on the New England asters, first beggartick flower near the zinnias. Climbing false buckwheat (*Fallopia scandens*) curled in bloom around the gray milkweed stalks. At Ellis this afternoon, I found that *Bidens cernua*, the nodding bur marigold, had opened while we were in New York. In the pathway beside the arboretum, I found *Galinsoga quadriradiata,* a kind of quickweed, in full flower, along with dense patches of a speedwell-type of groundcover I couldn't identify,

2020: A flock of honking geese flew over the house a little after sunrise, the first flock of the season, announcing fall. On my early walk with Ranger, I found an Osage fruit, almost full size, on the sidewalk. In the morning zinnias, not a single butterfly, in spite of the sun. At noon, a great spangled fritillary and many silver-spotted skippers, and then a tattered Eastern black swallowtail, all of which stayed and foraged for hours. But the garden still seemed empty without the tiger swallowtails and monarchs.

2023: Time count: 23 canna blossoms. A few raspberries reddening in the north garden, To Pearl Fen in the afternoon: cup plants to seed there, but Jerusalem artichokes, goldenrods, jewelweed, boneset, field thistles, ironweed, wingstem, black-eyed Susans, aging Joe Pye weed and more were in full flower, the whole fen covered in flowers. Two monarchs and an Eastern black swallowtail smothered in goldenrod. Tonight, masses of katydids and tree crickets and ground crickets and field crickets and tree frogs filling up the space around with a wave after wave a of sound. Casey left a phone message: a large white egret (immature Small Blue Heron) seen feeding near Ellis Pond.

Like the trees, we had to let each new year shape, teach, and renew us until our unconscious habits fell like autumn leaves to the forest floor, and new, more conscious ways of doing things sprouted in their place.

Ken Carey

September 7th
The 250th Day of the Year

Out of the west the wind comes over,
over the yellow goldenrod,
over the drying rattle-box pod,
comes heady with corn and apple smell now.

August Derleth

Sunrise/set: 6:08/6:57
Day's Length: 12 hours 49 minutes
Average High/Low: 80/58
Average Temperature: 69
Record High: 99 – 1899
Record Low: 42 – 1962

The Daily Weather

Today is usually sunny or partly cloudy with little chance of frost. Totally overcast conditions occur only once or twice every two decades, and rain comes just 25 percent of all the years. Highs are in the 70s on 40 percent of the afternoons, in the 80s on 50 percent; there is just a five percent chance of an afternoon above 90 or below 70. Lows remain in the 60s four nights out of ten.

Natural Calendar

Wild cherries have disappeared from their branches. Squirrels scatter buckeye hulls along the trails; locust pods fall beside them. The rich scent of Late Summer pollen is almost gone by end of the week, replaced by the pungent odor of fallen apples and peaches and leaves.

The sweet potato harvest has begun in North Carolina, the potato harvest in Wisconsin, the peanut and sorghum harvest in South Carolina. Farmers are cutting corn for silage all across the nation's midsection, cutting spring oats and wheat in Wyoming, cutting spring barley in California, cutting hay in Alaska, bringing in tobacco throughout the South and the Border States.

Daybook

1983: Mill Habitat: One tall bellflower holds, and some purple-flowered wild lettuce. Spider webs everywhere, the river low and collecting leaves and scum. New wood mint grows back around the tall stems of its July flowers. Dead grass droops over the henbit. Wingstem is strong throughout, clustered snakeroot turning yellow, boneset past its prime, agrimony gone to seed. Touch-me-nots burst when lightly squeezed. Blue jays loud, common.

1985: Wild cherries purple and falling at Clifton.

1986: Robin calls increasing, migratory staccato. Cardinals quiet. Crickets still very loud at night.

1987: Crows in the back trees this morning. Robins give their clucking migration song.

1988: First small white asters found at South Glen. Wingstem past its prime, ironweed, oxeye, showy coneflowers still all right.

1989: First beggarticks bloom in the yard; a few last raspberries against the rose of Sharon.

1991: Squirrels and blue jays loud this afternoon.

1992: Crows passed through, stayed in the back locusts for half an hour in the late morning, left for the afternoon; then a flock of about twenty flew over just after eight o'clock this evening. Even more rapid decline now of the coneflowers at the south wall, hardly any left. The very last purple loosestrife today.

1993: At Wilberforce, my ash tree is completely green, having lost its yellow patches! I've never seen it so resilient.

1995: This week the asters have bloomed in the garden, the small-flowered ones and the purple New England asters. The fleabane is lush among the mums. The showy coneflowers are two-thirds gone, but the blue spiderwort keeps blossoming. Most yarrow heads are black. The very last purple loosestrife disappeared today.

A shower of black walnut leaves brought me a sequence of impressions that occupied my mind for most of the day. The images included the elm trees outside the window of my boyhood room, my father working in the yard, my mother in the kitchen, the smell of bread baking, the forced air heat on my skin in the mornings, walks to school in the cold, hunting squirrels, feelings of comfort and regret, nostalgia, sadness, contentment. I saw my autobiography in falling leaves: courtships, incidents with friends and lovers, flashes of success and failure, twinges of old restlessness, old longing.

I didn't hear cardinals calling today, but blue jays were loud this afternoon. Crows passed through the yard, stayed in the back locusts for half an hour in the late morning, left for the afternoon; then a flock of about twenty flew over just after seven o'clock this evening.

1997: Some of the Queen Anne's lace leaves have turned dusky red. The achillea of the north garden has died completely back, only a few in bloom, but foliage is returning. Showy coneflowers in the south garden now half gone. Pond plants are deteriorating, and the purple loosestrife is done for the year; the water lettuce has shrunk to maybe a fourth of its summer size, as have the hyacinths. The pickerel plant stopped blooming a month ago; its seeds have fallen into the water, and only half its long stems and leaves remain. The green frog croaked once yesterday or the day before. Now silence.

2000: Screech owl heard in the back woods at 7:17 p.m.

2001: The pieces of autumn continue to fit into place, the growing robin migration, the occasional showers of leaves becoming more frequent, the first goldenrod rusting, the particles of second spring (the resurgence of April wildflower foliage) increasing. Each fragment is an increment on the gauge of the year, measuring the relationship of the earth to the sun, and my relationship to the place in which I live. None of the notes or observations seems irrelevant; each moment of awareness, like each physical particle observed, is a seasonal cell, similar to a holographic segment, containing the psychic and cosmic whole.

2002: The warm and humid morning silent until 5:48. Then, a blue jay, two minutes later a cardinal.

2003: Monarchs, skippers, and a new generation of cabbage butterflies all day in the garden, but swallowtails have diminished. Goldfinches came to the nodding sunflowers late in the morning, the second day I've seen them. Did they come for the sunflowers, or are they on their way south? Three forsythia flowers seen in the front east garden.

2005: North on the bike path: Spots of yellow on honeysuckles, black walnut trees and locusts, fallen leaves scattered on the path, powdered by the tires of the bikers. Only a few flowers: a few tall goldenrod, great blue lobelia, orange touch-me-not, white snakeroot. One soybean field completely turned a rich burnt sienna, another field mostly green and gold. Cabbage butterflies throughout the ride, one dark swallowtail, one painted lady (Cynthia). A groundhog was about to cross the way, saw me and retreated. Throughout town, late hostas hold their flowers, white and violet. The cutback pink spirea continues to bloom in the south garden. The New England aster buds are showing color but are not opening yet.

2006: To Kidron in northeast Ohio today. Goldenrod steadily coming in, and the soybean fields, still so solid green a week or so ago, are starting to turn. Very few Judas maples or other trees changing.

2008: Crows near 6:00 this morning, one cardinal and doves about 7:00. A hummingbird moth came to the circle garden even before the sun came over the tree line. Blue jay off and on, and more dove calls later in the morning. The small-flowered asters have prominent buds now. Five deep golden leaves on one of Don's serviceberry trees. Two monarchs seen in the back yard. Three crows along Limestone Street when I walked Bella toward the park this evening. Jays heard, too.

2009: Dark aphids on the sow thistle in the alley, flushed burning bush. One tattered monarch in the dahlias, one hummingbird in the butterfly bush. Very last large red hibiscus flowered today.

2010: Pleiades overhead at 5:00 a.m., autumn moving into the morning. Crows early at 5:38, a cardinal at 5:48, crows continuing until about 6:00. The hummingbird was back every few minutes starting about 6:45, and the first monarch and yellow tiger swallowtail were on the butterfly bushes by the time sun just touched the upper flowers a little before 7:00. Skippers out in force again through the day, but I found one dead in the cup of a zinnia leaf – the beginning of the end for this brood?

2012: Just a short time outside: the last pink tea rose picked, the first New England aster opening nearby, butterflies all about the zinnias.

2013: The shed orb-weaver is back with a new web. A brief walk this morning, a dove, a blue jay and a cardinal off and on. No swallowtails seen today when I worked outside for two hours. First quince fruit found floating in the pond.

2014: Sun and quite cool, a major high-pressure system arriving over night. Inventory: A handful of violet phlox, full bloom tall goldenrod, very early New England asters, zinnias and Knockout roses very strong, Jeanie's yellow and red tea roses continue to produce blossoms, the dahlias and the ragged cosmos and heliopsis and a couple of Anna Belle hydrangea clusters in the southwest corner of the garden continuing to bring light and color to that area, the false boneset and the virgin's bower and the small clump of Shasta daisies holding, the red amaranth still orange, a few blossoms left on the knotweed, the giant hibiscus still making pink flowers, the ironweed falling across the spent Joe Pye, the late-planted gladioli starting to produce deep purple and red flowers, a long-jawed orb-weaver across the west end of the pond, Moya's moon flower still opening, her white-flowered hostas in decline now, and Peggy's Limelight hydrangea tinted green, outlasting all the hostas. The young sweet-cherry tree is shedding a few yellow leaves. Butterflies in the sun: cabbage whites, one azure, several painted ladies, one great spangled fritillary, a glimpse of a black swallowtail. Chickadees and house sparrows and gold finches and nuthatches and cardinals and hummingbirds feeding. Red aphids still at the heliopsis. Tonight: thunderous crickets at so many tones and levels, counterpoint by screaming katydids under the bright, bright full moon at perigee.

2015: A rare day in the low 90s. Everything so bright and clear. More monarchs. Judy writes from Goshen, Indiana, 200 miles northwest of here: "We're in that time of year when the evergreens take on a blackish hue and the mulleins are fading in the tall grass around the pond. Our marigolds are hanging in there in their pots, but the petunias are headed for the trashcan on Wednesday. The deck petunias succumbed to the aggressive potato vines that were planted with them—too many vines for the delicate flowers. Next year, grasses on the deck, and some sturdy New Zealand impatiens. I love my King Tut in the front, but he takes an enormous amount of water—I think the plant is related to papyrus. I have three lovely moonflower plants grown from last year's seed (gave one to Nancy). I adore the way they simply appear late at night and then trumpet through the day. I'm certainly ready to stop watering every day, though. Three months is enough. It's good fall is coming."

2016: The huge field of snowflowers north of town is still in full flower, people clustering there with their cameras. Skippers continue to dominate in the garden, one painted lady seen, too, but no swallowtails noticed today. I did see an albino squirrel ran toward the pine grove at Ellis Pond. A report from Rick and Ali about seeing four nighthawks during the day. They also told about how they have sometimes seen nighthawks flocking around the lights at Early Fall night soccer games at the high school.

2019: Few butterflies today, only one monarch at Moya's and one tiger swallowtail passing through the zinnias at home. One scorpion fly seen on the canna lily foliage. Geese flew over the west end of town around 9:00 this evening as we walked home from the movie. No large, fat orb-weavers found in the yard yet this fall.

2020: To Keuka Lake in New York: the landscape dominated by goldenrod, color and quantity intensifying the deeper we came into western New York. Many central Ohio soybean fields were turning. Great banks of Japanese knotweed in bloom along the southern highway. Occasional Judas maples, patches of rusting hillsides. At the lake, goldenrod, sundrops, rudbeckia, some white snakeroot, purple loosestrife, small white asters, chicory, yellow sow thistles. Before we arrived, a freak storm or thermocline disturbance ripped away Chris's boat and destroyed a neighbor's dock. By evening, the water was smooth. In southern California, record heat parallels runaway wildfires. In the Rockies, deep cold and up to a foot of snow. In the Atlantic, several storms are forming.

2022: Robin peeping in the honeysuckles this morning. California bakes under record 100 - 115 degree heat.

2023: Time count: 23 canna blossoms.

Just think of the illimitable abundance and the marvelous loveliness of light, or of the beauty of the sun and moon and stars.

St. Augustine

September 8th
The 251st Day of the Year

The physical domain of the country had its counterpart in me. The trails I made led outward into the hills and swamps, but they led inward also. And from the study of things underfoot, and from reading and thinking, came a kind of exploration of myself and the land. In time the two became one in my mind.

John Haines

Sunrise/set: 6:09/6:56
Day's Length: 12 hours 47 minutes
Average High/Low: 79/58
Average Temperature: 69
Record High: 98 – 1900
Record Low: 42 – 1898

The Daily Weather

September 8th is typically a sunny day with only a five to ten percent chance of completely cloudy conditions. Thundershowers, however, occur 30 percent of the time. Today's highs: five percent chance of 90s, forty percent for 80s, fifty percent for 70s, and five percent for 60s. Evening are pleasant, with lows in the 50s half the time, in the 60s the other half.

The Weather in the Week Ahead

Early Fall arrives along the 40th Parallel during the second week of September. Average highs fall below 80, and normal nighttime lows move below 60 until the second week of June. Chances of highs in the 90s hold at less than ten percent each day this week, the first time that has happened since the end of May. Highs in the cold 60s occur another ten percent of the time (with the possibility of 50s for the first time since June 4th), with 70s and 80s sharing the remaining 80 percent. The rainiest days this week are historically the 9th and the 12th, each having a 40 percent chance of showers. The other days of the period carry about half those odds. Frost is rare at this stage of September, but chances of a light freeze increase to ten percent on the 13th and 14th as the third high pressure system of the month comes through.

The Natural Calendar

Early Fall brings puffball mushrooms to the woods. Goldenrod, asters and Jerusalem artichokes dominate the garden, but most berries are gone from the wild cherry; berries are red on the silver olives, orange on the American mountain ash, purple on the pokeweed.

Cobwebs seem to be everywhere in the woods, and the number of butterflies swells in the garden: coppers, blues, monarchs, swallowtails, skippers, painted ladies. When the days are cool, the cicadas are quiet. On the colder nights, the katydids refuse to chant and the frogs are silent.

The Feed Outlook for Wild Game

Standing corn will tempt wildlife in many areas through the end of October, but the percentage of feed available from cultivated crops declines at the rate of approximately two percent per day beginning at the end of September.

Acorns increase in importance for whitetail deer between the first week of October and the first week of November. White oak acorns are typically consumed first, then the deer move on to the red oak acorns – some of their favorite autumn treats.

Wildflowers and grasses usually stop flowering by the middle of September, and nourishing seeds will be forming during autumn throughout fields and woods. Among the most common wildflower food, the nutlets of the goldenrod attract deer, especially after acorns are gone. Cranberries are popular as long as they last, and wetlands often provide other options for late fall feeding. Roadside foraging becomes extremely lean in November and December; early sprouting winter wheat, however, could bring deer to those tender green shoots well into the cooler months. Staghorn sumac fruit clusters stand out after leaf fall and can also be very attractive to game.

Daybook

1985. Covered Bridge: monarchs common, grackles in the trees, and crows along the river, cicadas constant. Steady trickle of leaves, some gathering in the backwaters of the quiet river. Most of the sycamore bark has fallen; the trunks are white and slick, ready for winter. Red Virginia creeper outlines some of the trees. Sassafras is weathering to a pale green-gold. Some boneset leaves are brown, willow herb almost gone. First blooms on the swamp beggarticks and zigzag goldenrod. Cobwebs everywhere. Second spring's catchweed blooming. Four huge puffballs found along the hillside on the way to Far Prairie, where the trillium and bluebells were strongest in April. Next year's purple deadnettle is sprouting just off the path. At Wilberforce, leaves are falling from my ash.

1986: Cold morning. Rich Late Summer scent is gone, replaced by the crisp scent of fall. Robins calling steadily outside the back door.

1987: Box elders browning. Maples deepening. Fogs increasing. Heavy odor of fall, of apples and leaves. Cicadas seem to be gone.

1989: Knotweed done along the roadsides. Goldenrod still early full.

1991: Bittersweet on sale at the nursery; and I cut some orange berry clusters from a vine along Jacoby Road. Twelve sparrows at the bird bath all at once today. Three robins later in the evening. Geese fly over at 6:31 p.m.

1993: No robins these quiet mornings. Finally the last balloon flower wilts, its season of one or two blooms ending after weeks of fragile survival. Mimosa tree done blooming at Wilberforce, probably complete near the end of August. Autumn crocus noticed full bloom in front of the brown house across the street.

1996: This is the second week of Early Fall. There is no longer any question Late Summer is gone. The number of trees turning and the number of colors in the canopy have increased day by day since the end of August, the steady accumulation of change actually countable. On August 27th, I went out into back yard and saw one large yellow mulberry leaf on the grass, the first of the season. The next day, there were two, the next day none, the next day three, and now there are new mulberry leaves every morning, so many I have stopped counting.

1997: The first New England aster opened today along the south border.

1999: On the way to the back shed, I walked through my first flurry of box elder leaves this morning.

2000: Autumn crocus full bloom across the street. Another spider in the bathroom.

2001: Katydids chanting until about 4:30 this morning. Cardinal sang briefly at 5:57. Almost all the coneflowers – purple cones and summer Susans – gone. A little more yellow seen in the cottonwoods along the way to Columbus.

2002: Cardinal at 5:55 a.m., blue jay at 6:15. Stillness and heat. Whenever there was a slight breeze: showers of locust leaves. Another perfect butterfly day: dozens of skippers, cabbage moths, several monarchs, four spicebush swallowtails, one tiger swallowtail. Virgin's bower started to blossom (its first year) on the trellis. The violet *Aster hybridium* reached early bloom, as did the New England asters.

2003: Monarchs and cabbage butterflies common today. Finches came to the sunflowers again.

2004: Hurricane Frances brought light rain all day, its giant anticyclone spinning lazily up the Appalachians.

2005: Tropical storm Ophelia threatens the east coast of Florida today. Last of the peaches brought in at home.

2006: Crickets and katydids were singing at 2:00 a.m. A screech owl woke me up at 4:30. In the woods with Bella this morning: the wingstem was maybe a third completed, and many plants in the shade were falling over into the path, too stalky perhaps from the canopy. No robin calls. At home, sitting on the porch, I heard cicadas and saw one monarch on the ironweed (monarchs have been abundant so far this fall), but the small folded-wing butterflies no longer play in the sun. Ironweed is beginning to go to seed along the north wall. In the pond, one arrowhead flower remains. Only a few Shasta daisies and black-eyed Susans are left, but the large Royal Standard hostas are still in full bloom. All the peaches are down.

2007: Three New England asters now open along the garden wall, the virgin's bower reaching early full flower. Three of Mateo's small white asters have blossomed overnight. Tall goldenrod is in full bloom. Great ragweed lost its pollen in the rain last night. Thin-leafed coneflowers are making a swift decline. A squirrel chattered in the trees late this morning as we sat out with our tea. Tropical storm Gabrielle moves toward the Outer Banks. This afternoon, riding to Springfield, I noticed how much ochre had appeared in the box elders and the cottonwoods. A few maples had turned, and one cottonwood was almost bare.

2008: The alley's tall coneflowers are done now. Mateo's goldenrod and Mrs. Timberlake's roses anchor the south end of the block, a few purple bindweed hold to the east fence, but their full bloom has passed, and the small white bindweeds may have disappeared completely. The apples continue to fall, fruit fat and red and green. No birdsong heard this morning. Small folded-wing butterflies speed back and forth in the north garden in the cool sunlight. Peaches seem to be ripening normally, relatively few dropping; I picked one for breakfast this morning – medium firm and very sweet. In the park, the hawthorn berries have lost their pollen.

2009: Four tall coneflowers left in the alley. Purple morning glories dominate the east fencerows. Goldenrod early full. One cardinal at 6:03 a.m. Skunk odor a little earlier. Two young female finches begging for food from a bright golden father on top of the finch feeder this morning. Lilac losing leaves, white berries on the panicled dogwood, black walnut and redbuds yellowing, orb-weaver by the back shed, white autumn crocus full bloom as last hibiscus flowers fall. High season of honeysuckle berries. Hummingbird seen at the butterfly bush.

2010: Only crows before dawn this morning, the first time I've heard no cardinals or robins. And at the butterfly bushes, two monarchs but no swallowtails seen (for the first time in weeks), and the skippers were greatly diminished in number. At dusk, a small flock of blackbirds flew over, going southwest, only crows calling vespers in the neighborhood.

2011: Tree and field crickets in the cloudy, misty morning. Sparrows feeding heavily, but no cardinals singing. To Goshen, Indiana in the afternoon, rainy and cool. At night, katydids and field crickets were loud, none of the katydid hesitancy I heard in Yellow Springs the past few nights.

2013: The orb-weaver repaired his web overnight, was waiting for me this morning. Another orb-weaver has set up its web in the dooryard garden. Crows at 7:00 again. Walking Bella at 7:30, I heard distant cardinals, a few robin peeps, and clucks from the Limestone Street chickens. Cicadas were loud by 8:00. In the yard, peaches are just about gone, yellow jackets eating the last ones fallen to the grass. At Ellis Pond, a great poison ivy plant, clusters of dirty-white seeds prominent, winding up a gnarly red mulberry tree, and hickory nuts are almost all on the ground. One brown butterfly noticed on the zinnias, but only one male tiger swallowtail seen today, his wings pale and tattered.

2015: Six monarchs on the tithonias in the northeast garden – the first time ever this many all at once!

2016: One monarch (maybe two), one great spangled fritillary, numerous silver-spotted skippers – some mating. Bittersweet berries still not blushing in the east redbud tree. Rick wrote this evening about finding firefly larvae glowing in the grass. He thought at first they might be ant lion larvae, but they are more likely part of a firefly cycle.

2018: Rains from Hurricane Gordon reach Yellow Springs today, heavy precipitation throughout the afternoon. Geese flew over in the evening twilight.

2019: Geese honking around 7:00 this morning. Several young cardinals at the feeder as we sat with our coffee, and several hummingbirds competed for nectar. When I went out to the garden in the afternoon, a saw half a dozen monarchs all over the zinnias and tithonias, the most I've ever seen. On the way to the Indian mound, we saw soybean fields in early turn. A huge murmuration of starlings swarmed a far pasture as we drove back. Katydids started to call at 7:25 this evening.

2020: Keuka Lake in New York: Jill and I saw crews getting ready to harvest grapes into long, wide, wooden boxes, the harvest just beginning.

2021: One tiger swallowtail in the castor beans today, one hackberry butterfly. The tall goldenrod in the yard is finally opening, just as the first New England asters are starting to bloom. In the green wall of vegetation that looms above the garden (maybe 12 feet above the zinnias), the honeysuckle berries are red and orange. The pokeweed berries are black and starting to wither now, the purple stems wrinkled and flabby. The petals of the Japanese knotweed flowers, once so lush and attracting so many bees, are twisting and browning. The most dramatic drapery of the wall, the prickly common hop, with its pale green overlapping bracts, creates an ornamental patchwork in the dense foliage. The dainty white clusters of the climbing false buckwheat with their winged calices twine throughout, reaching into the weathered tree-of-heaven leaves.

2022: The same inventory as last year. And I add, one small pumpkin and two small gourds, a few gladiola flowers, cup plants still blooming but wrapped with false buckwheat and gourd vines, the phlox holding on behind the hedges of New England asters (not blooming), a couple of canna lilies flowering, but most just foliage plants now, a few Maximillian sunflowers peering from behind the phlox, one patch of the garden fresh with new goldenrod, three New England aster flowers and new beggarticks, the spiderwort leaves growing back thin and sparse, the Autumn Joy sedum in full rich flower along the back porch, the spindly wild lettuce (*Lactuca canadensis*) varieties, some grown up to the gutters, starting to seed, the volunteer red castor beans giving needed brightness where the gladiolas failed, the tall green castors six to twelve feet tall, saving the garden from its September tangle.

2023: Time count: 22 canna blossoms. Casey reports another egret sighting.

Here
is what I want to know. Here
is what I am trying to say.

Wendell Berry

September 9th
The 252nd Day of the Year

How rich in color, before the big show of the tree foliage has commenced, our roadsides are in places in early autumn, -- rich to the eye that goes hurriedly by and does not look too closely, -- with the profusion of goldenrod and blue and purple asters dashed in upon here and there with the crimson leaves of the dwarf sumac.

John Burroughs

Sunrise/set: 6:10/6:54
Day's Length: 12 hours 44 minutes
Average High/Low: 79/58
Average Temperature: 69
Record High: 99 – 1900
Record Low: 39 – 1883

The Daily Weather

Odds for rain are higher today (40 percent chance) than at any time in the first third of September. Still, the sun comes out 90 percent of the days; and highs reach 90 ten percent of the afternoons, reach 80 on 35 percent, and 70 on 55 percent. Frost is quite unlikely through the 12th, but nighttime lows drop below 60 one night in two.

Natural Calendar

The landmarks of August continue to disappear. In warm years, the late trefoils and wild cucumbers are already gone. Burdock and ragweed are decaying. Joe Pye weed has lost its color. Boneset is past its prime. Japanese knotweed blossoms darken and fall. Field thistles go to seed. The blooms of the giant yellow hyssop have wilted. The great flowers of the American lotus disappear. Resurrection lilies have collapsed, and coneflowers are in full retreat.

After the sky becomes dark, Delphinus, the Dolphin swims due south. Above it, near the North Star, Cepheus is between Cassiopeia (to the east) and Draco (to the west). Just below the southeastern corner of Cepheus, the star cluster of Lacerta lies in the Milky Way. The Big Dipper is low in the north, and the Milky Way dominates the night, Cygnus, Lyra, and Aquila, the constellations of the Summer Triangle, forming its brightest stars. At dawn, Orion stands in the middle of the southern sky; bright Capella shines high above him. Regulus, the spring planting star, approaches from the east in Leo.

Daybook

1983: South Glen. Touch-me-not pods explode now when I tap them with my fingernail, the plants and flowers old. Beggarticks, white snakeroot, yellow hyssop, goosefoot, horseweed, clearweed, smartweed, and goldenrod full bloom. *Solidago tenuifolia* identified, the slender-leaved goldenrod. The trefoils are completely done. Great ragweed has lost its pollen, and many of the wingstem and ironweed plants have passed their prime. A few bouncing bets, a few great mullein flowers, one moth mullein, some daisy fleabane, lobelias, a little catnip left. Slippery elms tuning yellow brown, poplars fading, some Virginia creeper is red. Hops clusters heavy. Most berries gone from the wild cherry. Migrating cedar waxwings seen along the river. Damselflies still here, butterflies everywhere: swallowtails, monarchs, blues, coppers. Geese flew over about 3:00 this afternoon.

1986: Robins calling, short peeps; they're sending signals back and forth. Cicadas quiet.

1988: When the woolly-bear caterpillars finally showed up this year, they were dark, some reddish, others black or brown. Last year's winter a mild, dry one after a September of lightly colored caterpillars. At South Glen, only a few tall bellflowers left.

1989: Light morning rain, robins clucking, crickets strong. A squirrel that lives in the back trees started its autumn calls at 8:00. Along the shore of Caesar Creek, the trees still not turning. Locusts have browned, but the shoreline is green. Arrowhead has gone to seed, big heads the size of acorns. American lotus mostly gone.

Beggarticks, large and small, are in full bloom along the beaches and on log habitats. On the way south to the lake, fields and waysides full of bright helianthus. Peaches have all fallen in the yard. The blue Asiatic dayflowers are growing weaker.

1991: Geese fly over the house honking at 8:05 this morning. At the Covered Bridge, a whole field of wingstem is done flowering. Asters and goldenrod full. Heavy odor of September, spice of seeds and decaying foliage. Gray stalks of garlic mustard and summer brome scattered, tipped like straw from the wind. River down lower than even in the drought of 1988, bottom visible all along the path. Swamp beggarticks and orange jewelweed full. Three-seeded mercury is reddening. Sedum reappears in the undergrowth, stalky from the canopied summer. Empty buckeye hulls along the trail. Locust pods common. Some ash and cottonwoods have lost nearly all their leaves. Elm and sycamore leaves on the low pebble shoreline at Far Hole. Dozens of fruits down under one Osage. Purple deadnettle sprouting, new sweet Cicely. Crickets loud. I walk through showers of ash leaves. Blue jays restless, noisy all the way from the bridge to Jacoby, apparently migrating. Caught in the rain, I crossed the river at the shallows north of the canoe launch, holed up at the Jacoby outhouse, and then set out again back through the showers of rain and acorns and buckeye hulls and leaves.

1993: Geese fly over at 6:30 a.m. Tall coneflowers noticed almost done at the corner of High and Limestone.

1995: Walking Buttercup down Limestone Street at dusk, Jeanie and I saw two or three dozen robins feeding, calling, flying back and forth in the long yard next to McKee's. The full autumn flocking has begun.

1996: The asters planted from seed in the spring have passed their best now, but they've brought pinks, whites and violets to the south garden since August.

1997: Cloudy rainy morning, temperature in the low 60s. No bird song, only crickets.

1998: Sparrows chattering this morning early in the pear trees downtown. The mother-in-law's tongue is full bloom in the greenhouse.

1999: Along the bike path, the jewelweed is wilting from drought. Ragweed is dry and empty, leaves crackle underneath my wheels. The canopy is thinning overhead. Ironweed is finished in the yard. In the Caribbean, Hurricane Floyd moves towards the East Coast as the hurricane season reaches its center.

2000: Half the leaves gone from our front maple, the most precocious of the High Street trees.

2001: At 5:35 this morning, a single repeated call, probably from a blue jay. Then at 5:40, full jay vocalizations. No other birds until a cardinal sang close to 6:00, then more jays. Then silence, then clucking and chattering from a squirrel and maybe starlings. No doves heard today.

2002: A long, bright day for butterflies: sulphurs, monarchs, skippers, swallowtails. One golden finch: still summer.

2003: Morning fog, the smell of autumn, fallen leaves. A cardinal sang at 5:50 a.m., then wrens took over.

2005: To South Glen with Mike: The woods is wearing out. More than half of the wingstem has completed its cycle, ironweed far less common. Under the canopy, the rich green glades of wood nettle are losing their color. Zigzag goldenrod is now open, tall goldenrod reaching early full bloom. Wild cucumber has large fruits. One pileated woodpecker heard, small flock of gold finches seen.

2006: Bittersweet berries are definitely orange (very pale orange) today. One of Mateo's Jerusalem artichokes has finally budded. A few tall coneflowers continue to bloom in the alley. Lilac pods are dark, redbud seeds drying, browning. A quiet morning at the back porch, fewer butterflies. One cardinal at 6:00 a.m. .

2007: After last night's rain, the garden looks especially tattered, some of the hosta leaves yellowing, complementing the mottled coleus. The buds are bigger on the Jerusalem artichokes; they should bloom any day. The last of the phlox are gone, but the clump of false boneset that I cut back in July is reaching full flower and provides a solid, fresh accent to the fading plants of middle summer. My winter greenhouse tomatoes (the Cobra variety) I seeded at the end of July are about three feet tall now, and one plant is blossoming.

2008: Rain last night, at least an inch. I almost stepped on a small toad, a little more than an inch long, out by the woodshed. Ben, the reporter who interviewed me last month sent me the name of a milkweed beetle watcher who has been seeing beetles every year for the past 30 years but said the insects were two weeks late this year. In the back yard, no bright yellow finches seen for two or three days. Have the males left or changed color? Hurricane Ike batters Cuba, heads out into the Gulf.

2010: Only crows again this morning. (As I drove home from buying muffins, I swerved to avoid a crow in the street. It was pecking at what I thought was road kill, but when I got close and the crow flew off, a young bird it had been holding flew off too.) In the countryside, corn and soybean fields are a golden brown, fencerows reddening with poison ivy and Virginia creeper. One large flock of starlings swirling down into a pasture. At the butterfly bushes, two monarchs, one spicebush swallowtail and one female tiger swallowtail seen over the lunch hour – but no swallowtails seen in the morning. Skippers are still about, but fewer than last week.

2011: Goshen, Indiana: Field crickets and monarchs on my walk this afternoon.

2013: Peggy's New England asters have started to open now. Mine are just showing purple on their buds. Peaches gone except for a handful. In the alley, the bittersweet berries are getting a little dusky, and the knotweed is in full flower. A few pale violet spiderworts are blooming beneath the peach tree. More maple leaves falling on the Lawsons' lawn. Maples with patches of color on the way to Dayton.

2014: Cool and foggy morning, patches of gossamer in the grass, orb-weaver webs empty, a sluggish scorpion fly, a painted lady (Cynthia), wings spread, warming on the stones at the edge of the garden.

2015: When I went out to the car this morning, I found a huge orb weaver waiting for me, its web strung between my windshield and the bushes beside it. The pond had a long-bodied orb weaver over it. The heat wave breaking. More monarchs in the garden. Jerusalem artichokes, white snakeroot, goldenrod all early full in the roadsides and at Bryant Park. Throughout the countryside, leafturn clearly underway, some soybean fields yellowing, some cornfields fully dry and dark. In the north garden, a few New England asters have opened.

2016: In the rain tonight, two quince fruits struck the tin room above the bedroom, sounded like rocks thrown hard against the surface. Soybean fields south of town suddenly turning. I saw a sizeable flock of Canadian geese feeding in the vacant lots at the west edge of town this afternoon, and a honking flock flew over the house in the dark around 7:30 this evening. At the gym, Rick told me about seeing fireflies a few nights ago, like a resurgence or late-summer hatch, congruent with what I saw at John and Louise's house a week ago.

2018: All-day rain from Hurricane Gordon.

2019: Sunny and warm, only a few cabbage whites seen in the garden, one spicebush swallowtail at Ellis Pond. The New England asters are showing purple at the center of their buds. Katydids heard at 7:23. Leslie and Mark report a huge flock of grackles visited their yard, then flew off.

2020: Jeni called and sent photos from Portland: The night sky is red from the uncontrolled wildfires fires south of her, and the morning sky is dusky gray with smoke. The town about an hour away where she worked a few years ago has been evacuated, and her favorite restaurant there was destroyed. The entire west coast is besieged by fire storms. Here at Keuka Lake, light rain and a cold front approaching: screech owl conversations after sundown, just like two nights ago.

2021: Blue jays, one monarch, and a flock of geese over the studio at dusk.

2022: Hurricane Earl, the first hurricane to threaten North America, skirts the East Coast, bringing heavy rains to the Southeast. Only a couple of cabbage whites in the yard today. Geese flew over honking at 7:25 this evening.

2023: Peter Hayes reports the egret still in the fields near his house, the same egret Casey saw the other day, I presume. It has been in the area most all of September. Time count: 24 canna blossoms. Hurricane Lee hovers above the Caribbean islands, a Category 5 at this point, threatening to move west into the States.

But on the hill the golden-rod, and the aster in the wood,
And the yellow sunflower by the brook in autumn beauty stood...

William Cullen Bryant

September 10th
The 253rd Day of the Year

*The garden air is full of the sound of crickets, the year's clock
made audible, ticking off the days.*

Robert Finch

Sunrise/set: 6:11/6:52
Day's Length: 12 hours 41 minutes
Average High/Low: 79/57
Average Temperature: 68
Record High: 98 – 1897
Record Low: 39 – 1883

The Daily Weather
The sun almost always shines today, and temperatures are
typically slightly warmer than yesterday's: 55 percent chance of
80s, and 35 for 70s, ten percent again for 90s. Half the nights fall
below 60, but frost almost never occurs. Early autumn, however,
often arrives by the end of the day with a cool front and a storm.

Natural Calendar
As Ragweed Season disappears, Red Berry Season begins
for silver olive shrubs, Orange Berry Season for the American
mountain ash, and Purple Berry Season for the pokeweed. Yellow
Soybean Leaf Season and Corn Silage Harvest Season change the
fields as Puffball Mushroom Season grows in the woods. Now the
High Season of Blackbird Abundance coincides with the end of
Dove Calling Season. And this week ushers in the Season of Early
Fall, which lasts until Peak Maple Color Season announces the
Season of Middle Fall.

Daybook
1984: Tulip poplars and cottonwoods have large gold patches of
leaves now. Crab apples have lost much of their foliage.

1987: Robins and starlings in the yard this morning, and crows, blue jays in the distance. The ash at my window is three-fourths turned and losing leaves. Some foliage of the maple in front of the house has come down. Woolly bear caterpillars common as I came home from work, all of them light or dark orange, no black stripes. Katydids still strong tonight. Large flock of geese lands on the college green.

1988: When the woolly bear caterpillars finally appeared this year, they were dark, some reddish, some dark brown. Last year's winter was a mild, dry one. Will this year be different? Vern Hogans, the local cat fisherman who forecasts by the thickness of the catfish skins, says cold.

1989: Crickets and katydids still strong in the warm evenings.

1993: Boneset has rusted in the swamp and false boneset along the highway in just the last few days. In the yard, some white and red phlox hold. The pink spider plant continues to come in. The ironweed planted from seed this spring is still early full bloom. Most cosmos killed by the drought, zinnias holding pretty well. Spiderwort still strong.

1996: The iron plant (mother-in-law's tongue) has finished blooming after having flowered for about two weeks.

1999: The sun continues relentless, the earth so dry in the drought, everything withering prematurely. I haven't cut the grass in over a month. Pond koi still active at their summer level, feeding heavily. Two monarchs seen today.

2000: Screech owl in the back woodlot toward Limestone Street at 7:07 p.m. .

2001: Two black swallowtails seen today. Full bloom of New England aster in the south garden. Late purple-flowered hosta full bloom in town as Royal Standard hosta continues late bloom by the apple tree. Queen Anne's lace is definitely gone. Goldenrod early bloom. Horseweed still prominent. Butterfly bush still all right. Artichokes full. Still long rows of blue chicory. At school, my red maples are stable, mostly green.

2002: A monarch butterfly at 7:00 a.m.

2003: Monarchs seen throughout the day in the zinnias. The flowers of the earlier virgin's bower have turned gray, but the later plants are still bright and in full bloom.

2005: To Amish country northeast of Columbus: Many patches of orange and gold on maple trees along the highway, several maples completely turned. Most of the soybean fields and the stands of tall goldenrod are turning. At home, a few serviceberry trees have lost all their leaves. Together with the black walnuts, the serviceberries make up the first tier of leaves to fall.

2007: Buds on the Jerusalem artichokes are straining now, will open any day. A cardinal sang at 5:53 a.m. – only one call, then silence. Crows heard briefly at 8:20 as we walked Bella through the alley. Mateo's black walnut tree is about 90 percent down.

2008: A low of 48 this morning, the first 40s of the fall. Doves strong at about 7:00 a.m. A cardinal heard at 8:30. A flock of starlings seen on the way to Fairborn, and again on my return.

2009: Several red maples in town have turned completely red-orange. Very last hibiscus flower by the back porch.

2010: Crows at 5:45 this morning, one faint cardinal call at 5:55. Lil's burning bush is deep red on the north side. The white autumn crocus on the northwest corner of the back veranda has started to bloom. Mateo's black walnut tree is about bare.

2011: Return from Goshen, Indiana beneath patchy clouds, high cirrus undercut by fair-weather cumulus and then threatening stratus, a few raindrops, temperatures into the middle 70s, cornfields browning, bean fields turning gold, some corn cut for silage in the drier areas of northern Indiana. A few monarchs seen, long drifts of goldenrod, full bloom of virgin's bower in the villages, several great flocks of starlings. At night in Yellow Springs, full chorus of tree crickets, a few field crickets, katydids in front of Gerard's and down near Lawson Place, but none along my section of High Street.

2012: The zinnias, New England asters, the false boneset, the fresh, white autumn crocus by the back porch, the virgin's bower (newly blooming this year, climbing, volunteering through the trellis above the wisteria and into and up Janet's redbud) all full of small butterflies, especially painted ladies now. I have not been able to watch for hummingbirds, but their sugar water continues to go down. They are still here.

2013: Katydids calling until 5:15 this morning, just as the sky was starting to lighten. A brown and a monarch in the garden at about 9:15 this morning, one more monarch late in the afternoon. Along the road to Wilmington, goldenrod is in full bloom, more and more cornfields brown, more soybean fields yellow, a deeper weathering of the woodlots. One small murmuration of starlings seen. Heat wave continues, highs in the 90s. Casey says that honeybees are swarming around the small flowers of the ivy plant that covers the side of his house. He reported something similar last year or the year before.

2014: Hackberry leaves have started to fall in the back yard, joining the cherry tree leaves. Black nightshade still blooming in the front hedge, full of green berries. Diana called: She saw a white goldfinch (black around the eyes, black markings on wings and tail) at her feeder at 1:00 this afternoon.

2015: Doves were calling when I went outside this morning at 5:45. I heard crows at 5:50 and one short cardinal warble about 6:10.

2016: Yesterday's rain seems to have loosened foliage from a few trees, ridges of walnut leaves gathered along Davis Street, a wide scattering of brittle cottonwood leaves on Greene Street near Jill's house. Hackberry leafdrop increases in the back yard. Another quince fell on the bedroom tin room in the middle of the night, the quince clock striking the early evening of the year. Leah came into the store today, said there had been hundreds and hundreds of little toads crossing her front yard this past week. This afternoon, a violent line of storms crossed the Midwest with heavy rain, thunder and lightning, bringing the first cold front of the early autumn.

2017: Returning from Hopewell, Virginia: One painted lady butterfly in the zinnias (only two butterflies of any kind seen on the drive and throughout my stay in Virginia). In the Appalachians, goldenrod and Jerusalem artichokes most common, many blanched sycamores and Judas maples along the freeway at upper elevations. At the fishing site along the James River: wild virgin's bower quite late bloom, beggarticks just beginning. Throughout the countryside from West Virginia into Ohio, soybeans fields show patches of gold.

2018: Cleaning up after the Hurricane Gordon rains: All the taller castor beans were toppled, and the Mexican sunflowers had leaned over the zinnias, covering them with orange. The circle garden's lush tangle of castor beans and zinnias, Mexican sunflowers and morning glories collapsed, and I had to cut away most of the plants. This cool, wet evening, no katydids heard, even though the crickets were screeching and buzzing. Geese flew over honking at 7:10.

2019: The hummingbird still comes to the feeder. One ragged Eastern black butterfly at Ellis. Driving to the shop, I almost hit two black buzzards that were eating a squirrel that had been run over on Dayton Street. Not only have the black buzzards moved into the area from Kentucky, they are becoming cityfied. The coffee trees downtown are shedding quickly now.

From a half hour north of Yellow Springs, Chris Walker writes: "I have been seeing nighthawks for the past two or so weeks. At first they were way high, but I recognized the wing profile and stripe. Yesterday I drove home for work and saw about a dozen of them, flying low over the road. I used to see these a lot when I lived in Nashville, but never up here. However, according to a range map, they're not unusual around here." His report supports the few other observations I've had at this time of year, the first one being from Rick and Mary on August 27 in 2009.

Carol Cuthbertson also reported seeing nighthawks at her property on Garrison Road north of town this evening, as well as a great cloud of dragonflies, the nighthawks swooping back and forth, feasting. A friend of Carol's in Yellow Springs saw the dragonflies tonight, as well. Is this the exact time (more or less), then, that the dragonflies appear in great numbers throughout central Ohio and that the nighthawks accompany them?

2021: Blue jays calling in the afternoon again. One monarch seen. Geese flew over the house near supper time and also an hour after sundown.

2022: One monarch glimpsed in the zinnias.

2023: Time count: 21 canna blossoms. One great spangled fritillary, the first New England asters open at the Glass Farm habitat. In the yard, the August Moon hostas are almost gone. Stonecrop in full flower. Peggy's magnificent Japanese knotweed cluster has gone to seed. Color continues from castor bean and zinnia blossoms. A Great Spangled Fritillary seen in a garden along High Street.

Autumn's onset means cooling breezes
and crickets that sing in bedroom curtains.

Juan Chi, 3rd Century A.D. China, (trans. C. Hartman

September 11th
The 254th Day of the Year

Grape clusters heavy under broad leaves,
powdery bloom on fruit black with sweetness
-- an ancient delight, delighting --

Wendell Berry

Sunrise/set: 6:12/6:51
Day's Length: 12 hours 39 minutes
Average High/Low: 78/57
Average Temperature: 68
Record High: 98 – 1897
Record Low: 40 – 1917

The Daily Weather

Chances of completely overcast conditions rise from yesterday's five percent up to 30 percent, and showers occur one day in three. Highs seldom reach the 90s (just five percent of the years) but make it into the 80s fifty-five percent of the afternoons, are in the 70s thirty-five percent, and in the 60s five percent. Evening temperatures dip below 60 sixty percent of the time, but frost almost always stays away.

Natural Calendar

This is the last week of the year in which normal averages drop only two degrees in seven days throughout much of the nation. Next week, the rate will increase to three degrees per week. A few days ago, at the end of August, averages were only going down at the rate of one degree every seven days. In town, the violet September crocus has opened. In the fields, goldenrod is peaking. New England asters are coming in, along with the *Aster pilosus*, *Aster lateriflorus*, Short's aster, and the *Aster cordofolius*.

Daybook

1982: False boneset still strong along the freeway.

1985: Clifton Gorge: zigzag goldenrod is in full bloom now.

1986: South Glen, late morning and windy, an autumn wind: Wingstem holds in the woods, mostly gone in the fields. River full of leaves. Dragonflies still hunting. Ironweed's brilliant purple turned to soft white seed above the goldenrod. Beggarticks now full bloom. Pollen count remains high, near 300, even after ragweed has gone to seed: Is it from goldenrod now? Three blues spiraling at South Glen, one cabbage butterfly on the path dying, two monarchs flying across the field. Many ragweed seeds gone, elderberries deep purple. Tonight a hard wind and rainstorm, at least an inch of water in the tomato flats.

1987: Blue jays, robins, squirrels chatter in the back trees all afternoon.

1988: At Jacoby: A great blue heron rises out of Jacoby Branch, feeding 8:30 a.m. Geese fly over south as I walk. White snakeroot is still early, delayed weeks by the drought; wingstem is very late too. But ironweed stayed on schedule, held up far better to the lack of water. Goldenrod still just starting. Tall coneflowers mostly gone. Huge patches of catchweed, in full bloom, second cycle. *Helianthus tuberosus* still full bloom. Pennsylvania leatherwing bugs still mating. Patches of poison ivy red and gold, but otherwise very little leafturn so far. At home, knotweed has faded. Last of the peaches picked and frozen. No cardinals heard this weekend. Light earthquake about nine o'clock in the evening. The 6th hurricane of the season caused quite a bit of cloudiness this afternoon.

1989: The ash at my window is maybe a fourth yellow, starting to drop its leaves.

1990: Roadsides of Grinnell are pink with smartweed. Pussy willow foliage fell in August; now it's growing back.

1991: Listing the changes, adding, subtracting notes, rearranging sequence, qualifying each day, adjusting the weather graphs, updating charts, reworking percentages, assessing the leaves, comparing years, taking stock, measuring asters, cutting back the hollyhocks, mallow, yarrow, queen Anne's lace, coneflowers, loosestrife, listening for geese, for blue jays migrating along the Little Miami, for the autumn robin staccato.

1992: At Wilberforce, my ash tree is almost completely gone.

1996: Instead of being invigorated by this September, I'm feeling lethargic. Instead of my typical excitement and anticipation about fall, in place of an urge to take stock and get ready for the cold, I'm experiencing a resignation and acceptance, a letting go of power instead of its collection, as though this winter were going to do something different to me than it usually does, as though I didn't need to fight it or resist it but let it blow over me and cover me up. There doesn't seem to be anything ominous or morbid in my nonresistance. It feels simply like abandon, without the thought or the hope of spring or any repetition or rebirth, into an unforeseeable end of this cycle, allowing whatever outcome has been chosen, obeying, obliging with curiosity and peace.

1998: A dozen cabbage moths in the garden this afternoon. Then in front, in the east garden, a skipper, a monarch and more cabbage moths. High tide of the *Lepidoptera*.

1999: Crows boisterous at 5:45 this morning. Again at 6:45 this evening through 7:00.

2000: Small herd of deer grazing on the Antioch School lawn at lunch time. Butterfly bush and Russian sage still strong in town.

2002: Powdery mildew has overtaken the zinnias just in the past ten days.

2003: A soft blush to many of the red maples in the area. Some of Don's serviceberry trees are turning quickly.

2004: One monarch seen today heading south across Dayton-Yellow Springs Road.

2007: Monarchs off and on this afternoon. One cardinal sang at 6:15 a.m. . The first real cold wave of the year moved in throughout the day. Expected lows in the 40s tonight and the next two nights.

2008: The skunk dug a number of holes in the lawn last night. The first small white aster was open behind Mateo's house this morning. A few feverfew flowers are left at Mrs. Timberlake's. Hurricane Ike heads for the oil rigs between New Orleans and the Mexican border. The peaches are dropping more now in the back yard. We froze twelve cups, filling three quart bags. At John Bryan Park, white snakeroot and wingstem in full bloom by the campsite, pileated woodpecker and downy woodpecker calling.

2009: Cardinals sang at 5:50 this morning . Geese flew over at 6:30, the second loud flock I've heard in the past week. Don's black walnut tree half down. Two chigger bites!

2010: Crows at 5:51, cardinal at 5:58 this morning, then quiet. Overcast and barometer dropping by midmorning, few sparrows or butterflies moving about, no swallowtails or monarchs. After lunch, the sky brightened a little, and the skippers and bees returned. One very small spicebush butterfly, one old and tattered female tiger swallowtail, one Eastern black came by. The snowball viburnum on the north side of the house is rusty red-brown on its east side. New England asters and Jerusalem artichokes are fully budded. Almost the last raspberries and peaches picked today. False boneset and the stonecrop in the dooryard garden continue to attract the most bees and skippers. One bright yellow finch at the feeder today.

2011: Crows at 6:00, one cardinal song at 6:02, then quiet. Finches, chickadees, nuthatches, cardinals, sparrows feeding in the yard. Two monarchs and one brown butterfly seen on my walk around the block with Bella, then about a half a dozen more monarchs and a great spangled fritillary worked the garden in the afternoon. Stonecrop and false boneset covered with large wasps, including the beautiful blue cricket hunters. A hummingbird moth came to the butterfly bush - I hadn't seen one for a while. In the park, Kousa dogwood leaves are rusting around the edges, red maples are tattered. One white aster at Peggy's has opened. Our peach tree has dropped most of its peaches, very few left hanging. Raspberries almost gone. The first two New England asters have opened along the stone wall. False boneset now full, stonecrop in the dooryard in early bloom, full bloom about town. A woodpecker tapped at the siding while Jeanie and I were reading the paper about 8:00 in the morning. This evening, all the crickets and katydids were singing, one particular tree cricket that sounded to me like an intense concert of castanets.

2013: Indian Mound park with Jeff: White snakeroot and orange jewelweed full and dominant, zigzag goldenrod, small white asters and great blue lobelias also in bloom, river very low from a month of drought, soybean fields mostly yellow between here and Cedarville. Behind Jeff and Kit's house, their ivy is in bloom – small white flowers like those on Casey's ivy. One monarch today, one spicebush noticed today as I went in and out. And I just noticed that the white autumn crocus is blooming by the back porch.

2014: The humidity and heat of the past week has ended: early fall is really here, light jacket weather.

2015: Lows expected in the 40s tomorrow night, summer ending. Monarchs still visiting the garden (three noticed today), but they and the cabbage whites are the only butterflies seen in many days. The sparrows feed heavily these days, but they make no sound.

2016: Over a dozen silver-spotted skippers in the tithonias and zinnias today, and one monarch passing through, Clear skies and bright sun following last night's arrival of early autumn. The very first violet coloring showed on the New England asters.

2017: Inventory on return from Virginia: the white autumn crocus has sent up its soft buds; the stonecrop here bloomed while I was gone, many pink flower heads; New England asters still not open, but the first buds show just a hint of purple now; the escaped virgin's bower that wanders through the north bushes is in full bloom; Japanese knotweed flowers disintegrating; pokeweed berries black hanging high up in the old peach tree; under the crab apple tree, the large, white-flowered August hostas (Royal Standard or August Moon) are still in bloom, as are the thin-leafed violet-flowered hostas; all the quince fruit appears to have fallen, all lying in a row behind the pond pump. Sitting in the yard after lunch, I saw a monarch, a painted lady, a yellow sulphur and several cabbage whites.

2018: Now Hurricane Florence, Category 4, moves toward the Carolinas. Mass evacuations ordered. I noticed sparrows on the front porch, pecking at the spaces between the bricks. I associate that with a winter pattern. The katydids were calling on schedule near 7:30 tonight, after being reluctant to brave the chill yesterday evening.

2019: Field crickets and buzzing tree crickets strong at first light. No birds, katydids or tree frogs. Jill and I came upon the first large orb-weaver of the season, just off Davis Street. Its web covered one whole side of the sidewalk. A heat wave settles in. Yesterday was in the 90s, more of the same today.

2020: Return to Yellow Springs from Keuka Lake: The landscape has rusted since we drove here on the 7th, and there are many more Judas trees that stand out. Many deep red leaves on the sumac, and goldenrod dominating the fields and roadsides. Jeni called from Portland: smoke has invaded her house, and the fires are all around in the city and suburbs.

2021:This morning, I was surprised to see that all the peaches had been taken from the peach tree, all the windfalls gone, too! Whatever took them was thorough; not a single fruit remained on the ground or on the branches Resting in the cool after work, 1 count ragged cumulous clouds racing from the northwest over the great. white mulberry tree. One monarch seen several, unidentified butterflies in the dusk.

2023: Cool weather continues with an extended high-pressure system. The time count this morning: 18 canna blossoms. I cut back most of the August Moon hosta blossoms.

The seasons revolve and the years change
With no assistance or supervision.
The moon, without taking thought,
Moves in its cycle, full, crescent, and full.

Kenneth Rexroth

September 12th
The 255th Day of the Year

Crows coming home to roost
at eight o'clock tonight,
comforting September
with constancy and clarity.

Sunrise/set: 6:13/6:49
Day's Length: 12 hours 36 minutes
Average High/Low: 78/57
Average Temperature: 68
Record High: 99 – 1897
Record Low: 38 – 1898

The Daily Weather

This is typically one of the two cloudiest days in September; a full 40 percent of September 12ths are overcast, and rain falls four days in a decade when the first high-pressure system of Early Fall nears. Sometimes hurricane remnants reach the Lower Midwest, increasing the chances of rain. Today also marks the beginning of a decline in percentage of daily sunshine, a decline that continues through December (the year's darkest month). There is a five percent chance of highs in the 90s today, 40 percent chance of highs in the 80s, 40 percent of highs in the 70s, 15 percent of 60s. Nighttime temperatures are typically mild for the next two days, with 60s occurring a little more than half the time.

Natural Calendar

Sandhill cranes start to arrive in Midwestern wetlands on their way to the Gulf Coast. Doves usually stop calling in the morning until February. Young toads appear more frequently in cooler evenings. As lake and reservoir water temperatures drop into the lower 70s and 60s, bass and walleye become more active. Fall raspberries and peaches end their seasons in the Ohio Valley and the Middle Atlantic.

Daybook

1982: Ragweed gone, soybean fields mostly yellow, cornfields motley brown, yellow, and green.

1983: Buckeyes falling to the ground near the market downtown. They were probably ready to be picked a week or so ago. Cabbage butterflies still mating on the zucchini. Leaves blowing down from the black walnut tree in the back yard. First small white asters bloom in front of the house.

1984: At the mill, the field along the river is filled with goldenrod, but a few have brown tips going to seed. Up river, the jumpseed is not quite ready to jump. Most asters haven't flowered yet. Thin-leafed coneflower is still full bloom, and some scattered agrimony. Dark orange touch-me-nots continue in late full bloom. Wood nettle is graying. Cobwebs and spiders everywhere. In the deeper woods, henbit and violets grow stronger. Canopy stable. Sweet Cicely coming back, and new mint. First zigzag goldenrod open. Helianthus flowers hold on along the road. Buzzards circling.

1986: Loneliness today. I feel lost, retreat again to Thoreau: "If a person lost would conclude that after all he is not lost...but standing in his own old shoes on the very spot where he is, and that for the time being he will live there; but the places that have known him, *they* are lost.... I am not alone if I stand by myself. Who knows where in space this globe is rolling? Yet we will not give ourselves up for lost, let it go where it will."

1987: Blue jays restless, and squirrels chattering off and on. Some ragweed stems bare. Patches of yellow on the Osage trees.

1988: Heavy rains from the hurricane today.

1989: A number of monarch butterflies seen heading south over Wilberforce-Clifton Road.

1990: Grinnell roadsides pink with smartweed.

1991: At Wilberforce, my ginkgo is fringed with gold. *Aster novii belgii* and prickly mallow full bloom today,

1998: Cardinals and crows came through about 5:50 a.m., then the cardinals stayed and sang on and off through the morning. The drought continues to deepen, all the highway grasses are as brown as in February. Squirrels have been chucking and whining a week or so now in the afternoons. A toad came to the sprinkler this evening as I watered the lawn.

2002: Full bloom of the new virgin's bower on the trellis for the past three days. Stella d'oro lilies still strong, and the New England asters are coming in steadily. Only a few blossoms left on the Royal Standard hosta, but the purple-flowered hosta is still in full bloom along the alley off Winter Street. Lots of skippers in the garden today, one black swallowtail, no monarchs.

2003: Mild and sunny: Monarchs were in the garden all day, four seen at one time. Cabbage butterflies were even more numerous. Skippers and tiger swallowtails came by, too.

2006: A camel cricket in the dog's water this morning; it was still alive and hopped away when I scooped it out. The Royal Standard hostas have lost most of their petals in today's hard rain, a sudden end to their long late-summer season. But in the front yard, the honeysuckle berries have become bright orange.

2007: Royal Standard hostas and Moya's August hosta are gone in our yard and in hers. They declined as the New England asters came into bloom. One cardinal sang at 5:57 this morning . False boneset providing a solid bank of foliage and color under the peach tree. I will spread the seeds around this fall, could use a full wall of their white and green. Like last year, the red and orange of the honeysuckle berries begin to stand out. Dozens of cabbage butterflies swarmed around the false boneset this afternoon in the intense sun. Jeanie reported seeing a small flock of crows on the way to Beavercreek. This afternoon, I noticed the new white autumn crocus by the wisteria vine.

2008: A warm drizzle this morning, a cardinal calling in the distance around 9:30. Hurricane Ike coming ashore near Galveston. Peaches continue to fall – maybe of third of them down by now, but the branches still bending low. Eight more cups – two quart bags - frozen this afternoon. The Red Baron hostas have produced bright purple flower buds, are becoming strikingly beautiful. Overcast sky throughout the day. The first Jerusalem artichoke is open along the north edge of the property. A large orb-weaver wove his/her web in the north window today.

2009: Cardinals at 5:50 a.m., geese at 5:30. First Jerusalem artichoke blooming, ten to twelve feet high. Still three tall coneflowers in the alley. Our ash tree starting to turn on the northwest side, the high branches of the hackberry are bright yellow in the sun, Ruby's redbud yellow. Baby sparrows begging. No monarchs for days.

2011: Crows at 5:58 a.m., cardinals making short "chit" sounds at the feeder by 6:00, then one melodious cardinal call at 6:05. Sparrows and a hummingbird at 6:30, then a small flock of geese flying over. Male cardinal song at 6:45. Woodpecker calls become more frequent now, probably our red-bellied one. A silver-spotted skipper and a large yellow sulphur in the morning, several monarchs in the afternoon. Thunderous katydids and crickets under the full moon tonight.

2012: So clear and quiet today, the day that Jeanie died at 2:10 this afternoon as I was rubbing her feet, the sky so very blue, the wind soft and warm, the garden full of butterflies.

2013: Drought broken today with a gentle rain all morning. Honeybees in the flowering knotweed in the alley. At home, the zinnias have definitely passed their first peak and continue to need to be cut to encourage new blossoms. The dahlias are getting ragged, but they too would respond to more care. Along the north garden, five of Jeanie's yellow tea roses have come into bloom, rich and thick, and her pink rose, eight feet tall, has two giant flowers. The very first New England aster has opened beneath them. On South High, the last blooms of the prairie dock hold on. The first river birch leaves are turning in the back yard, the redbuds are blanching like the foliage of the sweet cherry close by. Along the way to Wilmington, there is a definite increase in autumn color, dapples of yellow and orange throughout in many different woodlots and canopies, goldenrod brilliant, soybean fields losing their summer green. One bright yellow sulphur (like a cloudless sulphur, *Phoebis sennae*) in the late afternoon, one loopy, small black swallowtail, too, would not stay still at all. Across the street, Judy's purple-flowered hostas are still in full flower. Moya's white-flowered hostas full, too.

2014: Brisk and cloudy today. The last of the perennial hibiscus buds has wilted. Our virgin's bower and Peggy's are almost all gone.

2015: Brisk in the low 60s, light showers. A few more hibiscus buds hold on, and the virgin's bower is still in full flower. A handful of blossoms remains on Moya's rose of Sharon.

2016: A perfect day, sunny in the 70s, the garden full of silver- spotted skippers. One female hummingbird came to the zinnias while I sat on the back porch. The prairie dock toward the end of High Street has only about a fourth of its blossoms.

Looking back, I ruminate that the events in the garden are almost the same as they were on this day in 2012. The variations are not so important; it is the themes (like flowers and leaf coloration and butterflies and birds) that are important. As I look back at my daybook for September 12 of 2012 at 2:10 in the afternoon when Jeanie died, I see that all the notations for all the September 12ths before and since her death are essentially the same.

In the daybook, Jeanie's death is the only really different

event in my record for that day. And in a way, I can see my own death as an entry in the daybook, too, and can know that the day of my death, like the day of her death, will be taken up and blended with all the events of that same days forever before and after.

2017: The remnants of Hurricane Irma (which devastated Florida and caused major damage in Georgia and South Carolina) reached the Ohio Valley today: rain and gray. In patches of sunlight, a great spangled fritillary, a monarch, a painted lady, a sulphur and several cabbage white butterflies visited the garden this afternoon. Along the north edge of the property, hops and false buckwheat vines are still in flower.

2018: On foot at Agraria, I could see the cost of decades of monoculture and grazing. The fields appeared plain and empty. The woods of fat-berried honeysuckles and Osage, black walnut, hackberry, silver olive, red mulberry, locust and box elder that grew dense and wild along the narrow and shallow streams were wrapped in wild grapevines and blackberries, All around was the absence of care.

But I was not alone in my walk, and my companions were optimistic about the future of this neglected, damaged space. Robins, back from their midsummer molting, were peeping in the trees.

Field crickets chirped beside me all the way. Monarchs and Eastern black swallowtails, a giant swallowtail, an azure, silver-spotted skippers, cabbage white butterflies and a few great spangled fritillaries drifted in and out of the clusters of goldenrod, and other fare for pollen along the pathways and near the woods: an abundance of jewelweed, smartweed, horseweed, pokeweed and clearweed a few violet lobelias and small patches of Jerusalem artichokes and coneflowers, the first white asters, spent tall ragweed, false buckwheat vines in bloom and wild cucumber vines, a little red clover, jumpseed and chicory, one dandelion, dock and burdock, beggarticks, white snakeroot and Queen Anne's lace. Bright yellow swamp bidens surprised me at a sunny, low point of the brook, and I could see tiny minnows in the water.

At home, the pink-flowered sedum is in full bloom. One robin peeping in the honeysuckles. I talked to Ed Oxley, who said that he saw a sandhill crane flying over the golf course he was playing last week. This evening, geese at 7:15, katydids at 7:24.

2019: The third day in a row with 90 degree temperatures and sun. The first buckeye butterfly (*Junonia coenia*) I've seen this year visited the garden, one sulphur, many cabbage whites and many monarchs, too. I saw a second buckeye at Ellis Pond this afternoon. The first New England asters opened all the way in the night. This morning at 5:00, tree crickets, field crickets, tree frogs and a few katydids. At 6:00, one cardinal song and then crows called. Jill heard geese at 6:30. The hummingbirds are still here.

2020: Ruckus, crows versus hawk this morning about 6:15. Three monarchs and many cabbage whites seen today. Jill's black walnut tree has begun to yellow.

2023: Light rain this morning at 6:00, field crickets chirping along High Street.

September 13th
The 256th Day of the Year

The full-juiced apple, waxing over-mellow,
Drops in a silent autumn night.
All its allotted length of days,
The flower ripens in its place,
Ripens and fades, and falls, and hath no toil,
Fast rooted in the fruitful soil.

Alfred Lord Tennyson

Sunrise/set: 6:14/6:48
Day's Length: 12 hours 34 minutes
Average High/Low: 78/57
Average Temperature: 67
Record High 100 – 1897
Record Low: 38 – 1964

The Daily Weather

The 13th and the 14th are the last two days in the year on which there is a 15 percent chance of a high above 90 degrees. Eighties occur 40 percent of the time, 70s another 40 percent, with a cool high in the 60s coming the remaining five percent. Lows are usually close to 60; the third cool wave of the month brings a touch of frost, however, almost ten percent of the mornings.

Natural Calendar

A fourth of the corn is often mature by today, corn silage a fourth cut all across the Lower Midwest. Yellowing soybeans and drifts of goldenrod brighten the patchwork landscape. In northern counties, the planting of winter wheat gets underway. Throughout the South, cotton growers defoliate their cotton plants, a process that increases fiber quality.

Daybook

1982: South Glen: Wingstem still holding in the woods, gone in the fields. Touch-me-nots and jumpseed fading. Some white snakeroot has gray seeds, even green berries. More and more Queen Anne's lace turned to dark brown seeds. Wood nettle with big green seeds. Hog peanuts past their prime. Most burdock dying back, yellow and brown, only a few still flowering. One lone daisy, and a few daisy fleabane. Acorns common on the path. Some wild lettuce, much chicory holds. Some rose hips red. New England aster near full bloom, and heath aster, *aster lateriflorus*, Short's aster, *aster cordofolius*. Field thistles hanging on, and tall coneflowers. Leaves on the trails, the cover overhead spotted with new color. Sycamores a golden green. Dogwood yellowing. American mountain ash, fruit dominant, deep orange. Berries red on the silver olives. Purple berries on all the pokeweed. Scarlet Virginia creeper outlines the tree trunks at the east ridge. Spider webs across all the trails.

1984: The ash tree by my window at Wilberforce has begun to turn. Huge flock of starlings settles in the locusts at home, 4:30 p.m.

1986: Geese fly over at 7:54 a.m.

1988: Sharp leaf color change during the last three days. The trees, which faded in the drought are suddenly turning, cottonwoods most of all. Knotweed: quick loss of all its petals. No cardinals noticed singing for the last five days. Jerusalem artichokes still full bloom along the roadsides. Tonight: two cold, slow lightening bugs in the raspberries.

1989: Cardinal sings at 6:13 p.m.

1991: Cardinal waits until 7:37 a.m. to sing. Then quiet. The blue jay is loud at about ten, then everything's quiet again at eleven.

1992: Almost complete decline of the showy coneflowers, cosmos and zinnias thinning even more. Cardinals sing off and on today. Cicadas strong by noon, temperature warming into the 70s. Squirrel sitting high up in the Osage trees eating black walnuts, singing its screeching song, peeling off the soft green hulls, fragments falling a few yards from me.

1996: Jumpseeds are continuing to jump.

1998: Long-jawed orb-weaver spiders have disappeared from the pond. No more nightly web weaving. Robins chirp at 5:37 a.m. Cardinal and crows eleven minutes later. Wrens and starlings at 6:30. Baby wrens heard in the lilac yesterday.

2000: Cut back Queen Anne's lace and scattered seeds in the south and north gardens. All but two or three showy coneflowers gone. New England asters starting. Heliopsis/oxeye cut back, long past its prime. Ironweed seeds are soft, ready to plant. Pond weeded; water lilies are still very strong, producing five or six flowers a day from the single planting. Shasta daisy and veronica continue to flower, along with occasional achillea, butterfly bush, and Russian sage. The morning silent until 6:45 when one cardinal sang. Doves heard at 7:20. Flocks of starlings line the wires on the way to Springfield. Along the airport road, the tall Jerusalem artichokes are in full bloom. In town, the virgin's bower weakens in places. At 7:07 this evening, the screech owl in the back trees started to call, about ten minutes after sundown.

2001: Silver olive bushes starting to turn.

2002: Grass-leaved goldenrod (*Solidago graminifolia*) is open in South Glen, also fields of tall goldenrod (*Solidago altissima or gigantea*). Wingstem and blue monkey flower still full. Red-shouldered damselflies seen by the river.

2003: A cardinal sang at 5:52 this morning, continued off an on through the morning. The wrens began at 5:55. Dark woolly-bear caterpillars reported on the roads.

2005: A dozen cabbage butterflies in the butterfly bush this afternoon, a giant swallowtail in the impatiens, a monarch passing through. The virgin's bower on the trellis is about a third in bloom, and the New England asters have been opening for several days. The yellow coneflowers have disappeared throughout town, and the purple ironweed in the yard is almost gone. A few of the cutback Heliopsis are still flowering. A few chiggers continue to bite.

2006: A screech owl called at a little after 5:00 this morning.

2007: A cardinal sang at 5:58 this morning, otherwise quiet. Early purple crocus seen in the alley, the house next to Mateo's.

2008: Crows at 6:00 this morning. Weather muggy and gray. Three young cardinals seen with their mother in the honeysuckle bushes, and a male cardinal called off and on (around 8:00 a.m.) for about half an hour before I saw them. No yellow male finches seen for days. Peaches continue to come in heavily, and the alley apple tree seems to be dropping its fruit at about the same rate. One more Jerusalem artichoke open, more New England asters. The last of the late lilies is in bloom. Mateo's black walnut is about two-thirds down, no leaf fall on the serviceberry trees yet. Giant black cricket found sitting on the shirt I had placed on the back of my chair in the sunroom. Many cabbage butterflies, one bright yellow sulphur.

2009: Cardinal at 5:56 a.m., geese at exactly 6:30 again.

2010: Crows at 5:48 a.m. All the way to Dayton, increased leafturn, red sumac leaves, orange maples moving ahead of bleached cottonwoods, sycamores yellowing. Liz writes from Stafford Street: "The butterflies in the circle mowed around the field by the Covered Bridge have been so amazing! I saw a hummingbird moth spread-winged and vibrantly colored, but dead, clutched to a brown thistle flower, as multitudes of live hummingbird moths and butterflies sucked the nectar all around, oblivious to human presence. What a way to die! I had to wonder if the flower died when the moth died (I saw no other browned flowers), or if the moth, dying, chose a brown flower.... Is the dream dreaming us?"

2011: In Moya's yard, the late hostas are finally deteriorating. Across the way, Peggy's limelight hydrangea is reaching its best, as is her virgin's bower. The false boneset along our stone wall sets off the zinnias and the mums. I heard the cardinals chipping this morning at 6:00 a.m., on schedule. Tree crickets and field crickets call through the day. Jerusalem artichokes in full bloom, as are late tall sunflowers, along the highways. High of 86 today, clear skies, summer-like humidity. One yellow tiger swallowtail, two polygonia, two great spangled fritillaries, one buckeye, two monarchs, one red admiral, two sulfurs, in the garden today. Tonight - even without hearing aids - I could hear the katydids throughout the neighborhood. The black walnut tree by the church has lost most of its leaves, and it was hard to walk under the oak trees in my slippers because of all the acorns on the ground.

2013: Crows heard at 6:14 this morning. When I went out to get the paper, I found a white-lined sphinx moth (*Hiles lineata*) near the porch light. This afternoon on the outside geraniums, I found several tussock moth caterpillars, *Lophocamae*, white, hairy with black markings like a stripe down the back.

2014: I surprised a polygonia in the zinnias when I went out back this chilly afternoon – the only butterfly I saw. Throughout the day, occasional robin peeps. They seemed to have come back about a week ago out of their Late Summer sequestration.

2016: The silver-spotted skippers are still relatively common, but their numbers were down today. One smaller fritillary seen in the zinnias. No monarchs or swallowtails today even though the sun was bright and the weather warm. Jill reports murmurations of starlings every day on her way to work. Field crickets loud and steady all the way to Ellis Pond this evening.

2017: The prairie dock at the corner of High and South-West College Streets has maybe ten to 20 percent of its flowers left. On the way to Xenia, some maples are turning. At the Mills Lawn school yard, one red oak is shading deep scarlet. Across the street from my house, Lil's burning bush is blushing all across its crown. At home the viburnum is way ahead of the burning bush, a violet-rusty-salmon red.   Butterflies: a great spangled fritillary and several cabbage whites.

2018: The first New England asters opened in the night. Milkweed-type bugs are all over a few milkweed pods. Ironweed completely done. A monarch or two always in the garden whenever I go out to check. The prairie dock at the corner mentioned in 2017 has just a few blossoms left.

2019: Storms across the Midwest. Tat was stranded in her car in the middle of a flooded street in Madison, Wisconsin! In the Caribbean, more tropical depressions. Here sampling the garden zinnias: monarchs and hummingbirds in the hot sun.

2020: Hurricane Sally heading to New Orleans, two more systems forming in the Caribbean. In my zinnia garden, one monarch, about four cabbage whites, another monarch at Jill's tithonias. One exhausted bumblebee draped across a yellow marigold. No skippers or swallowtails. The first small white asters are opening near the porch. In the east garden, the thin-leafed violet-flowered hostas are in full flower. The virgin's bower has climbed high into the rose of Sharon, drapes across the honeysuckles and the weedy growth of tree of heaven. At Ellis Pond, bur marigolds (*Bidens cernua*) and maybe even some larger bur marigolds (*Bidens laevis*) have replaced the arrowhead. In the alley, beggarticks (*Bidens frondosa*) budded.

2022: Noting that the great flocks of birds that once used to settle in the back trees in the fall no longer come or appear over the fields. Still, however, the birds gather along the high wires.

2023: Getting ready for a trip to Italy, I trim the decaying garden. Only a dozen canna blossoms today, and I cut the last August Moon hosta back. Still, the beggarticks are filling in around the cannas like they do in the nearby fens. The October hostas with thin leaves and blue flowers have opened some. The first New England aster has opened in the yard and at the Glass Farm habitat. The Endless Summer hydrangea finally had two blossoms last week, slightly pink.

The first signs of fall have already made themselves noticed in the garden. The smells were first to change, the perfumes sweeter and heavier. Next will be the colors as they turn to the reliable shades of crimson, saffron, orange, and scarlet. There's something more serious about the fall than any other season. Maybe it's the light that gradually grows darker, making everything seem less trivial, forcing you to look harder to find your way.

Gail Tsukiyama, from *The Samurai's Garden*

September 14th
The 257th Day of the Year

For nothing exists nor happens in the visible sky that is not sensed in some hidden manner by the faculties of Earth and Nature....

Johannes Kepler

Sunrise/set: 6:15/6:46
Day's Length: 12 hours 31 minutes
Average High/Low: 78/56
Average Temperature: 67
Record High 101 – 1897
Record Low: 34 – 1902

The Daily Weather

As the sun moves to within a few degrees of equinox, Late Summer's grip grows measurably weaker. From now on, it is more likely that highs will occur in the 70s than in the 80s, and an afternoon in the 60s is four times as likely to be recorded as during the first week of the month. Although highs in the 90s occur 15 percent of September 14ths, the same percentage applies to 80s, odds not seen since May 24th. Rain falls 40 percent of the time, and the sun does not appear four years in ten. Odds for frost are one in ten.

Natural Calendar

In the final two weeks of September, a rapid deterioration of all the wildflowers, except the goldenrod and asters, occurs. And after these last flowers go to seed in early October, there is no major generation of blooming plants to replace them. Except for the few varieties that open during second spring, the final species that grow to maturity within most of the United States and Canada are in the process of bearing fruit.

\

Inventory

Wildflowers still in bloom (the number will shrink quickly through the month): wild mallow, chicory, bindweed, Queen Anne's lace, smartweed, trumpet creeper, heal all, touch-me-not, Asiatic dayflower, showy coneflower, ironweed, field thistle, tall coneflower, white snakeroot, clearweed, Japanese knotweed, white boneset, tall goldenrod, great blue lobelia, rose pink, hog peanut, beggartick, bur marigold, love vine, autumn violet, small white aster, New England aster, heart-leaved aster, Short's aster, zig-zag goldenrod.

Leaf-turn and leaf-drop: fading slippery elms, poplars and cottonwoods, rusting buckeyes, locusts deteriorating from leaf miner damage, scattered streaks of orange in the maples, a few red leaves on Virginia creeper, sassafras and poison ivy, browning edges on some box elders, mimosa blossoms falling.

Daybook

1985: Geese flew over the yard at 6:02 this morning.

1987: The land is dry, very few asters or zigzag goldenrod. They were aborted or delayed, I think, by the lack of rain.

1988: Cardinal sings 7:30 a.m. Birdsong is rare now, morning or afternoon, doves quiet too.

1989: Telephone lines filled with birds.

1990: In the damp mornings and evenings, toadstools in the lawn. Starlings in the back trees this afternoon, birds on the wires in the countryside.

1992: At dusk, bats still flying. When I walked the dog, the moon was rising, and crickets were still as loud as in Late Summer, katydids still strong.

1993: Warm, hard wind all day, barometer falling. I noticed that a large patch of leaves on the north side of the big maple in the yard had turned in the past few days. Most trees holding well; my ash at school is keeping its color better than I ever remember, not even a streak of yellow.

1996: Across the street, the patch of violet autumn crocus has come into bloom. In the east garden, the sedum, dead nettle, and a few spiderwort are still in full bloom, keeping color in the perennial bed. Other parts of the garden going down, the purple coneflowers turning black.

1997: Virgin's bower is still in full bloom. Ironweed is half done, but it still shines in many fields. Sundrops full bloom and seven feet tall in the south garden. Cicadas quiet this afternoon, but katydids strong tonight.

1998: Cardinal 5:50 a.m. and 7:30. Eight cabbage butterflies in the north and south yards this morning.

2002: Cardinal at 6:00 a.m. One Milbert's tortoiseshell butterfly seen in the butterfly bush.

2003: Four monarchs counted again in the zinnias today. And several painted ladies (*Vanessa cardui*) – which have been common throughout the past several weeks. Along the road south to Lebanon, scattered maples and ashes are turning. Tall goldenrod, false boneset, white snakeroot, and Jerusalem artichokes are prominent.

2005: Albert, the green frog in the pond, was croaking this morning around 7:20 .

2007: One painted lady (Cynthia) seen this afternoon as Jeanie was leaving for Indiana.

2008: The white autumn crocus is blooming now at the northwest corner of the patio.

2011: The white autumn crocus didn't come up this year in our yard, and across the street, the Danielson's violet autumn crocus must have been dug up in the latest round of landscaping. Crows at 5:55 a.m. this morning, cardinal "chit" calls and hummingbirds fighting around 6:00. Cardinal "chrrrr" calls around 6:30. Tree crickets loud in 62-degree pre-dawn temperatures, some field crickets when I walked Bella through the alley. Bright blue morning glories there and still some tall coneflowers in bloom. Through town, many maples and serviceberry trees have started to turn, box elders shedding - as well as the black walnuts. White snakeroot is in full flower along the Arboretum Trail at John Bryan Park, but few other blooming plants there besides false boneset and goldenrod. The great field of cosmos, red, white, yellow and pink, more than made up for the absence of wildflowers. Walking around the planting, Jeanie and I watched the finches rise together and then settle back into the flowers. We listened to the bees humming. This afternoon at home, two monarchs and one mourning cloak butterfly seen. A cool night expected, even cooler in the middle 40s forecast for tomorrow night. Crows very active in the neighborhood between 4:00 and 5:00.

2012: The mid-September high-pressure system came in on schedule today. This morning was soft and sunny, in the 60s, but skies darkened with altostratus clouds by noon, then stratus, then a cold north wind throughout the afternoon, butterflies disappearing into the safety of the leaves.

2013: A second morning with lows in the 40s, bright sun, bright moon at night. No large butterflies seen, in spite of a cloudless day. The sphinx moth stays by the front porch light, its third day. The orb-weaver was gone from the shed door, his place in the center of the old web empty.

2014: Cold morning in the 40s. A painted lady (*Cynthia*) butterfly was sunning herself in the zinnias midmorning. The afternoon warmed to the 60s, and I counted five painted ladies in the north zinnias, the most I've even seen at one time this year. Plus one

Eastern black, some silver-spotted skippers and numerous cabbage whites.

2015: Cool last night under the mid-September cold wave. Bright sun and mild today. No painted lady butterflies seen this autumn. Cabbage whites lively, three monarchs and one male (yellow and black) tiger swallowtail, several silver-spotted skippers in the garden.

2016: A male tiger swallowtail visited the zinnias in the middle of the morning, a monarch late in the afternoon. A few cabbage whites and skippers in the garden, but fewer than yesterday and the day before. The first New England asters opened around noon. Peggy's virgin's bower now is losing petals. My northwest-garden ironweed has gone to seed.

2017: Orb weaver beneath the porch light gets all the moths. Through the mist and clouds this morning, the world has turned ochre.

2019: From Madison, Wisconsin, Tat writes about seeing dozens of monarch butterflies, and a friend nearby saw what she thought was a thousand! When I drove by the field where the geese have gathered in the winter, I saw several hundred geese there for the first time this fall. But when I drove back after walking Ranger around the pond, they were gone.

2020: Black walnuts crushed on Limestone Street by passing cars. Flurries of black walnut leaves as I walked Ranger. At Ellis Pond, I picked up some of the pecans that had fallen, still in their green hulls. Walking home from Jill's, I saw three crows watching in the tall, dead pine tree. At home: one tattered hackberry butterfly, occasional hummingbirds, one monarch, one old great spangled fritillary, half a dozen cabbage whites, one scorpion fly in the zinnias. Milkweed bugs, still half size, huddle together on the milkweed leaves and pods. Chris reports a bittern at his pond, loons on the nearby lake. Hurricane Sally comes ashore near New

Orleans tonight. Air quality in Portland, Oregon, is still literally the worst in the world, and Jeni hunkers down indoors. Feel of autumn in the wind here in Yellow Springs. Makes me want to go around taking notes on everything that is happening.

2021: Portland, Oregon, visiting Jeni: The landscape has been severely affected by lack of rain. Suburban plantings are stressed, lawns brown. New England asters, however, are in full bloom, pacing their progress in southwestern Ohio.

2022; Driving from Xenia today, skies cloudy, cool temperatures, soybean fields gold as goldenrod: I noted for the first time, a vague ochre tint to the tree lines along the highway.

2023: First morning in the 40s. Through the countryside, many soybean fields still deep green, others almost completely golden. In the yard, the time count is 13 canna blossoms. It seems now tht the beggarticks and the false buckwheat have taken over the garden, backdrop for the stonecrop and the asters.

Like dew drops
on a lotus leaf
I vanish.

Senryu

September 15th
The 258th Day of the Year

A garden or nature journal becomes an autobiography. The act of watching becomes watching the self and forms the self out of and in front of the world. The journal affirms that I am this person who is observing leaf after leaf, field after field. Following and recording these seasons, I change into myself.

bf

Sunrise/set: 6:16/6:44
Day's Length: 12 hours 28 minutes
Average High/Low: 77/56
Average Temperature: 67
Record High: 99 – 1897
Record Low: 35 – 1902

The Daily Weather

Today is one of the more decisive times in the movement toward autumn. Overnight between September 14th and 15th, the chances of a cold dawn in the 40s or 50s leaps from the early September average of 40 percent up to 80 percent. The 15th is one of the dryer September days, carrying only a 20 percent chance of rain. Highs in the 70s come 60 percent of the time; temperatures rise only into the 60s twenty-five percent of the time. One afternoon in four warms above 80 degrees. Once or twice in a century, hurricane-force winds bring down the trees.

The Weather in the Week Ahead

This third week of September brings one of the most radical autumnal swings so far in the season. Not only do the chances of highs only in the 60s move from ten percent to 30 percent, but cold afternoons in the 50s become possible for the first time since June 4th. The likelihood of warm 90s or 80s falls sharply throughout the period, with September 18th bringing only a 20 percent chance of highs above the 70s, the first time that has happened since May 6th. Each day this week brings at least a 30 percent chance of showers, with the 18th having the highest chance: almost 50 percent. The mornings are chilly, and the possibility of a light freeze grows steadily. Two weeks ago, the odds were high against frost. Now the chance of freezing temperatures to occur in a seven-day period is up to 40 percent. Next week it will be 50 percent. In two more weeks, it will be 75 percent, and in three weeks almost 90 percent.

Natural Calendar

Along the Ohio River, tobacco plots are almost bare. Near Yellow Springs and along most of the 40th Parallel, cornfields are brown or gray. Soybean fields are yellow and shedding, and some fields have lost all their leaves. Grapes and fall apples are about a third picked. Commercial tomatoes and potatoes are just about harvested. Sunflower fields are starting to blacken.

Daybook

1985: Indian Mound and Upper Trail: The first goldenrod is fading in the woods, New England asters, small white asters, showy coneflowers, and white snakeroot still in full bloom. Only a couple of Joe Pye plants left. Sneezeweed discovered in full bloom, and large-flowered bidens. One puffball mushroom found near the river cliffs. Most field thistles deteriorated. Most wingstem have lost their petals. Horse nettle has yellow fruit as big as cherries. Geese flew over 6:30 p.m.

1986: Geese flew over the house at 6:30 a.m. More and more leaves turning. The tree line in much of the county is fringed with yellow and brown.

1987: Three fireflies lying in the night grass, blinking, creating a soft glow. Crickets intense. Apples thumping to the ground every few minutes; once in a while, one clatters into the potted plant below the tree.

1988: Cardinal sings near dawn.

1991: One dove calls in the late morning. They must have stopped their early morning songs just this past week. The coming winter's tiny craneflies seen swarming over the picnic table in the back yard this afternoon. It seems they have just emerged. A few katydids heard last night.

1993: Rain this morning, then cool and sun. The late-summer smell is gone now, the rich basil and pollen smell. Instead, the north wind brings in a different, less pungent scent. The trees remain green, but the feel to the air is autumnal. Uncle Bill called tonight from Gentilly, Minnesota. There had been a few other very light frosts so far, he said, but this morning, all the grass was "white as could be."

1996: Ride down the bike path, temperature in the 50s, clear blue sky: The tree line was green from Yellow Springs down past Jacoby to the Little Miami. White panicled asters, violet Short's aster and heart leaved asters, dark purple New England asters and tall goldenrod were all early bloom to full bloom. Ragweed was mostly gone, seedpods forming below its flower clusters. A few violet domestic phlox were still strong. I saw a last lobelia, lots of white snakeroot just on the other side of its peak, scattered dandelions and chicory, great mullein, Jerusalem artichokes, small flowered rudbeckia. Pokeberries are mostly purple now; a few purple elderberries hold on.

1998: Cardinal at 7:49 this morning. Eastern swallowtail butterfly at 7:45. Ten cabbage butterflies in the garden after lunch. Middle season for the New England asters.

1999: Hurricane Floyd bears down on the Carolinas. Two million people evacuated Florida yesterday, but the storm went north, ravaging the Bahamas, missing Jacksonville. In Yellow Springs last night, it was so cold that the katydids wouldn't sing. First time this fall.

2000: Full silence at 6:00 a.m., not one bird. Very last rudbeckia dies in the yard. About a third of the phlox are left. The New England asters are in early full bloom. Cornfields are browning quickly, the soy fields a bit ahead of them. In the south garden, it's obvious now that, in the course of just a month or two, the ranunculus have choked out most of the daisies.

2001: Jay, crows, cardinal, and the chatter of a wren at 5:55 a.m., then silence in between scattered calls. No doves calling. Forty-six degrees this morning. First time in the 40s this fall.

2002: Starlings cackling in the back trees this morning before noon.

2003: Driving to Columbus today, I saw few trees with autumn color. Only the cottonwoods were aging. The corn harvest had started, however, and most of the soybean fields were turning gold. Monarch butterflies seen from time to time along the highway. In the Caribbean, Hurricane Isabel threatens to move against the Outer Banks of North Carolina.

2004: Two monarchs seen flying south across the freeway this afternoon. One of them flew right into my truck.

2005: Screech owl repeating whinny before dawn.

2007: A cardinal sang once this morning at 5:56, the sky clear and temperature in the 40s. An hour later, I drove to Sharonville near Cincinnati. Ashes, cottonwoods, hackberries, catalpas, yellow poplars, sweet gums and box elders were fading and yellowing just enough to define the first phase of the Early Autumn leafturn. Next week, there should be dramatic changes. Three small flocks of starlings seen along the highway. One yellow tiger swallowtail seen at home in the north garden this afternoon. Large flocks of sparrows are coming to the feeder now. Before dinner, I brought in a little wood for the stove. I will make the first fire of the season tonight, keep the gas furnace off until the cold wave moves east and milder temperatures return.

2008: "It's such a beautiful afternoon!" Jeanie declared. "You're crazy if you stay inside playing with your computer. There's a wonderful breeze, too. Come on out and do things in the yard!"

Indeed, it was an extraordinary day. The sun was bright and warm. A southwest wind swept mare's tails and mackerel scallops above the village. The wind was light and cool, perfect for cleaning up the woodpile and for clearing off the back patio.

Hurricane Ike had struck Galveston and Houston the day before and was heading north, but the computer radar showed most of the rain staying to the east of Yellow Springs, and there was no sign of rain in the sky. So I gave in to the fine weather, put aside what I should have done inside and went out and rearranged the wood, took inventory of what I should split, set the kindling to one side, and estimated how many more truckloads I would need before January.

By three o'clock, the wind was growing a bit stronger and the cirrus and altostratus clouds thickened. Gusts came from the south and then the west, and the trees and honeysuckles that encircled the yard were starting to sway back and forth. I went to the covered porch to rest a little, and soon my wife and I decided it was better to watch the afternoon than to be outside in it. There was so much to see and feel. Cabbage butterflies and small, orange folded-wing butterflies continued to visit the dahlias and butterfly bushes. The sparrows had fed sporadically earlier in the day; now they flocked to the swinging feeders, descending from the unstable canopy, down by the dozen, sometimes, I thought, up to a hundred birds fighting for a place on the perches and literally covering the ground to forage for seed. A family of cardinals – a male, female and four fledglings – joined the frenzy off and on, then chickadees, finches and nuthatches.

By four o'clock, leaves were coming down into the backyard, and small branches from the locust trees were landing close by our vantage point. The more the leaves blanketed the grass, the more the sparrows loved it, abandoning the feeders to find insects. The orb-weaver spider that had spun a giant web below the roof was forced to retire, its web cut away. Our peach tree let all its peaches go. The tall Jerusalem artichoke plants I had been nurturing fell flat into the herbs below them.

Now the sound of sirens and cracking branches started to accompany the squall. A tree collapsed in the woodlot behind our property. A terrified squirrel clung flat against the trunk of our Osage tree, scrambling up and then down, then just hanging on. Small branches clattered to the roof of the porch. The cushion on the lawn chair next to me flew by, landing against the back of another chair.

But we sat there, mesmerized, unwilling to move until the air grew a little cold. Then we went in for supper, and while we were eating, the lights went out and the wind shifted to the north, bringing down three great white mulberry branches and a box elder tree at the northwest corner of our property.

We told one of our daughters about our afternoon, but she wasn't impressed with our reckless watching. She lives in Miami Beach and has seen a few hurricanes.

"You're just like the crazy people who go out surfing before the storm," she said.

2010: Two male tiger swallowtails came by today, monarchs, too, and swarms of skippers. A young cardinal fed by its mother. New England asters are beginning at home today, and the first Jerusalem artichoke is opening. Casey called, left me a message: "Hey, Bill! Got black vultures on the bridge at Grinnell Road, got turkey vultures on Glen Street eating a dead squirrel! Hope you all are well." The black vultures are a rarity here; they usually stay south of the Ohio River.

2011: Cool morning, 45 degrees. Walking Bella at 8:00 this evening: The tree crickets were more subdued, as were the field crickets. It seemed I went in and out of fewer sound pockets as I walked. In the yard, the zinnias and mums are brilliant in the bright afternoon. Many cabbage whites, one great spangled fritillary, one sulfur in the sunny afternoon. When I went out with Bella at night, no katydids in the cool 45 degree evening, and the crickets were thin, far fewer song windows, far fainter sound within them.

2012: A chilly morning, clouds then sun, then mild and quiet. Tat weeded in the garden for hours, clearing the edge of the flowerbeds for winter mulch.

2013: Weeding and clearing the garden spaces for winter. Inventory: scattered phlox, false boneset, some spiderwort, late hostas, an autumn crocus, final Shasta daisies, full zinnias, roses, full Jeanie's yellow rose. New England asters are coming on strong, but without the zinnias and roses, the garden would be dull and tattered. In the honeysuckles, red and orange berries shine through the blackening hops. False climbing buckwheat is tangling in the large east rose bush. Only cabbage white butterflies seen in the flowers today.

2014: A cool morning and early afternoon full of sun: Seven painted ladies (*Vanessa (Cynthia) virginiensis)*, a monarch and an Eastern black in the zinnias all at one time today. Rob says their abundance is either from a recent hatch or a migratory group or from a wedding (painted ladies being the butterfly of choice, he says, for releasing after vows are spoken). Clouds and rain in the afternoon, a cold, damp evening.

2015: Sun and mild, a perfect, bright day: One skipper and several monarchs passed through, and cabbage whites played. The New England asters continue to come in along the north garden edges. Jeanie's yellow rose put out one bright flower. The Shasta daisies are down to a handful of blossoms. The remaining color in the yard comes from tithonias and zinnias. The hummingbird still visits the feeder, but Karen reports from Milwaukee that hers seem to have left for the year. Last night, katydids and crickets were steady and harsh, undeterred by the cool air.

2016: Cool and sun. One tattered male tiger swallowtail, still an abundance of silver-spotted skippers, many mating on the zinnias or in randori above the north garden.

2017: At the art center downtown, their prairie dock has multiple tall stalks in full bloom. Yesterday I noticed honeysuckle berries had started to come down, just a few by the driveway. Green acorns from a white oak tree were all over the sidewalk at the college. One tattered great spangled fritillary and four cabbage whites stayed in the garden much of the afternoon. The female hummingbird still visits the zinnias.

2018: Sun and dry and hot here, Hurricane Florence flooding the coastal Carolinas. A few honeysuckle berries dropping. The zinnias and tithonias still host multiple monarchs, silver spotted skippers and cabbage whites throughout the afternoon. A great flock of starlings seen swirling into a grove of pines along Trebein Road near dusk. A few minutes later, above the grocery store parking lot, an even larger flock much higher and in an unbroken line north to south for several minutes.

2019: Female cardinal making call notes as we sat on the back porch about 7:30 this morning, the hummingbird coming back and forth, robins clucking south of the yard, crows to the southwest, one male cardinal song at 7:45, then silence. Honeysuckle berries have started to fall on the car through the nights – I park under a spreading honeysuckle bush.

2020: First morning in the 40s, on schedule, sun and clouds, an autumnal breeze in the honeysuckles. Geese flew over, honking, at dawn. Two itchy chigger bites on my left leg from sitting in the grass and brushing Ranger. Hurricane Sally inches ashore with thick rainfall and waves of twenty feet, Mobile, Alabama, in her eye.

2022: A note for the *Yellow Springs News*:

Decline in Butterfly Numbers and Species

It was the leanest butterfly summer for my yard in over forty years. As in the past, cabbage white butterflies were relatively common from spring to fall. Small blues and golden fold-wing skippers were often present. For a while in August, a few monarchs, male tiger swallowtails (the yellow and black ones) and two zebra swallowtails visited the yard. Other types, however, were almost completely absent for the first time since the 1980s: red admirals, pearl crescents, painted ladies, fritillaries, silver-spotted skippers, hackberries, question marks, mourning cloaks.

People with a greater variety of flowers most likely had a greater number and variety of butterflies. And people who spent more time outside watching for butterflies in more locations probably saw many more than I did. My experience, though, does reflect what I have heard from some other villagers, and it parallels the findings of the North American Butterfly Association. The July 4 butterfly counts that were carried out by members of that Association show a 36 percent drop in the total numbers observed over a ten-year period, and the number of butterfly species also fell, especially since 2017. The Ohio Lepidopterists have had similar results in their counts.

Probable causes for the declines are the usual suspects: insecticides, climate change, loss of habitat. Local, personal solutions may be temporarily possible in yards and fields by thoughtful plantings and by stopping the use of pesticides. It seems possible, though, that this decade could see the end of butterflies as a familiar part of our summer world.

2023: First day with a high in the 60s, day before a trip to Italy: Time count...almost out of time for canna lilies: only ten flowering. I expect to come back on the 25th to find most all of them gone, but the New England asters should be in full flower. Two cabbage whites seen. Webworms in the crab apple tree near the dooryard, and the North Carolina viburnum has turned reddish brown. A brief walk at the Covered Bridge: wingstem, ironweed, white snakeroot, powder blue lobelias, jewelweed all flowering, wood nettle lanky and to seed, the river clear and low. As I walked the familiar paths that have not changed at least in the past half century, the last 45 years of my life in this habitat swept across me, an electric or spiritual field of time in place connecting me again and again to what and when I have been here, place evoking and drawing together time, self joining both time and place.

And in fine, the ancient precept, "Know thyself," and the modern precept, "Study nature," become at last one maxim.

Ralph Waldo Emerson

September 16th
The 259th Day of the Year

Fayre Summer droops, droop men and beasts therefore:
So fayre a summer look for never more.
All good things vanish, lesse than in a day,
Peace, plenty, pleasure, sodainely decay.

Thomas Nashe, 1600

Sunrise/set: 6:17/6:43
Day's Length: 12 hours 26 minutes
Average High/Low: 77/56
Average Temperature: 67
Record High: 99 – 1897
Record Low: 38 – 1902

The Daily Weather

Today is typically one of the coolest and wettest days in Early Fall. Chances of clouds and rain: 40 percent. There is a 15 percent chance of temperatures in the 90s, 15 percent for 80s, thirty-five percent for 70s, and a 30 percent chance of highs in the 60s - the greatest chance of that since spring. And for the first time since June 12 there is the possibility of afternoons warming only into the 50s. Four mornings in ten drop below 50 degrees.

Natural Calendar

The second week of Early Fall brings an end to the first period of leaf fall along the 40th Parallel. Within the next fourteen days, most of the black walnut and serviceberry trees lose the remainder of their leaves. The next tier of foliage includes ashes, hickories, box elders, tulip trees and elms. Now the deciduous trees are almost bare in northern Canada. In New England and in the Rocky Mountains, they often begin to approach their brightest colors.

Daybook

1983: Touch-me-not, wingstem clearly declining along the roadsides.

1984: Forsythia leaves darken.

1985: Huge flock of geese on the golf course at the college.

1986: Geese fly over honking, 9:13 p.m., across the full, white moon.

1987: Hardly any geese this year, cardinals and doves quiet. Robins calling softly in the honeysuckles this afternoon.

1989: Robins clucking steadily at 6:30 a.m. Starlings on the wires, squirrels loud. Edges of rusty yellow on the ginkgoes. Mums half open. Patches of yellow on the lindens and gingkoes. Cardinal sings 8:27 a.m. At 8:30, more robins pass through the yard, their calls sounding urgent. No katydids heard last night. (It was wet and cold.)

1991: Red berries fall from the magnolias by my side door.

1992: A couple of forsythia flowers seen at the side entry. Rudbeckia almost all gone.

1993: Butterflies everywhere today. And I ran into one large cluster of monarch butterflies on the way home; although I swerved and put the brakes on hard, I couldn't avoid four of them. The afternoon was bright and cool, the rain that usually falls today having come yesterday. In the garden, white and red phlox still hold. At the mill, the river is down a foot, all the wingstem and ironweed gone, the asters in full bloom, the first goldenrod beginning to rust. At the dam, small blues fluttering by my feet, two bumblebees (the male quite small) mating in the sun at the water's edge.

1995: The first New England aster has bloomed today in the yard. Across the street, violet autumn crocus is in full bloom. Jeanie said that two of her kindergarten students had found toads in the last week. Yesterday, a toad hopped past me by the bench in the backyard, the first time all summer. Migration has apparently begun.

1997: This morning, I heard a downy woodpecker tapping on the cedar siding outside my door. This afternoon, blue jays were loud. And four flew over the house before supper. Full moon tonight - but no geese come across the sky. I haven't heard or seen them much this year. Where have they or I been? On High Street, the stalks of autumn crocus have emerged fully, but the flowers are just opening.

1998: Squirrel running through the yard with a black walnut in its mouth. Chicory still blooming. Cutover crown vetch flowering by the roadsides. Early leafturn noticed south along the highway to Xenia.

1999: Buckeyes are on the ground downtown. In the back yard, one black walnut hull wedged on the sharp edge of the outdoor grill. Autumn crocus still blooming across the street. This afternoon I went to the Jacoby swamp with our bulldog, Gus. The woods was so dry from the months without rain. Leafcup was shriveled. Zigzag goldenrod was struggling. White snakeroot, however, was unaffected by the weather. I saw robins for the first time since August, heard their migration clucking. They were flocking, eating honeysuckle berries, clustering around the stream. Then I sat by the swamp and looked out over the wetland. There the drought was harmless. Orange jewelweed stretched to the far wood line, bordered by purple Joe Pye weed. In winter, this place offers green and running spring water; in summer, protection from the uncertainties of the heat and rain.

2000: Long line of blackbirds crossing above the freeway near Middletown.

2002: Monarch at 9:00 a.m. Very last white Royal Standard hosta flower in bloom. Virgin's bower season is ending. Scattered yellow Osage leaves on the ground contribute to pre-autumn.

2003: Autumn crocus blossoms still holding under the maple a few houses down on High Street. Purple-flowered hostas still blooming in the alleys, but the Royal Standards are almost gone, only two flowers left. Monarchs still coming to the zinnias, chasing each other back and forth.

2004: The tea roses bloom in the south garden now that all the Japanese beetles have gone.

2007: Driving north of Yellow Springs, Jeanie and I saw several large flocks of starlings on the wing and starlings gathering on the telephone lines.

2008: After 48 hours in the dark, the power has come back on. Hurricane Ike brought winds of 70 miles per hour in the area, a freak storm, according to the meteorologists. Thousands are still without electricity. The cardinal family fed throughout the day, and 6:00 a.m. brought brief cardinal song and crows. No doves heard. Squirrels played in the broken white mulberry this afternoon. In the garden, the New England asters, the Red Baron hostas, and false boneset are in full bloom. A few spiderworts and Shasta daisies are left. The Knockout rose is still producing multiple blossoms. The peaches are almost all down, the same with the apples in the alley. No monarchs in several days, but one bright yellow male finch seen yesterday.

2010: Overcast and rainy: crows late this morning, 6:05, one male cardinal sang at 6:20. Two young cardinals being fed by their mother at the bird feeders before 8:00. Lots of skippers, two male tiger swallowtails, two monarchs when the sun came out. The first Jerusalem artichokes are flowering in the yard, a little behind the New England asters, which are in early bloom. Beggarticks are open beside the hobblebush and the volunteer virgin's bower.

2011: A little more than 40 degrees this morning, and I was not able to hear any crickets at 6:00, although Jeanie was able to hear them faintly at 7:00. When I walked Bella at 8:00, I was only able to catch fragments of cricket song in a few places, a field cricket and a high tree cricket. The peaches and the raspberries are completely done in the garden. The heliopsis has only a few flowers left. In the woods, the jump seeds are brittle and jumping, but here they are still soft. Along Dayton Street, chicory is ending its three-to-four-month season. Leafturn is accelerating in the village: ashes, box elders, maples, locusts all showing color. Miriam at the bookstore wanted to know about locations to find buckeyes. She said some little boys had collected bags of the nuts from all the trees in town. Bella and I walked again after dark, the crickets louder than last night, the temperature a little milder, maybe in the low 50s. Field crickets and the intermittent, ghostly, whistling tree crickets.

2012: The sky was so clear, the wind soft. I went out to South Glen along the water, taking inventory to keep the day: great fields of goldenrod at the height of bloom; the first white small-flowered asters, zigzag goldenrod beside them; new chickweed sprouts with two to four leaves spreading across the ground; bare buckeye trees, new buds showing; aging smartweed and snakeroot; blanched wood nettle; seeded wingstem, leaves bleached with powdery mildew; summer-green ginger leaves; gray brome; dry leaf cup; agrimony seeds crumbling; wood mint dry, still fragrant; field thistles puffed; burdock brittle; steady drizzle of locust leaves; last tall coneflowers, last lobelias, last woodland sunflowers and last orange jewelweed; new beggarticks; new burr marigolds bright as April cowslip; low, low drought river; downy woodpecker chirr and blue jay bell call and kingfisher rattle and nasal "peent" of the nuthatch and a robin peeping its migration song.

2013: Trumpet creeper vines still in bloom along Limestone. Peggy's virgin's bower is maybe a half done blossoming, most of the rose of Sharon shrubs have ended their flowering. Male goldfinches that came to the feeder this morning had lost their summer brilliance. The sphinx moth that had stayed by the front porch light for several days was gone this morning. I sat outside in the cool late afternoon, no butterflies, not even a cabbage white, and only one hummingbird at the zinnias.

2014: Another cool day. Peggy's virgin's bower is about nine-tenths gone. Along Phillips Street, an autumn azalea was showing its first violet flowers. I look back at the abundance of monarch butterflies on this date many years ago. And not a one today.

2015: Still hummingbirds at the feeder. A lethargic cardinal call, so late at 7:00, crows rowdy at 8:00, everyone sleeping in despite the sun and warmth. Monarchs in the tithonias throughout the day, one Eastern black, an azure, a small fritillary, a silver-spotted skipper.

2016: Sunny and warm, a female hummingbird at the tithonia this afternoon, and monarch off and on, many silver-spotted skippers. Moya's rose of Sharon still has some blossoms, as does my trumpet creeper. Knotweed, stonecrop, Jerusalem artichokes and hops still full, goldenrod in bright plumes, New England asters slowly coming in. At the northwest corner of the back porch, the first small white asters have opened, and the white autumn crocus is starting to bloom. Next to the parking lot near the grocery store, dusky pink persimmons lie all about the ground.

2017: Sun and warm in the high 70s: The white autumn crocus at the northwest corner of the house is in full bloom, and I saw a monarch in the zinnias close to noon. No New England asters in the yard yet, probably because I cut them back too much and too late in the summer.

Out for inventory with Jill in the later afternoon: Past the Art Center on Corry Street (and the biggest prairie dock plant in the region full of tall golden blooms) to Ellis Pond: some leafturn taking place; reddening on the dogwoods; red-purple virgin's bower climbing a telephone pole; an ochre shade to a few maples;

a hawthorn full of berries, leaves withering from drought; the ash grove paling and thinning; black walnut trees bare, walnuts all around on the branches and on the ground; faded touch-me-not foliage; fat green hickory nuts, some dropped to the grass, others holding among summer green leaves; tall, young smartweed and foxtail grass; a clump of full-blooming black-eyed Susans; bright honeysuckle berries.

Along the highway to Springfield: the great field of low sunflowers, in late full flower, filled with people touching and picking and photographing, rows of fat, heavy blossoms literally spreading out to the woodland horizon.

Near the Covered Bridge, August was more obviously in retreat, most ironweed gray and soft, most wingstem bare topped by prickly seed heads, tall goldenrod and white snakeroot (one stalk graced with a newly-emerged red admiral butterfly) all the way open, pokeweed with its violet stems tangled and weighted down by clusters of black berries, old mint that had been cut over weeks ago growing back and flowering, seven-foot-tall field thistles with heavy violet inflorescence; indigo lobelias stark against the beige grasses; clumps of woodland sunflowers, small white asters coming in, and for the last few hundred yards, a monarch butterfly followed us up almost to the road. Beyond the Birch House near Jacoby, some staghorn sumac with blood-red leaves and horns, a last tall bellflower plant in bloom almost swallowed up by the dying grasses.

At the Women's Park, the massive cup plants were no longer in flower, but the New England asters had come in. At home, the Danielsons' maple had a wide streak of orange. It is the first tree on the block to turn, like it has been since the turn of the century.

2018: At John Bryan Park with Jill: A huge flock of starlings and blackbirds together clucking and chirping and settling in and then out of the high oaks (and knocking down acorns) in the late afternoon. In the Carolinas, Hurricane Florence stalls and continues to flood the low country with record rainfall.

2019: Monarchs and cabbage whites in the zinnias and tithonias through the day. At Jill's, a painted lady and a skipper when I went out toward the dahlias. Excited blue jay calls as I walked back from downtown this evening. The jays have become part of the Early Autumn song.

2020: The garden seems so empty these days. One hummingbird, one monarch, one sulphur, a handful of cabbage whites as firestorms continue in the West and Hurricane Sally inundates the Mississippi Valley. Jays heard off and on. The prairie dock plant at the corner of High and South West College Street is still in bloom. Tangled banks of hops to seed and climbing false buckwheat in full flower lie draped thick across the honeysuckles like kudzu on the banks of the Santee-Cooper reservoir.

2022: Drive to Gethsemani in northern Kentucky: The trees are fading to ochre. Patches of goldenrod, boneset, Jerusalem artichokes flower along the way, purple-headed grasses shading the roadsides. Young large-flowered magnolia trees have started to flower in the graveyard. Two sulphurs and lots of hummingbirds at the monastery.

2023: Arrival in Rome, Italy, the landscape mostly late-summer green. The most common wildflowers were like varieties of hawkweed and chicory. Butterflies common (whites and a brown-orange type) . where Neysa lives in Campello mounysind. Like Ohio, the land was dray after weeks without rain.

Or it has come to be September
and the blackbirds are flocking.
They pass through the riverbank trees
in one direction erratically
like leaves in the wind.

Wendell Berry

September 17th
The 260th Day of the Year

See, Anarda, Fall is coming home,
bringing all its fruits.

Manuel de Navarrete

Sunrise/set: 6:18/6:41
Day's Length: 12 hours 23 minutes
Average High/Low: 77/55
Average Temperature: 66
Record High: 92 – 1931
Record Low: 39 – 1959

The Daily Weather

Highs in the 80s come one year in four. Seventies occur 40 percent of the time, 60s twenty-five percent; and from now through the end of the month, the chance of highs just in the 50s remains steady at ten percent. This morning, for the first time in the fall, low temperatures fall into the 40s about half the time. Chances of rain: 35 percent.

Natural Calendar

In the third week of September, Wildflower Season lingers, but most of the major late-blooming plants gradually close their flowering cycle for the year. Light Frost Season gathers momentum in the North. Katydid Season weakens in the cool nights, and Black Walnut, Buckeye, Cottonwood and Serviceberry Leaf-fall Seasons gradually come to a close in town just as Winter Wheat and Barley Planting Seasons commence on the farm.

Daybook

1982: Mulberry and Osage begin to get yellow leaves. Small white asters are prominent in front of the house.

1983: Trumpet creepers still strong. Grackles in the back trees all afternoon. Fall raspberries (Fall Red variety) are still coming in, about a pint every few days.

1984: Grinnell Swamp: Touch-me-not pods come to their peak of popping. Nodding bur marigold (*Bidens cernua*) found. Lobelia still full. Zigzag goldenrod early bloom. White snakeroot still full. Boneset faded. Poplars yellowing, sycamore leaves browning at the edges. Black and gold striped caterpillar of the milkweed tiger moth identified.

1986: Many catalpas almost gone. The ash by my window has lost most of its leaves.

1987: Honeysuckle branches heavy with red berries. Farmers' Market selling squash and late melons, mums, tomatoes, zucchini, gourds, apples, concord grapes, and the last peaches.

1988: Cardinal sings off and on all day.

1989: No cicadas this afternoon. Red berries on the spicebush. Bright New England asters seen today. Dozens of *Helianthus tuberosus* full bloom in a soybean field. A flock of geese has come to the field by Antioch again. No katydids last night, a few chanting tonight, one right on the front porch.

1990: Every event of fall adds to the momentum. The acts accumulate like leaves in the backwaters.

1991: Magnolia seeds are coming down, box elders shedding, small cottonwoods three-fourths gone, my ash tree almost all fallen.

1993: Still no asters blooming at home, only a few at South Glen. The drought has kept them back, as it has the mums. At the Covered Bridge, a cardinal sang once as I crossed over into the woods. Swamp bidens were in full bloom at the swamp, a few goldenrod and small white asters. Wingstem, protected by the canopy, was still bright. The river was as low as during the drought of five years ago, and it had a dank smell, a faint odor of sewage, the drought and the quiet air exposing the village's pollution.

1995: This past week, the weather shifted into the cooler 70s, and the clear sun that had dried out late August and early September was diluted with clouds and rain. At the park, the box elder is paler, rustier; the red maple's scattered deterioration has increased to a few minor patches now. In the south garden, the sunflowers that sprouted from birdseed in late July are in full bloom. Along Limestone Street, black walnut trees are half bare.

1997: Virgin's bower and tall violet sedum are still in full bloom around town. Yesterday, I saw a bed of August Moon hosta in full flower. Last peaches coming in at the orchard. More jays this morning, but no cardinals or sparrows, no robin calls. Crickets strong. Katydids loud last night. Berries on the hawthorns outside my room are starting to turn red.

1998: Artichokes and goldenrod still full. Redbud, locust, yellow poplar, ash, sumac, buckeye all turning here and there.

1999: Five silver-spotted skippers working one pink sedum in the east garden.

2001: In the chilly 47-degree morning, crickets are quiet except for just a few that sing so slowly it seems they are whining, crying over the cold.

2003: The zinnias have been attacked by powdery mildew for the past few days, are beginning to lose their beauty. In the Women's Park along Corey Street, almost all the coneflowers are black. Monarch and painted lady (*Cynthia*) butterflies continue to pass through the garden. My ash tree at Wilberforce has two huge splotches of gold. One Japanese beetle found on the roses. A few dead Asian lady beetles noticed on the roof.

2004: Virgin's bower and New England asters are still at the height of their bloom, but their slow decay has begun. False boneset is about half gone.

2007: Virgin's bower, New England asters and false boneset are still in full bloom. The Jerusalem artichoke flowers are just beginning to unfold. Another flock of starlings and a first flock of blackbirds seen in the countryside today. Nothing inside Yellow Springs, though. Walking through town tonight with Jean: we saw two milkweed pods that had opened early.

2010: Crows at 5:52 this morning. In the alley, robins peeping, starlings feeding and chattering. On Dayton Street, black walnuts cover the side of the street like mulberries. In the yard, the cardinal fledglings are feeding without their parents. Small white asters coming in at Peggy's and in the alley.

2011: When I walked out the door this morning a little after 6:00, crows were calling, and a male and female cardinal were on the platform feeder. Some tree crickets in the early morning, then a growing chorus through the afternoon until the evening - although still cool - roused even Gerard's katydids along Dayton Street. In the garden this afternoon, one tiger swallowtail, one Eastern black, one mourning cloak, one small fritillary, two buckeyes, a few silver-spotted skippers, many cabbage whites, no monarchs. At the northwest corner of the porch, the white autumn crocus that I had thought dead the other day suddenly rose to produce three giant blossoms. And in the alley, hidden at the back of Frank's old house, a clump of violet crocus was blooming, too.

2012: Preoccupied with other things, I forgot to notice when the Danielsons' Jerusalem artichokes came in to bloom - but they are full now.

2013: Crows at 6:10 this morning. On my walk with Bella, at 7:30, I could hear the steady distant chattering of starlings in the high trees, and along Limestone Street, the clucking of chickens behind honeysuckle bushes. The small-leafed hostas with violet flowers are still blooming in front of Don's house and Judy's. On the way to Wilmington, I saw the very first silage cutting, the first goldenrod rusting. On the way home: The whole sky was filled with magnificent wispy cirrus, and they stayed throughout the evening as the full moon was rising.

2014: Walked outside after lunch: one monarch, one painted lady (*Cynthia*) in the zinnias. My short visits to the garden often let me see what I am looking for. Under the giant beggartick plant, the white autumn crocus plant is coming into full bloom. At the corner of High and South West College Streets, the last prairie dock flower is blooming. Today Jonatha wrote: "I have seen three monarchs this year (so sad, only three), and all last Sunday. Two were on the flowers by Dayton YS Road, in front of the Little Free Library. The other was on the Glass Farm."

2016: At the St. Clare Monastery, lush white snakeroot throughout the woods, and Jumpseeds common and jumping. Throughout the drive from Yellow Springs to Cincinnati, no leafturn noticed, the woods as green as in Deep Summer, one power line with blackbirds side by side for yards and yards. A blue jay was calling when I arrived home in the middle of the afternoon.

2017: Warm and bright sun: Two hummingbirds (one brilliant green), a monarch, a tattered great spangled fritillary and many cabbage whites in the zinnias. In the Caribbean, Hurricane Maria moves toward Puerto Rico. In the northeast Atlantic, Hurricane Jose travels north near the coast.

2019: Continued warm and dry. This morning at 6:40, one clear cardinal call, then silence except for the buzzing of the tree crickets. In the garden midmorning: only cabbage whites and fluttering hackberry leaves. In the afternoon, three hummingbirds and half a dozen cabbage whites. No monarchs seen today. The virgin's bower, flower, climbs up into Janet's redbud tree. In my yard, Moya's and Judy's, the large-leafed white blossomed hostas are ending their flowering seasons. The thin-leafed late hostas with violet flowers remain in full bloom, as in years past. Honeysuckle berryfall gains momentum. At Ellis Pond, two blue jays were calling continually and flying back and forth between two trees.

2020: A flock of geese, honking, flew over the house as I sat on the porch watching the sunlight break through the trees. Mild and bright today, one monarch late morning, one Eastern black swallowtail in the middle of the afternoon. I noticed powdery mildew on some of the zinnias for the first time this year. On the east end of the north garden, in front of the tall marigolds, the first New England asters bloomed. Before supper, Ranger and I walked the Covered Bridge habitat for the first time since last fall. In the field (solid with goldenrod), the New England asters were open. In the woods, wingstem was almost gone, the blue lobelias were down to a few blossoms per plant, zigzag goldenrod was full, wood nettle all gone to seed, its bare umbels like antlers reaching above the tattering undergrowth. Crows, hawks, blue jays occasionally on the other side of the tree line, far off. I looked closely at the river and the far shore, knowing it was the same river and shore I had first walked along over forty years ago. The water was low and clear, most of the stones at the bottom visible. My sensations were nostalgia, familiarity, loss, returning home, gratitude, confusion, peace. The future seemed part of that landscape, too, unimaginable in the same way that the decades of memories were indistinguishable, the repetition of walks blurring the past, closing it pores, making the present so dense.

2022: Gethsemani: Heat and silence. Dry sun. I walked two hours into the hills, accompanied by numerous large grasshoppers (*Lubbers*?), small to mid-size butterflies, some like rusty hackberry butterflies, others banded like buckeye butterflies, pale sulphurs but no cabbage whites. Purple long-budded grass, about three feet tall, was dominant, probably the grass that I saw so much of when I drove along the Bluegrass Parkway. Some ironweed and many areas of white snakeroot seen, some small-flowered woodland sunflowers. But the habitat was really quite foreign to me, my botanizing getting sloppy with my sagging mood. I didn't feel at home there this visit, the fields appearing full of foreign plantings, creating a sense of alienation.

And a then a note from Chris Walker gave a welcome, redeeming blessing of home:

"I finally sat down on the pond porch at about 4:30. Debbie joined me. We watched groups of white butterflies dancing on the prairie, some in pairs, some in clouds of six or more. (Debbie called them "sets"—terminology from her square dancing days.) We noted a few monarchs enjoying thistle blooms here and there.

"After a while, one Monarch fluttered close to the porch, around a post, then back and forth in front of us. Debbie was standing, I was sitting. The butterfly flew in under the porch roof. I extended my hand silently. She fluttered around Debbie once, twice, maybe three times—and then suddenly lit on Debbie's finger. Such a beautiful look of joyful wonder on Debbie's face. I said quietly, 'What a gift.'

"The butterfly sat still on Debbie's hand for a minute or two. I slowly reached for my phone to take a picture—and she suddenly flew.

"We watched her flutter around the porch, around a post, out, back in, investigating the table between our chairs—and then she lit again on Debbie's finger. The very same finger. This time I did not move, and she tarried 3-5 minutes. Then she was off again.

"Again she fluttered around the porch, weaving in, out, around, over, back in, toward us, around the back of my chair— and onto <u>my</u> hand.

"She stayed still on my right hand for about 45 minutes. It was butterfly meditation. We were able simply to be with the lovely creature. Occasionally I would whisper a word of welcome and rest to her. Once I stroked the side of her wing. She stayed. Eventually, I moved her gently to the table to my left. She turned to face me, and sat still on the table for another minute or two, then flew.

"I stood to say farewell and extend my blessing. Again we watched her flutter around the porch, around a post, up over the roof, back down, in . . . and back to my hand. The same hand.

"I let her sit again for a while. I asked her quietly, "What is the meaning of this visit, friend?" Then I coaxed her gently free of my finger. She flew.

"That time, she fluttered off over the thistle, the milkweed, the goldenrod and aster. We bid her thanks, and blessings, and a good journey.

"What _is_ the meaning of that visit? If there is some hidden meaning, I can't know it in this life. Maybe she recognized us in some way. Maybe she was attracted by our benevolence. Maybe it was some simple biological factor—some smell or taste—that drew her and caused her to tarry.

"Or maybe there is no meaning other than that, for that hour, we were together. Perhaps that is all the meaning we need.

"I will never forget."

Sometimes hath the brightest day a cloud;
And after summer evermore succeeds
Barren winter, with his wrathful nipping cold:
So cares and joys abound as seasons fleet.

William Shakespeare

September 18th
The 261st Day of the Year

As we lay awake long before daybreak, listening to the rippling of the river and the rustling of the leaves ... we already suspected that there was a change in the weather, from a freshness as of autumn in these sounds. That night was the turning-point of the season. We had gone to bed in summer, and we awoke in autumn; for summer passes into autumn in some unimaginable point of time, like the turning of a leaf.

Henry David Thoreau

Sunrise/set: 6:18/6:39
Day's Length: 12 hours 21 minutes
Average High/Low: 77/55
Average Temperature: 66
Record High: 96 – 1895
Record Low: 37 – 1959

The Daily Weather

There is a five percent chance of highs in the 90s today, and a ten percent chance of 80s; most of the days, however (65 percent), are in the 70s. The remaining days: 15 percent chance of 60s, five percent for 50s. Skies are totally cloudy 45 percent of all September 18ths, with rain occurring 40 percent of the time. Nights are typically cool, with lows below 60 occurring more than half the time.

Natural Calendar

In the woods, Middle Spring's sedum is growing stronger. Henbit, mint, and catchweed revive as the canopy thins. Waterleaf has fresh shoots. Snow-on-the-mountain has recovered from its mid-summer slump and can be as thick and as beautiful as in Early Spring. Sometimes forsythia even responds as though it were April violet time instead of autumn violet time, whole bushes breaking into bloom. Praying mantises make egg cases (oothecas) for their eggs.

Touch-me-nots continue to burst to spill their seeds. Wood nettle, wingstem, clearweed and ironweed complete their cycles. The huge pink mallows of the wetlands have died back, heads dark, leaves disintegrating. In the pastures, the milkweed pods are ready to open.

Daybook

1983: At Ellis Pond, most wildflowers are gone, but arrowhead still blooming, bur marigolds, small helianthus, blue bindweed. This afternoon, we drove south to Serpent Mound. Zigzag goldenrod is common there, and Short's aster with its heart-shaped leaves. Touch-me-nots are still popping. Red woolly-bears seen, also red and black ones.

1986: Rain deepening the Early Fall colors.

1987: Boneset and knotweed almost gone.

1988: Black seeds on the wood nettle. New showy coneflowers still full. False boneset and goldenrod still hold along the freeways. First zigzag goldenrod blooms. The rest of the tall goldenrod is still not completely open.

1989: Robin migration calls near seven o'clock this morning. Buckeyes starting to fall from their hulls. No cicadas.

1993: On the way to Springfield, the first flock of autumn blackbirds seen flying southwest along the Mad River, both the western and eastern ends of the flock lost on the horizon. South into Kettering: the tree line has started to shift just a little into gold.

1995: The snow-on-the-mountain along Dayton Street has recovered from its Dog Day decay and has grown back thick and beautiful as in early spring.

1997: There are reports in the media that El Nino is bringing warm waters up along the Pacific coast, that tropical fish are being caught off the coast of northern California. This is supposed to be the strongest El Nino ever, more powerful than the one of 1982-1983. I will watch the winter and compare. In the yard, the sedum holds and a few last hosta are blossoming, but the heliopsis has never come back from its late August decline. The showy coneflowers of the south garden are almost gone.

1999: To Zanesville for the art fair: sunrise over the rolling hills at 6:15. Fog in the hollows, land dry and brown, goldenrod full throughout. At the rest stop between Columbus and Springfield, I found a patch of *Bidens coronata*, a tickseed sunflower. Also *Coreopsis tinctoria,* a yellow bidens-like plant with a dark maroon coloring to the petals near the center. And the hawthorn berries were heavy and bright red.

2000: Dogwoods are turning pink, and there are patches of red in the gum trees. A few locust leaves are yellow. Sparrow hawk found dead in front of the school door. Mike says he might have been migrating to Ohio.

2003: To Washington Court House: I drove east into the cirrus clouds that were preceding Hurricane Isabel (which was coming ashore at that moment on the Outer Banks of North Carolina). Monarchs flew across my path, and woolly-bear caterpillars were common on the road. Most of the soybean fields were yellowing or rusting, and the corn was browning. Goldenrod filled the pastures. Sycamores and cottonwoods had an ochre tint. The whole landscape glowed in the sun.

2006: This evening Jeanie said she heard a car make a loud screeching noise, and it was answered by the screech owl in the back woods.

2007: Jeanie saw a hummingbird at the Mexican sunflowers this afternoon. The first Jerusalem artichoke flower in the back yard is more than half open – the highest flower, maybe ten feet above the ground. At Wilberforce, my ash tree is completely green, but along the road to Wilmington, the ashes and maples, locusts and lindens are showing large patches of color. Almost no robin migration calls heard this summer, and very few robins seen in the area since the end of June.

2008: In the south gardens, the toad lily continues full bloom, along with the Red Baron hosta, New England asters and false boneset. Some patches of rudbeckia and spiderwort complement the bushy roses. An autumn perennial garden: late hosta, roses, asters, false boneset, Jerusalem artichokes, virgin's bower, variegated Japanese knotweed, and annuals, maybe all in their own September area.

2010: One male tiger swallowtail, one female today, two monarchs. The skippers continue to swarm.

2011: 5:55 in the dusk, crows started to call. Then at 6:00, the chipping of the cardinals and the arrival of a hummingbird. The cardinals came in to feed and then flew off at 6:07. Only faint tree crickets off and on. At 6:45, crows flew over the house screaming, and a cardinal gave its melodious territorial song as a younger male ate at the feeder.

Walking Bella at 8:00, I passed through far fewer windows of crickets than I have in past mornings; perhaps it was the cool (52 degrees), or maybe there has been a thinning of the insects or a closing of the mating cycle. This afternoon, overcast, the mourning cloak butterfly was back at the fallen peaches, and a sulphur and a polygonia were in the north yard. This evening, temperature at about 65, humidity high, the crickets produced a tremendous volume: field crickets, high tree crickets, intermittent crickets and "castanet" crickets. I could hear katydids throughout the neighborhood, not just at Gerard's. So tonight, the window of sound was the entire block.

2012: To Columbus: Cottonwood trees losing leaves all along the highway, and many were altogether bare. Goldenrod was in full bloom, and it was hard to tell the goldenrod fields from the yellowing soybean fields. Crows heard from my bedroom this morning about 6:15 .

2013: Virgin's bower in rapid decline throughout the village. The violet crocus is blooming at Mrs. Timberlake's. Red berries noticed on the star magnolia across the street.(I missed when they formed and turned.) Tree color has been holding, poised, for the last week or so. I picked a few raspberries from the bushes tangled in bindweed, and as I ate lunch this noon, several cabbage whites careened around the zinnia bed and a striped-bodied sphinx moth (from the late-summer hatch) hummed from flower to flower. One hummingbird came by, but no swallowtails seen. The sphinx moth stayed all day, and late in the afternoon, a lone, dark monarch joined him (or her) in the zinnias. At 8:30 tonight, the full moon was so bright and clear due east, katydids and tree frogs thunderous.

2015: Crows at 5:58 a.m. The bur marigolds in the pond have suddenly become dark. In the circle garden, their cousins, the beggarticks, have also lost their color. Underneath the beggartick tangle at the northwest corner of the porch, I found the white autumn crocus, strong and blooming. Through the day, at least one monarch, several skippers and cabbage whites, one polygonia. Tonight beautiful Megan told me that monarchs had been abundant at her farm throughout the month.

2016: An hour after dawn, fog throughout, a female hummingbird came to just the white zinnias. Then a robin peeping in the honeysuckles, the first I've heard since they departed after raising their fledglings. Is this the pivot week for their return?

2017: Hummingbirds active in the zinnias and castor beans this morning near dawn, temperature cool upper 50s. In the zinnia garden in a warm afternoon: a great spangled fritillary, a monarch and several cabbage whites. Downtown, persimmon fruits squashed on the grocery store driveway. Hurricane Maria heads to

Puerto Rico, Category 5.

2018: Sun again and hot: one monarch, a few cabbage whites. At the shop, the Kentucky coffee trees are yellowing. Near Jill's the cottonwood tree is half down. At home, a few cherry tree leaves are turning, Jeanie's river birch a more profound ochre. On the roof, the trumpet creeper vine has lost most of its leaves, its green beans prominent. New England asters coming in throughout the north garden, but smartweed is crowding them out. Katydids began to call in the neighborhood at 7:15 this evening. The chirping crickets and the tree frogs came on strong much earlier.

2019: Dry weather continuing. More blue jay activity off and on throughout the day. A few butterflies in the garden, a monarch, cabbage whites, a painted lady.

2020: New moon and perigee brings the first afternoon in the 60s. Freeze warnings for central Michigan and the Adirondacks. Light frost possible in northern Ohio counties. One silver-spotted skipper, one small brown fold-wing skipper, three cabbage whites. At the quarry, scattered, short goldenrod spikes, some white snakeroot, some stiff or lance-leaved goldenrod, no butterflies. When I got home, I found a note from Kate saying that she had seen a green heron at Ellis Pond this morning.

2022: Three very large murmurations of starling seen on the 230-mile trip from Kentucky. In the Caribbean, Hurricane Fiona, the first major storm of the year to reach the Americas, ravages Puerto Rico, then goes northwest to Santo Domingo.

A vast similitude interlocks all,
All spheres, grown, ungrown, small, large, suns,
moons, planets....

Walt Whitman

September 19th
The 262nd Day of the Year

The year growing ancient,
Not yet on summer's death,
Nor on the birth of trembling winter.

William Shakespeare

Sunrise/set: 6:19/6:38
Day's Length: 12 hours 19 minutes
Average High/Low: 76/55
Average Temperature: 66
Record High: 95 – 1908
Record Low: 34 – 1901

The Daily Weather

While the 19th can be one of the warmer days in middle September (highs in the 90s occurring one year in ten and with 80s coming three in ten), mild 70s are recorded thirty percent of the time, and chilly 60s thirty percent, as well. The possibility of rain declines to 25 percent, and skies are clear to partly cloudy 80 percent of the time.

Natural Calendar

Buckeyes start to burst from their hulls. More black walnuts, more hickory nuts, more acorns and persimmon fruits come down. Mullein stalks stand bare like withered cacti. In the perennial garden, varieties of late hostas, like the August Moon and the Royal Standard, discard their petals. Woolly bear caterpillars appear more often, crossing warm roads in the sun.

Daybook

1985: Grinnell Swamp: A few late blue lobelias, full bloom of zigzag goldenrod, boneset fading. Black walnuts common on the ground now. Sycamore leaves crunching underneath my feet. At the Covered Bridge, April sedum growing stronger, catchweed blossoming, coming back as the canopy thins. Virginia creeper has been red for a week. Crows loud out by the road. At the river past the bridge, a huge school of suckers or carp spread for maybe fifty feet in front of me.

1986: Yellow jackets swarm around the small white asters in front of the house. Wasps hug the goldenrod. Silver-spotted skippers move through the huge New England asters. Some black walnut trees have lost their leaves. The first woolly bears of the year seen today. Very last raspberries and a few everbearing strawberries picked.

1987: South Glen: Wasps working the goldenrod, skippers and honeybees in the small white asters.

1988: Several black woolly bears seen today. Tree color accelerating.

1989: Jacoby East: Spider webs everywhere. White snakeroot late now, touch-me-not a few last seeds popping still. Wingstem and Joe Pye weed almost complete. Clearweed gone to seed. Buckeye and hulls and acorn shells on the path. Hickory nuts are green, a few fallen. Spots of gold on the yellow poplars. A last *Helianthus lateriflorus* picked. Some tall coneflowers still intact, and many bull thistles. Squirrels chattering. Fresh waterleaf continuing to grow back, and new sweet Cicely. Hundreds of bees in the patches of small-leafed asters. First autumn violet found blooming. Some box elders bare. Garlic mustard sprouts are about a week old. Katydids, cicadas, crickets still strong. A cardinal sang at twilight.

1993: Along the Mad River, another long flock of starlings, and two huge flocks of geese, one flying north, the other south. In the garden, some red and white phlox are still holding, and pink spider plants, blue spiderwort, and the purple ironweed started from seed. Along the roadsides, the tall artichokes are still in full bloom.

1997: The green frog that lives in the pond was croaking off and on this morning between 5:45 and 6:30 a.m. He was quieter during the earlier cooler days of this month; with the weather warming, he is starting to call again. Now at 9:15 a.m., the squirrel is squeaking in the back locusts. Four monarch butterflies seen in the yard today.

1999: North along the bike path, the landscape is withering from a month without rain, honeysuckle leaves drooping, trees drying up instead of turning. Asters hold in the bud, without enough moisture to bloom. A robin heard, but just one. A patch of bouncing bets hold on down by the junkyard. The frog has been quiet for a week or so.

2001: White snakeroot, late goldenrod, and Jerusalem artichoke prominent now. The maples are gathering momentum. Small patches of gold in a few ashes. Some box elders half brown. Burning bush is turning redder. Last night a screech owl at about 7:15. This morning, another at 5:15. On the way to Columbus: several soybean fields completely rusty brown, cottonwoods deepening into ochre, fence rows of Virginia creeper and poison ivy are darker maroon. At school, the red maple and the white oak show little change from last week, still holding green.

2003: At South Glen, all the wingstem and ironweed are gone. Only goldenrod, Jerusalem artichokes, white and violet asters remain in bloom. A small flock of crows seen as we came back toward the bridge – the first crows I've seen close to town all year. Monarchs in the yard again today, and one aging tiger swallowtail.

2004: Gethsemani in Kentucky, 200 miles southwest of Yellow Springs: A decided gilding to the woods throughout the trip. Here, the undergrowth is tattered and old, sweet gums turning red round their edges. One monarch seen here (and only one other when I was driving cross country), one painted lady (*Cynthia*), and three yellow sulphurs. Several darners noted: one large pale blue, one green, one thin blue. Many Asian ladybugs. Pollen all gone from the ragweed. Field thistles still have a few blooms, but their foliage has withered. Goldenrod, hedge bindweed, *Aster vimineus* (small white aster) and *Aster lateriflorus*, black-eyed Susan and white snakeroot still seem strong. I failed to identify the most dominant plant in this habitat: about up to six-feet tall, five white petals in clusters, winged stalks and flower stems (but some of the same flowers without winged stalks or stems), alternate mostly entire leaves – untouched or barely toothed. One sneezeweed, several lobelias, purple loosestrife, boneset. Orchard grass, yard grass (*Eleusine indica*), Johnson grass, yellow foxtail grass and green foxtail grasses (a larger and smaller *sertaria*), umbrella sedge (*Cyperus strigosus*). Chestnuts had just recently fallen to the monastery paths, their large, prickly hulls broken open, round nut exposed. Some chestnuts still hanging on the tree. At the pond, frogs and toads noticed, and I found a small, thin, black and white striped snake perched on the side of a dead sapling. On the way home, some milkweed pods seen open, Jerusalem artichokes tall and bright. Tobacco fields were golden green.

2006: My ash tree at school is a fourth yellow, and other ashes on campus are starting to turn. Mateo's Jerusalem artichokes are budding, one starting to unravel. Jeanie found a large camel cricket in the dog's water this evening while I was gone.

2007: At 5:32 a.m., a cardinal gave one melodious, warbling call. Then silence, and no later calls. A hummingbird came to the impatiens as we ate breakfast, stayed a long time, then visited the butterfly bush. A Jerusalem artichoke was full open this morning in the back yard. Mateo's artichokes are at the exact same point they were last year on this date. During lunch, we watched at least two red-breasted nuthatches coming and going at the feeder. One monarch passed through in the middle of all the nuthatches. Another hummingbird at 4:00 p.m.

2008: To Wilmington yesterday afternoon: One bright red-orange Judas maple, golden fields of soybeans, many plants shedding, corn fields brown and some corn already cut for silage. One large flock of starlings. Dusky summer green holds in the tree line. In the alley, Mateo's artichokes are not budding yet, his goldenrod has started to rust, and his small-flowered asters full bloom. Katie has some very tall perennial helianthus in her side yard, probably Jerusalem artichokes. Shasta daisies down to one in the north garden. One bright yellow male finch seen today, one yesterday as well. Squirrels have been chattering constantly the past few days, and chasing each other through the high branches.

2009: I went down along the Ohio this past weekend of equinox, stayed at a retreat center near Melbourne, Kentucky. I slept in a room on the third floor of a nineteenth-century convent. My windows, almost eight feet tall, faced southeast toward the river, and I opened them out onto oaks and pines and cirrus and the sounds of the distant highway and the railroad that followed the water.

The land, like the calendar, lay at the edge of fall: scattered cottonwoods, ashes and locusts rich gold and yellow, streaks of orange and red in the maples. Leaf fall was just beginning, mostly from sycamores, buckeyes and hickories: withered leaves tangled in green honeysuckles, some coming down onto acorns and hickory nuts.

There were spots of decay on undergrowth maples, holes eaten, trails left by leafminers, disease spreading across elm leaves, discoloration pushing out from penetration by insects or wind, scarlet veins eating through the paling summer greens, sometimes the change occurring from the outside fringe, invading to core. There were random, pure white leaves on honeysuckle bushes, pale orange bittersweet berries, bright red rose hips, arbitrary blanching of spicebush foliage, magenta Virginia creeper, all mixed like stained glass windows when the sun came out,

Around the buildings, long drifts of white snakeroot stood between the lawn and the woods. Down the hiking path, I found waves of late-season wildflowers, sometimes hundreds of yards of the same variety: communities of tall, yellow touch-me-nots in full bloom up and down an entire hillside, lowlands full of wood nettle going to seed, rows and rows of smartweed along dry streambeds, clusters of dark ferns across an eroded bank. As I came back, I wondered at the graveyard of nuns, perennial stand of gray crosses clustered tight, shoulder-to-shoulder like the wildflowers.

Late in the moonless evening, the societies of katydids and crickets repeated the chants of the retreatants. In the middle of the night, the trains howled and rumbled west along the valley toward Cincinnati, and in the morning Venus shone through the branches. (I thought of Thomas Wolf: *"The rails go westward in the dark. Brother, have you seen starlight on the rails? Have you heard the thunder of the fast express?"*)

2010: No swallowtails or monarchs noticed today, a warm partly cloudy Sunday. The young cardinals continue to come to the feeders – they do it all by themselves now, having become independent from their parents in just a week.

2011: Cloudy and mild this morning, strong tree crickets, crows at 6:00, cardinal chirps at 6:07. Rain through most of the day, no butterflies noticed. The crickets were very strong at night, however, and even though Gerard's katydid was not calling, I heard others across the street. Still, it wasn't as wild as last night's chorus.

2012: A monarch in the garden.

2013: High grating crickets and lower, more melodic crickets at 5:15 this morning, no loud tree frogs. Cardinal chipping at 6:15, crows at 6:24 – quite late. Then rain. Virgin's bower completely gone now on the north trellis. The cottonwood near Lawson Place has lost half its leaves. They lie crisp at the side of the street. One monarch seen flying south along the freeway this afternoon. One hummingbird came to the feeder near suppertime.

2014: Painted ladies, sulphurs, cabbage whites, a brown hackberry, two Eastern blacks visiting the zinnias in the bright sunlight today. One hummingbird came to the feeder this morning. A few days ago, I saw the first robin in the yard since they disappeared after the fledglings were raised. Then yesterday and the day before, isolated peeps, and now in the early afternoon there is steady robin peeping in the honeysuckles.

2016: Peggy's virgin's bower down to maybe a tenth of its flowers. Rick reports a great cloud of lightning bugs rising up from a yard as he walked this evening.

2017: Rain throughout the day bringing down honeysuckle berries and leaves on top of the car. Throughout the neighborhood now (and in the east apple-tree garden) the large-leafed August Moon and Royal Standard hostas are down to their last blossoms. In the north garden, the New England asters are struggling, several buds trying to open, but it seems a disease is weakening some of the plants, killing others. Some burning bush shrubs are fully red.

2018: Monarchs scarce, only one seen in the tithonias today. A full Judas maple in Xenia, corn fields all dry and ready for silage, soybean fields at least half yellowed. I haven't seen a male tiger swallowtail in what seems like weeks. The hummingbird still comes to the feeder.

2019: Heat and sun. Dry weather affecting many trees and lawns, browning leaves and grass. A monarch, a hummingbird, half a dozen cabbage whites, a glimpse of one small fritillary in the zinnias. Several male goldfinches, their plumage mottled from molting, no robins seen or heard; they have remained hidden since the young fledged. At Ellis Pond, jewelweed fading, the last two bright yellow sundrop blossoms at the very tip of their stalk, the shore lined with golden bur marigolds in full flower. In east Texas, the Houston area, Tropical Depression Imelda brings several feet of rain, flash flooding.

A Note for the Yellow Springs News: Yellow Springs Climate 2035 – 2050

The certainty of nature…is what frees us to be fully human, to be more than simply gatherers of food. But what will happen – this summer or next summer or some summer soon – when that certainty falters?

Bill McKibben, *The End of Nature*

If I were not connected electronically to the outside world, I would have no idea that a climate Armageddon might be approaching. My backyard notes of the past decades, as well as Dayton records since the 1880s, offer few clues that indicate the coming storm.

The other day, I talked to a man who had been growing corn and soybeans near Yellow Springs for about forty years. When I asked him if he had noticed the climate changing, he shook his head.

"Some years are wet, some dry," he said. "Some are hot. Some are cold."

Like an isolated settlement of hominids, unaware that invaders are about to destroy them, we live our lives as we have always lived them. It is difficult to imagine radical local change.

But depending on what sources you read, Ohio climate is expected to undergo a significant transformation in the coming decades. According to some scenarios, Yellow Springs weather may be similar to that of Baton Rouge, Louisiana, or Dallas, Texas, by the end of the century.

Perhaps of more immediate interest is the likelihood of the village developing a climate similar to that of central Tennessee by 2035, northern Alabama by 2050. High heat and humidity will accompany that shift, and the chances of bitter cold winter months will fall relatively quickly. The Yellow Springs of 2035 will have many more summer afternoons in the 90s, fewer winter nights below freezing. Will the river or Ellis Pond freeze over in fifteen years? Not likely.

Models also indicate that the winter and spring months will be characterized by greater precipitation. In the Yellow Springs area, that could mean later planting times for farm and garden crops. Local flooding will become more likely, as well. At the same time, it appears that odds for summer droughts will rise since higher temperatures will increase the loss of moisture from the soil.

Among other dangers, "Tornado Alley" (the region, like Oklahoma, associated with high numbers of tornadoes) seems to be moving east, bringing with it an increased possibility of severe storms like the one that struck the area this year. And, like the surprise of a tornado, other changes are likely to occur with little warning.

2020: A low of 39 this morning, full sun and breezy as the day progresses, high in the 60s. Nadia and Steve came by, and we had brunch on the porch, and I got cold, came in and turned the heat on in the house for the first time since spring. At the Glass Farm wetland habitat, goldenrod full, small white asters full, New England asters early. Many cabbage whites, two sulphurs in the fields, one great spangled fritillary lumbering through the Catholic graveyard. A hummingbird wandered in the zinnias today.

2021: Return to Yellow Springs after a week in Portland, Oregon: more New England asters blooming, fewer canna lilies, full goldenrod and pink-flowered sedum. Only a cabbage white butterfly seen today, and a few hummingbirds. I heard a flicker call in the bushes this afternoon, and a blue jay over near Moya's. We left Portland in the first significant rain in four months. Gillian reported seeing very few butterflies this year, and no spiders. Rain is forecast here tomorrow and the next day, the full moon of the 20th once again, appearing to bring a decided shift in the weather.

> *women and men (both dong and ding)*
> *summer autumn winter spring*
> *reaped their sowing and went their came*
> *Sun moon stars rain*

> e.e. cummings

September 20th
The 263rd Day of the Year

Look to the Great Harvest
When all Things will bear Fruit and
Will be ready for the Gathering.

Paracelsus

Sunrise/set: 6:20/6:36
Day's Length: 12 hours 16 minutes
Average High/Low: 76/54
Average Temperature: 65
Record High: 95 – 1908
Record Low: 37 – 1962

The Daily Weather

Five percent of today's afternoons rise into the 90s; thirty percent warm to the 80s, fifty percent to the 70s, 15 percent to the 60s. Rainfall occurs one year in three on this date, and the sky is clear to partly cloudy eight years in ten. Morning lows dip below 60 degrees 80 percent of the time, the first time in the fall that such cold is so likely.

Natural Calendar

In Oregon and Maine, foliage colors are often approaching their brightest. Along the 40th Parallel, the smoky tint of last week's canopy becomes clear and crisp. The summer green of a few sycamores, locusts, elms, box elders, maples, poplars, cottonwoods and redbuds is breaking down. Patches of deep scarlet in the sumac and Virginia creeper highlight the changes in the tree line. There are streaks of amber on the lindens, ginkgoes, tulip trees, locusts, mulberries and Osage orange.

Robin migration calls complement the chatter of the crows and jays and squirrels in the early mornings. Grackles and starlings flock in the fields. Sometimes katydids keep silence after dark, leaving the whole night to the great chorus of crickets. In the

Rocky Mountains, bull elks are mustering their harems, and snow is falling.

Daybook

1983: Catalpas are turning pale along Stevenson Road. Some white snakeroot becoming brown. Small flowered asters in full bloom everywhere.

1984: Maple seeds falling. At the Antioch School, maybe a fifth of the chinquapin oak leaves are turning yellow, began the first week of September.

1985: Between the 13th and the 20th, a decided change in the tree coloring. Yellow predominates in this dry September. Sycamores, locusts, hackberry, box elder, some maples turn, some cottonwoods and red buds, too. In the arboretum and throughout the area, the ash trees show their changes, some red, some gold. Judas maples are everywhere. At the same time, the goldenrod is in full bloom, and the soybean fields are solid yellow. Scattered in the pastures, the milkweeds have all turned yellow too.

1992: The same acceleration of color this year as last. And the garden mums are coming in full, the purples first, now the reds opening. The volunteer pumpkin is completely orange, and its stem is almost dry. First of the autumn radishes pulled last night, a little thin, bet they have fine flavor. Lettuce and spinach still not full enough for salads. Beans and tomatoes still strong.

1997: The frog croaked this morning, air temperatures mild in the 60s. Cicadas strong all day, katydids at night. Cats are catching crickets in the house. On a brown stem of horsetail in the water, I found the hollow skeleton of a dragonfly, which must have emerged within the past few days.

1998: Major ash turn now. Some false boneset and goldenrod rusting.

1999: Crickets and katydids were strong this morning at three o'clock. In Wilberforce, my ash tree is mostly golden, but it is holding its leaves well. The parking lot ashes have just started to turn. Soybeans are yellow throughout. In the pond, the arrowhead leaves are yellowing too, and all the plants are dying back. But the koi are still hungry, still eat excitedly even with the water cool.

2000: As a low-pressure system approaches town the afternoon carries warm gusts of wind, sun, showers of leaves. The first heavy snow in the Rocky Mountains was reported this morning. The burning bush on High Street is almost completely red. Chicory is still in full bloom along the roadsides. Ash turn is accelerating.

2001: Low whinny of a screech owl this morning toward King Street at 5:15 . On Limestone Street and on Walnut, the virgin's bower is almost done for the year. At 8:45, one cardinal call.

2002: Long flock of blackbirds seen crossing Grinnell Road today. Don Wallis said he saw a flock like that last week. Fewer butterflies in the yard today.

2003: Only a wren and chickadee chattering in the yard at dawn.

2004: False boneset and virgin's bower are almost done blooming for the year. The ash by my old office window in Wilberforce is more than half bare, the remaining leaves yellow. In the parking lot there, locusts and ashes are starting to turn. No monarchs seen on my drives today.

2006: Big camel cricket found in the bathtub this morning. I put it out in the shed. The day is cold and gray.

2007: In the alley, almost all the seeds are gone from the great ragweed. Near Limestone Street, the bittersweet is blushing pale orange.

2008: Very quiet morning. I walked Stella in the dark – no

cardinals or crows or doves. In the yard, our volunteer virgin's bower has been gone for a couple of days. Peggy's still holds full. A few serviceberry leaves are falling, a few more turning orange. The land is dry, coleus foliage wilting, the pond low. High stratus covered the village this afternoon, cooling my work on the brick sidewalk to the street.

2010: Crows at 5:56 a.m. Sudden decline in the numbers of skippers at the butterfly bush and the false boneset. No swallowtails or monarchs seen today. Last peaches from our tree for breakfast.

2011: More duskiness to the tree line, more maples turning to sharper oranges, more ashes gold. In the alley, one rose of Sharon bush is almost completely yellow, the great knotweed half finished, Jerusalem artichokes strong and bright. Crickets steady when I went out at 9:30 a.m. At least three monarchs in the garden this afternoon, and a hummingbird came to the feeder several times. Tonight, the tree crickets were strong; Gerard's katydid was loud as ever, and Peggy's field crickets were in full voice.

2012: More monarchs, more hummingbirds in the garden today. On the way to Dayton, a patch of dandelions. At Ellis Pond just outside of town, beggarticks and goldenrod and small white asters (*laterfolia*), swamp bidens, jewelweed, bindweed, horseweed, ragweed seeds all gone, one parsnip in bloom, black walnut trees almost bare, cottonwoods going, very last sundrops and white vervain, some white clover, a little watercress in bloom, all the hickory nuts down, just two thistle buttons, steady cricket song. And two white ducks shadowed me all around the pond.

2013: Sylvia sent me an effusive note about finding a toad in the grass. She was "feeling lucky," she said. And she went on: "Oh yes, lucky, so I got down on my hands and knees...I didn't want to miss a single detail...such serious eyes for one so young regarding me with great solemnity."

Toads are relatively common in Yellow Springs, and

sometimes they mate in my garden pond in April or May. The young tadpoles reach land in Early Summer and grow to at least an inch or two long by about the time Sylvia saw hers in late June. After that, according to my notes, they wander on cooler days and nights, hiding from drought and heat in dank corners of the woods, eating the insects that frequent those places.

I find them most often between the last week of August and the third week of September, and the increased frequency of my backyard sightings at that time coincides with the toad migration which occurs between Late Summer and Early Fall here in Yellow Springs and throughout the region.

2014: A slight warming today. Early morning brought one painted lady (*Cynthia*). A monarch came by at 9:45, and then there were cabbage whites and several monarchs and painted ladies in the zinnias throughout the day. A red-tailed hawk cried off and on when I was outside in the garden; I have heard red-tails for the past several days. In the arboretum across the stream from Ellis Pond, the buckeyes are down from the yellow buckeye tree, splayed open on the grass, the buckeye foliage ochre now, the first of the turning on this side of the pond. And the Sweet Hart chestnut has also dropped its fruits.

2015: Bright sun, cool. Goldenrod rusting, virgin's bower and prairie dock almost gone. A brilliant Eastern black in the tithonias this morning, cabbage whites and a polygonia in the afternoon. The New England asters are solid full bloom along the edge of the north garden, only interrupted by zinnias flopping over on top of them. The purple thin-leafed hostas have finally closed their seasons, but the latest variety (Red October) is still lush. I note last year's comment about hearing red-tailed hawks – and it seems I have been hearing and seeing them more and more from early September.

And another note – this one about toads. Yesterday I saw a fat American toad squatting under the bike rack at the post office, reminded me of Silvia's message on this date in 2013 and of my previous sightings of toads in mid-September. Coincidences? Of course not. (After Ed Oxley's toad sightings of October 2, 2013, I have had no toad sightings or reports, and I presume that not too long after that, they have dug their hibernation burrows and are ready to sleep away the winter.) Apropos: a chilly north wind is picking up in the afternoon: I started the day with a fire in the wood stove and have kept it cooking throughout the day.

2016: The days continue bright and warm, dew on the grass each morning. But suddenly almost all the silver-spotted skippers have disappeared from the zinnias. Only one or two of them still play here, along with a handful of cabbage whites. No larger butterflies seen, no swallowtails or monarchs or great fritillaries. Now the box elder leaves have withered but haven't fallen. The hackberries are weathering, some pale, others curling. The serviceberry trees have thinned but keep much of their foliage. Locust leaves come through the bushes every few minutes.

2017: Hackberry leaves fluttering to the zinnias, tricking me into thinking they are butterflies. Along Greene Street near Jill's house, the road is slippery with fallen cottonwood leaves. Jill's maple is cluttering her yard now, the great leaf fall beginning in earnest. As we walked down Davis Street, several black walnuts clattered onto the roof of what used to be the old fish market decades and decades ago. Two monarchs, a couple of painted ladies, a silver-spotted skipper, pairs of cabbage whites, one fold-winged skipper. The hummingbird still checks the zinnias. Along Dayton Street, the serviceberry trees are rusty brown and shedding. Halfway downtown, I almost twisted ankle on black walnuts. More red maple trees turning yellow and beige, starting to come down.

2018: One buckeye tree completely down on Elm Street. And most of the serviceberry trees have thinned to a few leaves, rusty, lace-like against the sky. From Italy, Neysa sends a photo of *Clathrus uber*, a red, sponge-like mushroom. She has a "little patch of them" now because, she guesses, of all the rain they have had recently.

2019: To Gethsemani near Louisville, temperature in the 90s, one fierce downpour then sun, occasional turkey vultures soaring overhead: The tree line was weathered from age and heat, soybeans fields yellowing and some standing corn completely dried out.

The New York Times reported that studies show the bird population of the hemisphere has declined by three billion birds since 1970. But Chris Walker talked about seeing flocks of nighthawks, an osprey and a bald eagle, and a giant swarms of dragonflies on his farm in Champaign County, about 40 miles north of Yellow Springs. At the monastery, Father Michael said his bees had had a pretty good summer, responded well to the medication for mites, and even produced some comb honey that had been relished by the monks.

In the evening I watched half a dozen hummingbirds competing for nectar and mockingbirds chasing each other through the chestnut trees outside the refectory window. Then I received a note from Leslie and Bruce, and they had heard calls of blue jays, pileated woodpeckers, downy woodpeckers, Carolina wrens, chickadees, white-breasted nuthatches, crows, red-shouldered hawks, red-bellied woodpeckers, cardinals, killdeers, starlings and titmice. They had a list of butterfly sightings, too.

So I put all that together with the turkey vultures, the hummingbirds and the mockingbirds I had seen myself. I read what Henry David Thoreau had written about how the world was well kept and how its undertakings were secure and never failed. What if, I thought, Henry David were still right?

2020: Another chilly morning, sun, breeze. I sat and watched for butterflies in the zinnias, but only three cabbage whites appeared. One green-bottle fly basked on a new spiderwort leaf. No bees seen, even on the knotweed. Hackberry leaves sailed down into the flowers, surrogate swallowtails, softening the impact of the scarcity of insects. A hummingbird came by in the late afternoon, tested the orange tithonias. At Jill's, the thin-leaved coneflowers have started to decline. At Ellis Pond, the *Bidens,* thick and bright yellow, line the shore (the water mostly covered with algae). In the ash grove, a handful of robins.

2021: Only one cabbage white this warm, mostly cloudy day. Thin-leaved coneflowers have started to decline as the New England asters flourish.

2022: Emily sent this message: " Hi Bill! I just saw 20 to 30 Broadwinged hawk's kettling over town. They're mingling with the black vultures. A really cool migration sighting!" And Jill told me about seeing a huge flock of grackles flying over town toward the northeast.

The world is well kept.... Her undertakings are secure and never fail. If I were awakened from a deep sleep, I should know which side of the meridian the sun might be by the aspect of nature, and the chirp of the crickets, and yet no painter can paint this difference. The landscape contains a thousand dials which indicate the natural divisions of time, the shadows of a thousands styles point to the hour.... It is almost the only game which the trees play at, this tit-for-tat, now this side in the sun, now that, the drama of the day.

Henry David Thoreau

September 21st
The 264th Day of the Year

He Himself in Heaven
placed the Stars,
and tells what Signs are best
for Men and Women Year to Year,
so that every Labor find its proper Time,
and all Things come to pass
in fruitful Order.

Aratos

Sunrise/set: 6:21/6:34
Day's Length: 12 hours 13 minutes
Average High/Low: 76/54
Average Temperature: 65
Record High: 95 – 1908
Record Low: 31 – 1897

The Daily Weather

Frost season begins today in Yellow Springs with the chance of a light freeze becoming a minimum of five percent per night until the first week of October – when odds quickly increase. Highs on the 21st are in the 90s five percent of the years, in the 80s thirty percent, in the 70s thirty-five percent, in the 60s thirty percent; one cold afternoon in the 50s fills out the spectrum. Rain occurs 35 percent of the time, as do totally overcast skies. "South wind today means a warm autumn," says traditional lore.

Natural Calendar

Average temperatures, which varied only one or two degrees at the height of Deep Summer, dropped a full four degrees in August, and now fall four degrees almost every week.

Nearly 200 species of birds have begun to leave the Midwest by equinox. Only about 60 remain, and those will be on their way at the close of October. By that time, insects will be disappearing, leaf color will have peaked, and all of the wildflowers except for a few asters, goldenrod, Queen Anne's lace and chicory will have gone to seed.

The second tier of trees, including the ashes, cottonwoods, box elders, hickories, and locusts, starts to turn quickly after equinox, reaching its most radical transformation in the second week of October. As the second layer of the canopy loses its leaves, the trees of the third tier, especially the maples and oaks, come in for ten to fourteen days; they usually pass their prime a week before Halloween.

A fourth tier that includes the ginkgoes, sweet gum, and white mulberries can hold out until the first or second week in November. The first front of late fall often brings a hard freeze and cloudy wet days in the 30s and the 40s, bringing down the leaves from these trees overnight.

Beech, honeysuckles, boxwood, forsythia and the strongest of the silver maples, Osage, pears, and sycamores keep scattered color in the landscape past Thanksgiving. When Early Winter arrives near December 8, however, it takes the almost all the holdouts.

Daybook

1984: Tree coloring increasing. Virginia creeper, deep red, accentuates the other losses as it winds up along the trunks. Soybean fields are yellow, blend with the goldenrod.

1985: One forsythia branch seen blooming today.

1986: A small flock of robins in the yard, all talking with their short migrating call. Buzzards circling South Glen. The ash outside my office window has lost almost all its leaves. Honey locust with patches of yellow. One whole forsythia bush is blooming today.

1987: Katydids definitely quieter this past week, and none heard tonight. No cardinals for about a week and a half. Woolly bears seen this week appear much darker than earlier in the fall, but still orange.

1990: South to Switzerland County along the Ohio River: I head west and south from North Landing into a thunderstorm. The soybeans are half yellow, and the corn is old. Most black walnut trees are bare, fruit exposed and swinging in the rain. Small white asters and goldenrod are in full bloom; chicory is still open.

The breeze is steady but gentle from the southwest, leaving intact the haze across the valley. Swallows are still diving. Buzzards circle. Poplars are weathered, the raindrops darken the remaining green, brighten the patches of yellow on the Osage. Queen Anne's lace is so thick in the fields that it looks like cotton. I pass boneset seeding in the creek, and hundreds of yards of thistles, down matted to their stems. Poison ivy red, sumacs red, purple New England asters.

Milkweed pods are getting hard and pale. White snakeroot keeps its flowers, as do the Jerusalem artichoke and wingstem, remnants of August. Tobacco is hanging in a few barns. I stop at Patriot landing, walk in the light rain through spotted touch-me-nots and small white asters. Steady chanting of crickets. The diesel grinding of a barge coming down river. Smartweed at my feet, pink and white. Smell of wood smoke, and wet leaves, river mud, and bittersweet old pollen, old wildflowers, and hay.

Sycamores are turning, two of their leaves fell right in front of me. Tattered blue dayflowers beside me. Summer spider webs almost gone. The purple loosestrife has ended its flower cycle along the water. The huge pink mallows have died, heads black, leaves decaying, stems dark. Wild cucumbers have formed, prickly like cacti. Beggarticks are open, and heal all, mistflower, heart-leafed aster. Later, up Bodey Hill Road: I came across a few sundrops. White campion here, a few late ironweed, large-flowered leafcup. West on the highway past patches of goldenrod: a few tobacco fields yellow, some green. Some tobacco stubble tangled with bindweed. Late wild lettuce. Some coneflowers still. Toward evening, crows in the trees across the Long Branch valley.

1991: Cabbage butterflies still mating in the broccoli. Red mulberry leaves thinned to maybe a half, the screen between the yard and the neighbors weakened.

1992: All the crickets still seem to be here tonight, katydids too. Yesterday in the warm afternoon, cicadas were still the dominant sound, even over the cars along Dayton Street.

1993: Three days in a row to Springfield in the late afternoon, each time a long flock of starlings seen over the old National Road route and along the Mad River.

1997: Green frog croaks at 5:45 a.m. Crows in the yard by 6:12 a.m. By 7:30, more birds about, a jay and a cardinal, others twittering.

1998: Darner at the pond. Bullfrogs: one about three inches long, one two inches. One brief frog croak, but no more.

2000: Half the burning bush in town has turned deep red. Ashes are accelerating. Chicory still full bloom.

2001: Fewer black swallowtails seen this week, no monarchs. The skunk keeps up his nightly digs around the yard. Virgin's bower flowering cycle has ended.

2002: A long flock of blackbirds flew over the house this morning between 8:10 and 8:20. I saw a hummingbird in the butterfly bush at 6:00 this evening. Another day without butterflies in the yard.

2003: Lots of butterflies in the garden all day: monarchs, cabbage whites, painted ladies, and orange fritillaries. No swallowtails seen at all. One darner seen.

2005: Albert, the green frog, croaked a little this afternoon. At the trellis, virgin's bower and New England asters are at their peak. No significant leafturn yet across the countryside.

2006: Jeanie discovered a praying mantis egg case in the north garden ferns this afternoon. In Wilberforce, the ashes are turning quickly.

2008: We ate the last peach of the year for breakfast this morning. In the alley, a few apples still are left on their branches. Leafturn is intensifying throughout the countryside. Lil's burning bush has started; locusts are fringed with gold; box elders and ashes are rusting and yellowing; the corn and soybean fields match the box elders. Mrs. Timberlake's pale fall crocus are tall and strong; the darker purple crocus that Frank's sister must have planted so many years ago are in flower, almost covered by the long grass by the alley fence. One monarch seen in the yard.

2009: It is often late September when I make my trip into Kentucky to meditate for a few days at Gethsemani monastery. Since I rarely see the monastery at any other time of year, my trip takes me out of the circular context of the world of Yellow Springs in which I normally live. When I arrive for my retreat, the same flowers are always in bloom, the same trees are turning, the same birds singing. Nothing has changed since the last time I came. Time has been held still by place.

At home, I find no such stability. Every day, the markers of the year change just a little. The anchor is pulled up with each sunrise. Nothing stays the same. But at Gethsemani, like a childhood memory of home or a distant summer of love, like an old photograph revisited, or a repeating dream, the season remains frozen to its context.

Before dawn, the sky spreads so deep above me, Orion always at the same stage of his ascent in the east, the Pleiades always overhead. Away from city lights, the sky is so dark and clear that I can always see the legs of Taurus, not just his red eye like here at home, and the Milky Way is almost as bright as a moon.

Inside the chapel, the sun falls through the tall stained glass windows at the same angle at Vespers as it did last year and the year before and the year before. The solar clock has stopped here, has not passed through winter or spring or summer.

I too am the same year after year, always looking for the same answers, always coming full circle back to where I began, always staying suspended in autumn, never finished. Maybe that is well and good. I will die, after all, in the world of circles, within the whole turn of some near or distant year. But in the few hours of retreat, I step outside the loop, hide from the inevitable, stand still in self-deception.

2010: Crows at 5:54 a.m. Accelerated leafturn on the road to Xenia: red leaves on some sweet gums, some ashes in full color, more bright orange maples. One female tiger swallowtail and one red admiral seen at noon.

2011: Crickets and crows when I went out at 6:00 a.m. in the soft rain. The male and female cardinals came to the feeder at 6:20. When Jeanie and I sat outside for a while after breakfast, the hummingbird came by. Maple, ash and box elder leaves have been pulled to the street in the rain.

2012: Mike Miller said he saw frost on his roof this morning. No bright yellow finches seen for several days.

2013: Gethsemani: Coming from Lauds, I saw a great orb-weaver web in one of the west windows of the monastery. In the woods, white snakeroot, tall goldenrod, New England asters, small white asters, the broad-leafed achillea, and a plant similar to sneezeweed with alternate, toothed, entire leaves, all still in full bloom. Very late zigzag goldenrod, a tall vervain-like plant with purple flowers all past their best. One black swallowtail sighted, one blue, one buckeye-like butterfly. One hummingbird seen at the feeder outside the refectory. Red berries and blushing leaves on dogwoods, bright scarlet and purple staghorn sumacs. Chestnuts huge, and a few fallen and open on the grass. All across the woods, the high trees are worn and blanching. It was the same all the way from southwestern Ohio.

2014: One hummingbird seen after sunrise. Painted ladies and cabbage whites throughout the windy morning, two monarchs and an Eastern black seen in the afternoon. The goldenrod has started its decline, the virgin's bower gone. The zinnias are leaning, still producing flowers, but need to be deadheaded much more than I have been doing. Local sunflowers are drooping and rusting, rudbeckia and stonecrop maybe half to seed, ironweed in the yard completely finished for the year.

2015: Sun, warm: One male tiger, cabbage whites. The white autumn crocus is tall, splayed, uninhibited.

2016: Sun, warm. A few cabbage whites, only a couple of skippers. The white autumn crocus is as exuberant as it was last year. A large Osage fruit on Limestone Street this morning. Late in the afternoon, a spirited monarch came through the garden. Bill Meers reported from Dayton: "We saw our hummingbird(s) again this morning-- the latest we have seen them at our window feeder. For me they are a marker for the end of summer. I doubt if we will see them again until spring."

2017: Two or three monarchs in the afternoon zinnias, a shining green hummingbird and even one tiger swallowtail. Throughout town, leaves of red maples, cottonwoods, black walnuts, serviceberries and hackberries clutter the sidewalks and make the streets slippery in the rain. Black walnut fruits thump to roofs and car tops. Jumpseed is yellowing, speckled. Rose hips are darkening. Poison ivy is gold, and blackberries have purple leaves. Milkweed pods stretch to open.

2018: Perfectly clear sky, mild 70-degree morning, soft east wind, sphinx moth near the porch light, beggarticks done blooming along Davis Street. Hummingbird still feeding. One monarch. Barometer dropping.

2020: Third night in a row in the 40s, clear and dry. Hurricane Beta comes ashore on the Texas-Louisiana coast, heavy rains.

At 11:30 in the morning, Casey called: "I got a pair of

bald eagles circling out above Ellis Pond," he said, "with very distinctive white heads and white tails. They're not flapping their wings at all. They're just gliding on the thermals."

Into South Glen for the first time in maybe a year: The paths are even more overgrown than at the Covered Bridge habitat, only white snakeroot in bloom, tattered wood nettle and wingstem collapsing, groves of honeysuckle covering many areas along the diminished paths, the way to the old butterfly preserve is almost lost in the undergrowth, dark from the overgrowth. Only two cabbage whites seen in the zinnias today. I weeded around the fresh leaves and flowers of the spiderwort row, took out some of the wire fences that separated the canna lilies from the day lilies, watered the thirsty ground.

This evening, Jill and I saw a cloud of bats circling the old school house, thousands of bats, it seemed, rounding and rounding the tower.

2022: Warm and humid, barometer dropping before the new moon cool front, murmurations of hackberry leaves driven south over the yard, gusts of puffy wild lettuce seeds. At five o'clock, Piston, my Australian Shepherd and I were sitting out in the backyard, hoping for butterflies. Then suddenly the cloudy sky above us was filled with dragon flies circling and diving and rushing erratically back and forth.

Nimbus moon
Ice white
Orange edge
Darkling sky
Feather fleece
O September night!

Dee Krieg

September 22nd
The 265th Day of the Year

When the bright Virgin gives the beauteous days,
And Libra weighs in equal scales the year;
From heaven's high cope the fierce effulgence shook
Of parting Summer, a serener blue,
With golden light enliven'd, wide invests
The happy world. Attemper'd suns arise,
Sweet beam'd, and shedding oft through lucid clouds
A pleasing calm; while broad, and brown, below
Extensive harvests hang the heavy head.

James Thomson

Sunrise/set: 6:22/6:33
Day's Length: 12 hours 11 minutes
Average High/Low: 75/53
Average Temperature: 64
Record High: 95 – 1895
Record Low: 33 – 1897

The Daily Weather

Highs in the 90s come once in a quarter century; 80-degree temperatures occur about 25 percent of the time, 70s forty percent, 60s twenty-five percent, and remain in the cold 50s on five percent of the afternoons. Morning lows are typically in the 40s or 50s, with mild 60s and chilly 30s the exceptions. Chances of rain and overcast conditions today are 45 percent. The season of severe pollen density usually closes near this day in the Lower Midwest but may continue into October before frost in the North.

The Weather in the Week Ahead

Equinox parallels a drop in extremes as well as in averages. Days in the 90s are rare after the 22nd of September, and even 80s will be gone in about three weeks. The odds for an afternoon in the 50s or 60s this week doubles over those odds last week. The season of light frosts deepens in Ohio, Indiana and southern Michigan; the 24th and the 27th even carry a 20 percent chance of a mild freeze - the greatest chance since May 10. On the 23rd and the 26th, chances of a high below 70 degrees are better than 50 percent, the first time that has happened since May 4. Precipitation is usually lightest on the 28th (just a 15 percent chance of showers on that date).

Natural Calendar
Libra weighs in equal scales the year.

James Thomson

The Libra Sun straddles the phases of autumn in Yellow Springs and the Lower Midwest, ending almost all the wildflower seasons and accompanying the start of the most dramatic phase of leafturn in the entire year. Although Scorpio (October 23 to November 22) shatters the last of the canopy, Libra takes the earlier trees, especially the ashes, box elders, black walnuts, buckeyes and locusts, then quickly colors the best of the maples.

The sun enters Libra as great crested flycatchers, blue-gray gnatcatchers, ruby-throated hummingbirds, eastern wood peewees and bank swallows move south. Buzzards gather to ponder migration. The cobwebs that blocked summer paths become rare. Osage fruits, persimmons, acorns, hickory nuts, buckeyes and black walnuts cover the ground. The wingstem bows to sets its seeds.

Daybook

1982: The cornfields are almost completely brown now, as are the grasses and many of the wildflowers along the roadsides. Some white snakeroot and Queen Anne's lace are past their best. Most tree lines are tinted. Only a few tomatoes and raspberries are left in the garden. Ragweed is yellow and drooping. Soybean leaves are brown, seem dry and brittle.

1989: Most Queen Anne's lace has gone to seed now. The

undergrowth is thinning around the back yard, making it less private on the south and west sides. First goldenrod seen dying back along Grinnell Road. Rains from Hurricane Hugo fell today, and the barometer dropped to 29.55. Frost followed with the arrival of high pressure. Leaves falling quickly from my ash at school. Most are yellow now, and more than half have come down. Will they be gone when I come back on the 25th? Box elders and black walnuts half fallen in places. Three small wood snails found at Mill Habitat under dead branches. Shells a mixed color, brown and light tan and yellow, with a soft luster, faintly ribbed, all three with dark stripes around the outer edge: *Polygyra* or *Polygyridae zonitidae*.

1991: Crows active at 7:30 a.m., no other birds heard until then. Crickets are quiet this morning, were subdued, along with the katydids, last night, sobered by the sudden cooling of the nights. Now, 7:35 a.m., the blue jays are here.

1992: At South Glen, fishing: The first cold front of autumn is moving in, but the air is still mild. Shiners or chubs steal my bait, biting from the minute the cast is complete. Nothing caught, however. This is just past the edge of summer, maybe just a handful of days past, the subtle decays of late August and the past few weeks building up until the change seems sudden to me now. I react to the obvious landmark of major leafturn, but each leaf falling seems a landmark, too.

1993: Rapid onset of color, the vague smoky tint of last week quickly becoming clear and bright, streaking the maples, the rusting of whole ashes. A flock of grackles seen on the way north from Xenia. Every day on my drives, more birds. In the garden, swallowtails and monarchs have disappeared. Early September perennials still hold. Seven-foot helianthus still strong along the way to Springfield and scattered throughout town. Asters still at their peak. First beggarticks aging now, white snakeroot along Grinnell finally breaking down.

1999: One cardinal at 7:45 a.m. One robin peep heard a little earlier. First frost on the roof, clear skies and a low of 38. The sapsucker came through, tapped on the siding at 12:21 p.m. Snakeskin found in the rocks beside the pond.

2000: In and around Yellow Springs, more ashes, sweet gums, maples, locusts, black walnuts, burning bush, tulip tree are turning, maybe a tenth of the tree line. On the way to Gethsemani in Kentucky: the Cincinnati trees seemed further advanced than the country trees: more maples.

2001: Cardinal at 6:05 this morning, fog thick through the back trees. At the Cascades, scattered leafcup and wingstem still in bloom. White snakeroot is starting to brown. The canopy is still dark and strong.

2003: Two monarch butterflies seen on the way to Wilmington this afternoon. One cottonwood tree yellow, two or three maples orange, my ash at Wilberforce shedding quickly, a few ash in the parking lot nearby with streaks of red.

2006: Mateo's Jerusalem artichokes are still not open – but that plant is in full bloom throughout the countryside.

2007: Mateo's artichokes still lag behind. Ours are in early bloom, and the north garden is full of New England asters, virgin's bower and false boneset. Three monarchs, a black swallowtail and a female ruby-throated hummingbird seen as Jeanie and I sat on the back porch after breakfast. Scores of white cabbage butterflies haunted the asters and the boneset. Yellow locust leaves fluttered to the ground in front of us. A cardinal sang at 8:30, the first one I had heard so far in the day. Black walnuts have fallen to Dayton Street, lie crushed by cars along the curb. Jeanie noticed that most of berries were gone from the pokeweed, eaten by the birds. Coming back from Dayton, we saw a long flock of blackbirds or grackles flying north high over the road, one of the giant fall flocks.

2008: A flock of grackles in the back trees when I went out to the shed this evening.

2009: No cardinals this morning, but crows at about 6:10 a.m. In the alley, the tall coneflowers are making a comeback, five in bloom now. All along High Street, the Jerusalem artichokes are in full bloom. In the east garden, our New England asters are all open, and the false boneset is still strong. The white autumn crocus by the back porch is drooping a little. Some of the new Heritage raspberry bushes have blushing raspberries. Ruby called to say she had heard Snowy Crickets (small, green "thermometer" crickets) singing on her ride today. A long flock of blackbirds or grackles flew over the house, cackling, as I arrived from downtown at about 4:50 this evening.

2010: Partly cloudy and warm in the 80s: Three monarchs at the butterfly bush around noon. Very few skippers now. No swallowtails seen today. Storm at 4:00, locust leaves raining down with the wind.

2012: Hard rain last night, cool this morning, starlings chirping somewhere off to the west, squirrels chattering in the alley, Osage fruits along High Street, fallen in the storm, one cardinal call before 8:00 a.m.

2014: The equinox cold wave blew in with Libra yesterday afternoon and last night. Clear and chilly now, but the painted lady (*Cynthia*) and cabbage white butterflies are up with the sun. A polygonia seen in the afternoon. Rick brought over an American lotus plant for the pond, and we placed it down in the shallow west end.

2015: A perfect day in the 70s with lots of sun, but only cabbage whites and a couple of skippers in the zinnias, and no hummingbird seen at the feeder. The prairie dock has completed its bloom time at the corner of High and West South College Streets. I cut back the swamp bidens from the pond, their flowers spent and leaves tattered.

2016: Warm and sun: cabbage whites and a few skippers. The New England asters are peaking, just as Peggy's virgin's bower loses most of its petals. All around the countryside, most of the trees are still late-summer green, and the goldenrod and Jerusalem artichokes are still strong and bright.

2017: And exceptionally warm day, the first of almost a week of heat. Jill noticed that a small snake had been run over on Greene Street, and Ed Oxley left a message saying: "I had an unusual sighting on Wednesday, the 20th. I was walking my dog, and it was getting to be dark, and I was coming back through the woods, and I saw a lightning bug about three feet off the ground. It was the only one I saw, and it just blinked once, but I thought it was pretty late in the year to see one, definitely not a glow worm because it was up in the air."

Firefly time usually ends during August in Yellow Springs, but Rick reported seeing larvae glowing in the grass on the evening of September 8, 2016, and I noticed glow worms in my lawn on September 23 of 2004 and on the 24th in 2009. Ordinarily, the larvae overwinter and come out as adults in the spring to mate (and blink). Ed's firefly may have been a larva that emerged as an adult out of season, fooled by the early September chill and Harvey's rains, followed by the heat wave of the past week.

I saw a hummingbird in the garden before I left for Gethsemani this morning, and the New England asters were coming in a little more. The white crocus was still tall. I drove through Early Fall on the trip through Kentucky, noticing that the tobacco fields were half-turned gold like the soybean fields. Sycamores were rusting far ahead of other trees.

2018: A chilly wind this morning, the equinox cold front arriving on schedule. A monarch this morning, braving the cold. This evening, a meditation walk with about twenty people at Agraria, and at the end, a great flock of blackbirds flew south overhead. As

Jill and I watched the sunset from the edge of town, formations of geese flew over toward Ellis Pond.

My notes for the newspaper from the Agraria meditation walk:

Community Equinox

On September 22, a few hours before the exact time of equinox, a small group of about twenty people, adults and children, came together at the Agraria farm, a Center for Regenerative Practice of the Arthur Morgan Institute for Community Solutions.

The activities, in which I was happy to take part: a walking meditation along a wooded trail and a potluck in the great barn near the Agraria offices. In search of an impression of the landscape at this particular time of year and at this particular time in the early history of the farm's regeneration, I gave out index cards and pens and asked everyone to write down anything they noticed as they followed each other single file in silence for about twenty minutes.

When I collected the cards, I saw that the group had created a detailed community description of this equinox moment in 2018. I wanted to share their notes with them and with others, and so I have put together a collage of their comments. The phrases in italics, separated by ellipses to distinguish different authors, are the observations of the meditators.

A high-pressure system had just come through, and air was chilly. *Blue gray cloudy sky with yellowish strip toward the horizon...65 degrees, light breeze.* At the barn: *momma cat and kittens climbing in and out of the wall, same colored markings momma small and thin...farm cat so soft and friendly padding slowly and deliberately...*

On both sides of the path a habitat of fields and woods: *Vast green plains, years of toil etched into their surface in neat lines, soft carpets of grass and mulch and moss... the soft green of meadow...*

Underneath the canopy: *between dark trunks, old vines crawling up crusted trees, clinging in a silent embrace... arching of honeysuckle framing the path, frail fingers of branches reaching, reaching, reaching...*

The walking evoked the sounds and smells of the landscape as well as the process of the walk: *crickets chirping, tiny spider, distant birds...soil wet ...the feel of fall...crunching gravel...fresh air...mud smell...cool air making the tip of my nose and fingers cold... everybody striding down the path...walking on crackling sticks and moist moss, dead fallen leaves light green and brown...mud sucking at my boots...oops! kids rushing ahead of others with energy... dog barking, caw like bird call...squirrel call...traffic noise, the ebb and flow of life in curious harmony with distant rumbling vehicles... birdsong, rasping insect song, jewelweed "pop"! .... A crow or jay says "watch out!"...*

And the notes revealed a long litany from many voices of all the things that lay about the meditators: *Raccoon scat... deer prints in the mud... a catbird seen, a pigeon, robin.... Carolina chickadee...cardinal, downy woodpecker, northern flicker, red-winged blackbird... grackle, starling, white-breasted nuthatch, broad-winged hawk, chipmunk, mosquitoes....people walking quietly in and through nature watching spiders in webs... insects fat and tiny, strong zigzagging overhead...tinnitus matching the crickets, nearly canceling each other out....*

Pokeweed stems are bright red, berries green, poison ivy is yellowing...touch-me-not flowers fading ...prolific bright red honeysuckle berries.... a majestic mushroom cupped upward growing from the side of a tree.... goldenrod framed by a green fence...

White clover...haven't seen a 4-leafer in YS yet...purple coneflower, trees still mostly with green leaves, ... large rocks partially buried in the path... mottled orange-brown leaf, dark red leaf bright... white, small fungi on sticks...

Coltsfoot...dandelion, plantain... mossy rocks...a hickory nut...stinging nettle, poison ivy...rusty wire fence...damn honeysuckles... rusty shotgun shell...a white moth ... crab grass, small white flowers with yellow centers before open fully... purple-red berries on shrub with opposite leaves...Virginia creeper...white snakeroot in bloom...hackberry galls but no berries... empty branches on short trees, wild berries low...

Cherry trees with holes in the leaves, Osage orange, wild rose, starlings overhead, robust mole tunnels, moss with spores, old walnuts, white lichen...
chickweed, silky dogwood, morning glory, oriental bittersweet, thistles, mulberry, chokecherry, sage, foxtail, oats, burdock, euonymus, box elder... greenbrier, clearweed... empty Baltimore oriole's nest... powdery mildew, a turkey tail mushroom...

To this list of things seen and heard, two participants added: *Smiles inside me celebrate the time in nature with people.... people I like and love...I am happy,, with lots of people all around, and now the trail beckons me, life ahead...*

2019: Gethsemani: A cool morning at last, the equinox front arriving here on time. From the refectory window at lunch time, I watch the hummingbirds twirl and spiral around their feeders.

2020: Once again, cool and sun. Watching for butterflies in the zinnias, I was surprised by a bright goldfinch filling in for the absent tiger swallowtails. The berries on one the pokeweed trees have started to shrivel.

2022: Driving to Keuka Lake in western New York, driving parallel to a windy cold front, the first really chilly weather of the autumn: field after field of golden soybeans throughout Ohio, goldenrod everywhere, many violet asters, small white asters. occasional Judas maples, many rusting staghorn sumacs.

Cricket, one-note song,
Lesson in simplicity,
Just what I needed.

Paul Quenon

September 23rd
The 266th Day of the Year

All about us, there was marked change. Mornings were cooler and crisper than before. The ever-lengthening shapes of afternoon shadows seemed drawn more irresistibly into the night. Fields were rough and tweedy, as though an old brown woolen jacket had been thrown over them to ward off the chill....

Vincent G. Dethier

Sunrise/set: 6:23/6:31
Day's Length: 12 hours 8 minutes
Average High/Low: 75/53
Average Temperature: 64
Record High: 93 – 1908
Record Low: 32 – 1974

The Daily Weather

Partly cloudy to clear 60 percent of the time with showers coming four years in ten. Lows are in the 30s on 15 percent of the mornings. Afternoon highs are in the 50s five percent of the years, in the 60s fifty percent, 70s twenty-five percent, 80s 15 percent, and five percent 90s. After today, warm 90s are not to be expected until next summer.

Natural Calendar

The temporal countryside of Yellow Springs takes on its autumnal contours from the increasingly violent movements of the Earth's atmosphere as it tilts away from the sun.

Graphs of barometric pressure reveal many of the topographical patterns of the season. August's barometric configurations are slow and gentle like low, rolling dunes. Heat waves show up as wide plateaus. Thunderstorms are sharp, shallow troughs in the mellow waves of the atmospheric landscape.

At the close of Late Summer, the year has begun its ascent to the steep cliffs of December. By the beginning of

October, the barometric waves are stronger; the high-pressure peaks become taller; the lows are deeper, with almost every valley bringing rain.

Tapering floral sequences and the gradual surge of leafturn occur amid the diminishing expanse of middle September. From the broad lowland of warmth with its six months of birdsong and its hundred days of insect calls, the sun pulls the land up into the foothills of the year where asters and goldenrod bloom and where trees are gold and red.

Middle Fall is the rough piedmont of another country, stripping foliage, putting buds into dormancy, burning away the undergrowth and revealing the dark hillsides. At the end of Late Fall, December's great range of cold and snow fills the horizon. Beyond it lies another immense upland, the frigid, high plateau of Deep Winter in which nothing ever seems to grow or change until the ground crumbles and gives way, shattered by thaws, and time tumbles down into the sudden, stormy gorge of March.

Daybook

1984 South Glen: Maple leaves begin to fall along the path. Jumpseed is yellowing, rose hips darkening. Poison ivy is gold, and blackberries have purple leaves. Milkweed pods are full size, straining, ready to open, foliage pale. Scattered coneflowers hang on. Black medic still open. Crickets strong. Wingstem is gone, most ironweed too. Smartweed full bloom. A few bouncing bets still flowering, their foliage deteriorating. Meadow rue leaves are tinted a faint violet. This is the height of goldenrod and New England asters. Osage starts to change color. One dandelion seen open.

1985: At the Cascades, oaks, ash, cottonwood are turning, ashes dropping leaves. Peach leaves suddenly on the ground by the garden wall.

1986: Half the pussy willow leaves are gone.

1988: A cardinal sang once this morning. Buckwheat on Grinnell finally turns, matted from the rain. Purple asters are common now, small white asters in full bloom. Starlings fill the trees at the dairy outside of town.

1992: The weather graph records the consistent arrival of the first real cold front of the season around this date. The breath of the world is steady, but with almost human variations. The years, like people, are of the same species, have different personalities: some are identical twins, some diametrically opposed, but all share certain characteristics.

1993: At the Mill, new-born water striders skating on the water, constant, playful movement.

1997: Virgin's bower has disappeared now, its petals having fallen in the past week. Rose of Sharon still produces flowers, but far fewer. No trumpet creepers noticed recently. The very last showy coneflower is blooming today in the south garden. Across from the pond, the New England asters are all blossoming, and roadside asters, violet and white, still appear to be completely in bloom. This morning at breakfast, I was looking out at the high locusts: two squirrels were mating thirty feet above the ground.

1998: Another thin-bodied blue-tailed dragonfly at the pond today. One silver-spotted skipper and a few cabbage butterflies, too.

1999: Yesterday, long flocks of blackbirds were crossing the highway. This morning, a cardinal sang at 8:39. We went north to Kelley's Island in Lake Erie later in the day, the weather warm, cirrus clouds sweeping up from the southwest. The trees were pre-autumnal 150 miles from Yellow Springs, vague, misty tones in the tree lines suggesting fall, but still keeping a deep green sense of early September. Near Sandusky, a long flock of red-winged blackbirds. On the island, everything was so dry. But the lake was rich with bass and sunfish. We sat on the rocks and caught something on almost every cast. It was wonderful to sleep with the wind on the tent, the air full of the smell of water and dried leaves and fish. I stayed awake a long time, listening and feeling.

2000: Gethsemani Monastery in Kentucky: A cardinal at 6:10 a.m., then migratory robin calls. Wrinkled, black datura seeds gathered from their dried calices. In the monastery pond, one lotus flower was left; I took one seed from a rotting pod.

2003: Along the north garden about 2:00 p.m., five monarchs seen together in the zinnias. Wooly-bear caterpillars and monarchs common as I drove to Wilmington this afternoon.

2004: One firefly glowing off and on by the peonies at 5:00 this morning.

2005: Albert, the green frog, was croaking this morning about 5:00. Along the bike path, many honeysuckle bushes yellowing.

2007: The first of Mateo's Jerusalem artichokes opened overnight. Autumn quickly deepening.

2008: No birdsong this morning except a few blue jay calls after dawn. To Wilmington: Warm and sunny, high in the 80s. My ash tree at Wilberforce is yellow and has lost more than half its leaves. The foliage there and throughout Greene and Clinton counties is turning quickly, with many sweet gum, early maples, ashes, hickory, locusts and box elders shaded with gold or orange. Most of the soybean fields near Wilmington are brown, almost all their shedding complete.

2010: Near record temperatures in the 90s today. One monarch, one spicebush swallowtail seen at the butterfly bush.

2011: To Gethsemani Abbey, Kentucky: Rain throughout most of the trip, then breaking clouds and blue sky once I turned onto the Bluegrass Parkway. Throughout the drive, early leaf turn was accelerating, with many ash trees completely gold or violet, many losing their leaves, cottonwoods ochre and shedding, locusts and grapes pale yellow, streaks of red in the sumac, deep red Virginia creepers revealed in the thinning canopy, specks of gold in the silver olive, the undergrowth weathered and rusting, the goldenrod in full bloom, corn and soybean fields turning, maples joining the ashes, even Osage orange leaves tattered and drooping. At the monastery, warble chatter of mockingbirds, "chit" calls of cardinals, far crows, blue jays, some tree crickets, and a cricket that seemed to chirp like a clock ticking, two chips a second. One monarch heading southwest through the courtyard. As the bell tower struck four o'clock, a giant prickly chestnut fell off the tree beside me, opened and spit out its burnished seed. Before Vespers, 4:10, the sun came directly in onto the altar. At 4:30, it had moved to the cross beside the altar. It will always do that at Vespers when I am here for equinox, linking me to this place at this particular time.

2012: Crows at 6:15 this morning. At Ellis Pond this evening, beggarticks were darkening, and their leaves purple with age. The last white vervain flowers were gone. The arrowhead leaves were mottled, and the ash grove was a deep autumn forest green, tinged with a hint of violet.

2013: Crows at 6:12 this morning, a cardinal singing off and on when I walked Bella at 7:30. A hawk/hummingbird moth was sitting on the porch beneath the light when I got up, and it is still there this noon. As I ate lunch on the back porch, another hummingbird moth visited zinnias, both in the circle garden and along the north border of the yard. Several hummingbirds vied for the feeder. Cabbage butterflies played in randori above the butterfly bush. The white crocus still blooms near the last giant flower of the pink hibiscus. In front of Annie's house, a bush daisy (*olearia*) has just produced its first blossoms. Along the highway to Xenia, the corn is mostly dry and brown. Whistle crickets started intermittent calling while I was outside at 4:00 this afternoon. No orb-weavers seen today.

2014: Again clear and cool: Painted ladies, bright sulphurs, cabbage whites, folded wing skippers. The hummingbird came to the zinnias but bypassed the hummingbird feeder. Throughout town, leafturn beginning, especially in the maples and the yellow buckeyes. Our viburnum by the north window has become rusty violet-red, and Mrs. Timberlake's maple is the first on the block to show color. Still one flower on the prairie dock.

2015: In the north garden, the New England asters are glowing against the high orange tithonias. One blossom remains on the High Street prairie dock. Tonight I walked with Kathy at the edge of town, moon above us, and the tree frogs were so loud there, and the katydids so intense.

2016: From Yellow Springs to Lake Keuka in New York State: From almost solid late-summer green in southern Ohio, we drove northeast for 480 miles into a gradual transformation of dusky ochre and then finally in the last 100 miles into more prominent bubbles of pale color in the hills, maples still just isolated flashes of orange and sumacs, fringed with bright red dominating many of berms along the highway. We were at the gateway to Middle Fall; if we had gone further into the northeast, we would have encountered the full breakdown of the year. Foretaste of middle autumn, lush roadsides of goldenrod and New England asters and tall pale violet asters and fields of white asters accompanied us all the way from the warm 80-degree weather of Yellow Springs to the brisk north wind and 60s at the lake.

2017: Gethsemani in the middle of a heat wave (highs in the low 90s and upper 80s): A few white snakeroot clusters and branches of small white asters. As I walked in the woods, suddenly about fifty feet from me: a clattering shower of leaves from a tulip tree.

2018: Before I left for Gethsemani, I heard crows calling right about on time, 6:00 a.m. Sweater weather here, and heavy rain from Cincinnati south all the way to the monastery in northwestern Kentucky, an ochre landscape throughout the drive, with only rare Judas trees and occasional goldenrod, small asters and white snakeroot.

2019: Driving to Gethsemani on the 20th, I saw only a dusky ochre to the tree line. Today, driving back in the rain, it seems to me that fall had come in just the past few days, mixing gold deeper into the ochre. When I arrived at Dayton-Yellow Springs Road, I saw a flock of crows in a cut over corn field, the first cut field and the first crow flock of the autumn. New England asters were flowering in clumps along the fencerows.

2020: Crows greet the dawn, and geese fly over honking as the sun comes through the back locusts and a great flock of blackbirds settles in the trees. A female hummingbird comes by to inspect the last canna lily and the new blossoms of the late-seeded tithonia in the circle garden.

2021: Chilly, clouds and sun, high of 60 degrees, wind gusts massaging the bamboo, no butterflies at all. At Pearl's Fen, the white snakeroot, Jerusalem artichokes, tall sunflowers (*Helianthus giganteus)* and all the goldenrods were still at their peak. the low, purple Joe Pyes had lost their color, jewel weed done except for a handful of orange blossoms, field thistles bedraggled and gray-brown, a few sneezeweed bright, the last very blue lobelias, high drifts of small white asters, full bloom of New England asters and a lower, paler violet aster with maroon stems, like an *Aster puniceus.* Overall, the fen had become awash in asters and goldenrod, having lost much of its diversity of two weeks ago..

Thomas Jefferson's Garden Book, *occupied as it largely is with notes on the weather, will never have the readership of the* Declaration of Independence. *Still, as Henry Mitchell points out in* The Essential Earthman, *"a gardener profits from small trifling facts, and the more of these he or she has observed, the more resonant, the richer the enjoyment becomes...it is not the fact that is important, but the gardener's awareness that a fact is being beheld.*

Charles Elliott, *The Potting Shed Papers*

September 24th
The 267th Day of the Year

This afternoon, walk slowly and remember:
Death comes quickly in the evenings of September
To the snakeroot and the goldenrod.

bf

Sunrise/set: 6:24/6:29
Day's Length: 12 hours 5 minutes
Average High/Low: 75/53
Average Temperature: 64
Record High: 94 – 1908
Record Low: 31 – 1897

The Daily Weather

The chance of a high in the 80s is 15 percent today (with a slight chance of 90s). Seventies come 40 percent of the years, 60s forty percent, 50s five percent. Lows fall below 60 seventy-five percent of the time, and there is a greater likelihood of frost this morning (20 percent) than on any other morning of September. Rain occurs 30 percent of the days. Sky conditions are clear to partly cloudy eight years in ten.

Natural Calendar

Black walnut, buckeye, cottonwood and serviceberry leaf-fall seasons are ending in town just as goldenrod, asters and beggarticks start to go to seed, everything seeming to unravel at once. Touch-me-nots are still blooming in the woods, but their foliage breaks down as their last pods burst. Late Summer's clearweed has green seeds. Wingstem and ironweed are done blossoming. The last jumpseeds are jumping. Boneset and white snakeroot darken. Beggarticks are almost ready to stick to your clothing. Roadside sunflowers and Jerusalem artichokes enter their final weeks. More crickets move indoors, mindful of the frost to come. Monarch butterflies become more numerous in some years, visit the late annuals in the afternoon sun; other insects, however, become less common in the field and garden as the number of pollen-bearing flowers dwindles.

Daybook

1982: Bottom leaves and stems of goldenrod turning brown. Osage fruit on the road. Goosefoot turns yellow, bends to set its seeds. Smartweed declining. Beggarticks still strong.

1983: First frost this morning. Geese restless all day.

1984: Most of the leaves on the ash outside my window have fallen since the 22nd. At the Cascades in North Glen, oaks, maples, ashes, tulip trees, cottonwoods turning.

1985: At the Cascades, oaks, maples, ash, yellow poplar, cottonwood are turning, a sudden change after an unusual ten-day spell of cool, sunny weather. Long acorns on the path.

1986: Katydids and crickets still strong. Fireflies still glow in the grass. Jerusalem artichokes faded now.

1989: First light frost. No cicadas yesterday or today. Cardinal sings sporadically. Crows fly over. Peach leaves suddenly accelerate their fall.

1998: End of false boneset bloom along the freeway.

1999: Kelley's Island: Light rain this morning, and dozens of robins all around us in the campsite, peeping and checking the ground for food, all of the birds moving south towards the mainland. Excellent fishing throughout the morning as we sat in the eye of the front. When the sky cleared, the fishing changed, the recklessness of the biting stopped. First the fish became cautious and fickle; then by mid afternoon, they refused to bite at all. I thought the cold front had already come through, since the clouds were gone. Still, the weather was mild through the day, and then as the sun went down, a hard cold wind came up and blew all night. I lay awake, listening and feeling.

2000: Coming home from Gethsemani in Kentucky: The ashes and locusts along the freeway, mostly green when we went down two days ago, have undergone a major transformation. Now the golds and maroons are prominent in long patches. The 23rd was the pivot day, or last night the pivot night.

2001: Susi's garden is done except for a few goldenrods, a few purple phlox petals. On the road to Columbus: black walnut trees are bare, more crab apples thinning, more spots of gold on the maples. The ochre of hackberries and catalpas seems to have deepened. Sweet gums are blushing. When I drove south to Washington Courthouse, I saw entire ash trees in full autumn color.

2003: Color growing so slowly and uniformly through the woods. Few monarchs, one woolly-bear caterpillar seen today.

2005: Albert the frog croaked in the dark this morning, just before a thunderstorm came through. One monarch noticed today. More cottonwoods and maples turning in the countryside.

2007: Hummingbird seen at the Japanese honeysuckle flowers. All of the autumn crocus have wilted now.

2008: Along the bike path with Jeff: White snakeroot decaying quickly, asters full bloom.

2009: One firefly seen blinking at the edge of the porch this cold and rainy morning.

2011: Gethsemani: Into the chilly, grey morning, swallows circling above the monastery, crows, blue jays and cardinals and mockingbirds, ground crickets and field crickets and tree crickets accompanying me on my walk. The pasture full of plants I could name and plants I could not name. Common ragweed everywhere gone to seed, dominant between the cracks in old cement and blacktop, ancient chicory and Queen Anne's lace, horseweed past its best, beautiful sugary pink smartweed in large clumps, sedge that was brown and ochre, healthy crab grass, blushing wild dogwood, small white asters, alternate branches (two tiny bees huddled- one on top of the other - on one aster blossom, tall goldenrod full. Japanese honeysuckle hung to the ruined walls of barn site. White-berry panicled dogwood, the tall mystery snakeroot or achillea tattered, one aged ragweed with maroon stems, thin bedraggled pokeweed, two dandelions in all, cardinals chipping around the ruins of the old barn, occasional tan moths frightened as I walked into the pasture. A pileated woodpecker called as I walked along the woods, squirrel chattering behind me, one blue and two buckeye butterflies the only butterflies seen on the walk. Under the canopy of oaks, greenbriar had lost all its leaves, sassafras was turning. Along the road to the farmland, a row of black walnut trees had lost their leaves. Around the monastery, yellow poplar leaves were yellowing, some falling. No katydids tonight the last night here.

2012: Frost on the High Street rooftops this morning, frost on the car windshields. A cardinal heard near 7:00 a.m. Peggy's virgin's bower is almost done for the year. Goldenrod is rusting, false boneset darkening along the freeway south. Although color is appearing at the edge of so many trees, the ashes have not started to dominate the leafturn yet. At Ellis Pond, the first red leaves on the scarlet oak, and one side of a small red maple has turned (and several full turn along Dayton Street in town). The swamp bidens have a few dark flowers along the water's edge, queen Anne's lace brown and dry.

2013: Poke berries dark and disappearing in the Phillips Street alley, and almost all the apples are down across from the tall knotweed that has lost all its blossoms. A hummingbird glimpsed through the bedroom's east window; she was testing the mallow for just an instant. Most soybean fields on the way to Wilmington have either started to turn or have lost their leaves, and the bean harvest has begun. Many ashes are turning, and many maples have developed patches of gold or orange. Goldenrod has slipped over the edge of its peak and is starting to turn. In Yellow Springs, one sweet gum tree along Xenia Avenue has become deep red-purple. Bella got full of small burs when we were walking at the nursing home's pond.

2014: Cabbage whites and a few painted ladies today, count is down considerably. Hummingbird food has been almost all taken by the bees. At the Antioch Farm, lots of yellow-gold sulphurs in the vegetable garden. Ruby Nicholson (age 104) reports a hummingbird at 2:30 in the afternoon outside the window of her nursing home.

2016: Peter Hayes reported seeing a hummingbird this evening.

2017: This morning in the dark: tree frogs far off in the woods, tree crickets buzzing so loud around the monastery. At about 5:30 I began to hear a bard owl, "Who cooks for you?" beyond the garden. After I came out from Lauds at 6:15, the sky was in twilight. Fog lay all across the hills. Crows were calling. I heard a robin whinny, and all around the cries of a great confluence of roosters rose from all the surrounding farms. Against the wall of the walkway to the chapel, the crickets still sang. At noon, two hummingbirds came to the feeder by the refectory, another at dinnertime. One black swallowtail glimpsed as I sat out near the graveyard talking to Bob Johnson, who, it seemed to me, had risen from the dead, having survived a mysterious lung ailment and whom I had given up for lost.

The heat wave continues here in Gethsemani, in Yellow Springs and all across the Midwest and the eastern part of the country. Hurricane Jose and Maria threaten the Atlantic coast with high winds and tides (Maria having devastated Puerto Rico).

2019: The jewelweed has stopped flowering at Ellis. Only the bidens and one new bull thistle brighten the shore. Black walnuts thump to the ground as I walk the west side of the pond. When Jill and I went walking at John Bryan Park, we came under a black walnut tree in which there was a large flock of birds, sending down branches and fruit. That happened to us one other year in almost the same place.

2020: Sun and warm, a monarch for over an hour in the tithonias, many cabbage whites, one silver-spotted skipper. At the Pearl Fen, an additional monarch, tree and field crickets, and the high canopy full of blackbirds. And an array of wildflowers in full bloom: tall goldenrod, white snakeroot, false boneset, New England asters, tall violet asters with red stems (Purple-stemmed asters - *Aster puniceus*), field thistles in their last bloom, Jerusalem artichokes.

Along Fairfield Road, a long hedge of burning bush in full early color, like the viburnum on the north side of my house. Throughout town, Judas maples multiply.

2021: Cool and bright sun. Yellowjackets in the sugar water feeder, bees and wasps all over the lush purple New England asters. One small fritillary in the asters, one sulphur, one cabbage white meandering, one monarch briefly at the zinnias. One hummingbird sparred with the yellowjackets at the feeder this afternoon. One fully black woolly bear caterpillar found as I restacked the woodpile. Only an occasional Judas maple seen so far in town. The green quince fruits at the corner of High and Limestone are as fat and hard as golf balls. In the middle of the ferns on the north side of the house, a tall (at least ten feet tall) wild lettuce plant (*Lactuca canadensis)* has put out white, puffy seed clusters that catch the last of the sun, are brighter than all the other flowers of the garden. Geese fly over at 6:00 p.m.

Here and there swamp maples are turning, the woods are lit up by these subtle changes, a single bright leaf here or there, the ferns beginning to pale, the bush-blueberries already bright-red in leaf. There is still goldenrod everywhere, and the asters are beginning.

May Sarton

September 25th
The 269th Day of the Year

*By the twenty-fifth of September, the Red Maples are beginning to
be ripe.*

Henry David Thoreau

Sunrise/set: 6:25/6:28
Day's Length: 12 hours 3 minutes
Average High/Low: 74/52
Average Temperature: 63
Record High: 94 – 1908
Record Low: 35 – 1903

The Daily Weather

There is only a 20 percent chance of rain today, with skies clear to partly cloudy nearly 90 percent of the time. Highs reach 80 two years in a decade (rarely 90), the 70s four years, the 60s four years. Frost comes only five to ten percent of the mornings, but lows are in the 50s one fourth of the time, and in the 40s more than half the time, leaving only a little room for milder 60s. Average temperatures, which varied only one to two degrees at the height of Deep Summer, now start to fall at the rate of four degrees every week.

Natural Calendar

Milkweed Pod Bursting Season reveals the passage of equinox. Insect Season slowly dissipates, and spiders weave fewer webs. Across the countryside, Ashturn and Hickoryturn Seasons color the ashes and hickories gold. Red Barberry Season spreads through the barberries, and Box Elder Leaf-fall Season deepens. Finally, the first days of the Season of Killing Frosts (which lasts through the middle of May) completes September.

At midnight, the Milky Way runs from east to west across the sky. The stars of the Summer Triangle are setting in far west, and Orion is climbing up from the eastern horizon. Hercules, which was overhead at 12:00 a.m. in the first week of June, is now setting in the northwest, and Castor and Pollux, the twins of Gemini are peering over the tree line in the northeast. By sunrise, Orion has shifted to the center of the heavens. January's Leo and its brightest star, Regulus, have come up in the east, and the Great Square is following Hercules into the Pacific Ocean.

Daybook

1983: Covered Bridge: Tree coloration has remained stable all month. Stands of brown mullein follow a more predictable pattern, foretell next month's sudden changes. There are a few tall bellflowers left here and there – the strongest will last into November. Touch-me-nots are still blooming, but their foliage deteriorates. Parsnips are growing back. Clearweed has its seeds. Older wingstem and ironweed are done. Wild lettuce leaves are yellowing. Some goldenrod is brown. Boneset flowers are rusting. Most seeds have fallen from the wood nettle. Henbit comes back in the garden, violets in the grass. No cobwebs noticed across the path. A flock of finches seen downstream.

1988: Jacoby: Now the goldenrod and asters are in full bloom. First autumn violet found. White snakeroot still full. Boneset gone. Coneflowers still hold, and artichokes. Trees not ready yet, still in early September transition stages.

1992: Frost has threatened for the past three nights, but we have escaped unhurt with a light wind. Cardinals and crickets silent this morning. Sky so clear.

1995: Covered Bridge: the high portions of Japanese knotweed were burned by the frost this week. I noticed burdock was brown, its seeds ready to stick. The canopy is still intact here, almost no coloration in the trees, and the paths are still relatively free of leaves.

1997: The pussy willow in the back yard has lost almost all its leaves to leaf miners. Out in the country, the turning of the landscape picks up speed. This morning, temperatures were in the 40s, Orion in the south, the sky clear.

1999: Kelley's Island. Cormorants back and forth across the inlet today. I've never seen them in their formations before. This afternoon I talked to a woman who was going to Florida for the winter with her family. But she was unhappy at the prospect of leaving the cold and the wind. "I love the seasons here," she said.

2000: Many dogwoods red now.

2001: Doves have been quiet for how long?

2003: One crow heard at 6:30 this morning; it seems to me it was the first one I've heard from the back yard all year. A small flock of crows at the mill habitat this afternoon at 1:00. To and from Washington Court House: at least a half dozen monarchs seen. Goldenrod, New England asters, small white asters, pink smartweed, Jerusalem artichokes and Short's asters are still strong along the roadsides and in the woods. At home in the north garden, three monarchs and maybe ten painted ladies seen. Virgin's bower has ended its season.

2004: A cardinal sang at 6:10 a.m. Afterwards, no birdsong at all until I heard a robin clucking in the back woods in the early afternoon. A small flock of geese flew honking over the village about 2:30 p.m.

2006: The ash trees at Wilberforce are full color today.

2007: Walking in the alley this morning, I heard starlings and looked to find the flock roosting in a dead maple over on Stafford Street. My ash tree at school is full yellow and has lost at least half its leaves. Most of the Wilberforce ashes and locusts are in early full, but some are holding back. On the road to Wilmington, many of the woodlots are reaching a stage of early turn. The coming week should be the best for all the first tier.

2008: Mateo's tree is bare today, and my ash tree at school has lost all its leaves, as well. The autumn crocuses are still strong and tall, and Jerusalem artichokes are multiplying even as the goldenrod is rusting. Peggy's virgin's bower has started to decline. On the way to Wilmington, the entire landscape is turning quickly, reaching the early side of the first tier of leafturn – much the same as last year at this time. Ash, maple, redbud, sweet gum, box elder are all falling into line. One of Don's serviceberry trees is about half down. Katydids and crickets loud every evening.

2009: Eight tall coneflowers in the alley, the plant making a comeback. Banks of violet and pink morning glories.

2010: Cool with sun, crows at about 6:00. No butterflies in the morning, then as the afternoon warmed, four monarchs at one time in the garden, one female and one mail tiger swallowtail, a small fritillary, two bright yellow and orange sulphurs, a handful of cabbage butterflies, just a few skippers, one red admiral and one painted lady (*Cynthia*). False boneset continues to draw the butterflies and bees, New England asters are in full bloom, as are the tall Jerusalem artichokes and the butterfly bush. Hummingbirds still come to the feeders. A green and black caterpillar was eating the Queen Anne's lace plant by the back porch (near the white crocus that is still blooming strong).

2011: Gethsemani Abbey, Kentucky: *"What is easier to discuss mutually with You, O God, the three crows that flew by in the sun with the light flashing on their rubber wings. Or the sunlight coming quietly through the cracks in the boards. Or the crickets in the grass?"* Thomas Merton, "Dialogues with Silence"

An afternoon walk, cirrus and broken cumulus clouds, a hot Sun but a mild southwest breeze. There was even more to see than I saw yesterday. The same birds: chickadees, jays, crows, cardinals. Well, I did see two killdeers, the first in a long time. But today there were so many more butterflies, a swarm of blues at a damp depression in the roadway, dozens of buckeyes, many smaller fritillaries and sulphurs, many many grasshoppers, most smaller green and brown, but some of the larger species with the black and gold wings. A cluster of buckeye and polygonia butterflies happily feeding on the scat of a raccoon or opossum. No cabbage whites and no monarchs seen.

And more wildflowers: partridge peas on the earth dam by the high lake, beggar ticks and swamp bidens along the lake shore, a new white-flowered, three-petal water plant related, I believe, to the arrowhead plant, but with rounded basal leaves. The crickets were strangely quiet for most of the walk today - in spite of the heat, only a few field crickets and then later some sound-windows of ground crickets or tree crickets.

Then I found a large drift of a variety of rudbeckia, took pictures in hopes of identifying it at home. And deeper into the pasture, three-leafed, purple-flowered tick trefoil, and some horse nettle with pale blue flowers, and then a patch of sundrops and some thin-leafed Asiatic dayflowers, bright blue three- petaled near the woods. Then coming back, wood sorrel and black medic in the abbey lawn. The trees: cypress, white and red oak, yellow poplar, sycamore, sassafras, dogwood, elm, walnut, ash, one deep black-red sweet gum. I returned to the monastery with my ankles and feet overrun by chiggers.

2012: Osage fruit down along High Street and in the alley. Violet-petaled asters are open now, Short's or heart-leaved varieties. On the trellis, one of Jeanie's clematis vines has a soft, purple blossom, the virgin's bower hanging on. At the bike path from Ellis Pond, many red-centered white asters. Gray, bleached skeletons of hemlock. Stinging nettle common there, still in bloom. Red maples are beginning to be ripe in town and at the park. Cardinals and blue jays seen in the alley, but only the blue jay gives its call. High crickets in the early morning, in the late afternoon and at dusk. Strong whistling cricket sound, often intermittent into the night.

2013: The garden continues to wear thin. Several large drifts of New England asters keep the center of the north border in color, and the zinnias and dahlias and the second bloom of roses and the butterfly bushes are still bright – even though they are shaggy and aging. The white autumn crocus still blooms. There are spatters of pink phlox and blue spiderwort, but the weeds are taking over all around them, invading and covering. Even Liz's garden is brown and old, her Joe Pye sagging and seeding. One hummingbird and one hummingbird moth seen today but no butterflies at all. In the east garden, a large orb-weaver set up his web.

2014: Bright, mild, sun: The hummingbird was here this morning at the zinnias and the feeder. Many painted lady (*Cynthia*) and cabbage white butterflies throughout the flowers. The very last tall, pink hibiscus flower opened overnight.

2015: The hummingbird came by this morning, one monarch seen in the afternoon, cabbage whites and a skipper. Shasta daisies down to three blossoms. Orb weavers still common. The New England asters keep the garden intact, framed by tattered zinnias and tithonias. An autumn violet uncovered when I was weeding the daisies.

2016: Arriving home from Keuka Lake in western New York: A giant swallowtail greeting us at the west side of Jill's house. Across the countryside today: the leaves are no longer hinting or suggesting; now the earliest leafturn has begun between where we started out near Rochester and northern Ohio. But back in central and southern Ohio and Yellow Springs, the temperature is over 80 degrees, and the trees are green as in summer. Throughout the 500 miles between here and Lake Ontario, the roadside vegetation is still red and gold and purple and white with sumacs, goldenrod and asters – and even still some blue from chicory.

2017: Gethsemani to Yellow Springs: Below Lexington, the trees are green. Above, and intensifying into Ohio, it is Early Fall, light coloring in so many wood lots along the road. Here at home, geese have gathered at the water feature near the university at the edge of town, the New England asters are in full bloom. One monarch seen when I looked out the window.

2018: Gethsemani in the rain: Walking in the courtyard, I saw a woman on her knees under the chestnut tree. "Chestnut time?" I asked, and she looked up at me with a big smile and said the monks had given her permission to take as many as she wanted, and she showed me all the shiny chestnuts in her basket. Large prickly hulls lay open all about her, the nuts peering out at us.

2019: A cold 52 degrees this morning. Perfect sun and mild throughout the day. Hummingbirds still at the feeder. Jerusalem artichokes seen tall and bold yellow behind the Baha'i church. Two silver-spotted skippers, three monarchs, two painted ladies seen in the garden while I was weeding. Jumpseeds very brittle, the stems easily emptied when I run my fingers down them. A small flock of geese in the field by Ellis. A small flock of ducks on a pond at the quarry.

2020: Geese fly over at sunrise. Windfall apples continue to fall to the sidewalk near Peggy's house. No monarchs seen today (but it was a perfect butterfly day, sunny and mild), only a very few cabbage whites.

2021: Cool, sun. Koogler Fen: one monarch buterfly, the undergrowth thinner, more cottonwoods becoming naked, great ragweed plants toppled, their seed heads prominent, drifts of goldenrod and red-stemmed violet asters, large-flowered bidens in full bloom. Bur cucumber fruits (*Echinocystis lobata*) one to two inches long beside the creek.

2023: A rare cloudy day. Inventory on return from Italy: The soybean and corn fields were uniformly brown from the air and along the roadsides. Leafturn noticed well underway on the drive home. In the yard, the time count produced 14 canna blossoms, and the tall goldenrod, the New England asters and small white asters had opened to full. The viburnum was deep purple, the Endless Summer hydrangea finally in full bloom with pink flowers, its first of the summer. The beggarticks had ended their season, as had the

Japanese knotweed and the virgin's bower. The hops clusters had lost their luster. One white snakeroot cluster surprised me behnd the back honeysuckles, its flowers tight an gright white. Stonecrop had kept its color, as of course the zinnias and the red-stemmed castor beans.had. When I checked the koi pond, I noticed that the fish did not move as I approached and gave them some food. The next morning, I surprised a great blue heron at the water, and the fish were hiding. I wonder how many, if any, the heron has gotten. The last time the fish hid was just after Jeanie died, and I wondered at the time if they would not respond to my voice the way they did to hers: September mystery resolved by seeing the heron.

We are born and placed among wonders and surrounded by them, so that to whatever object the eye first turns, the same is wonderful and full of wonders, if only we will examine it for a while.

Giovanni Dondi, 14th Century, Venice

September 26th
The 269th Day of the Year

I walked to the Mid-Meadow Trestle and stood watching the sunset, all copper and gold and mother-of-pearl in a mackerel sky. Over all the evening hung a kind of melancholy, for its sounds were all autumnal, presaging the absence of the birds.

August Derleth

Sunrise/set: 6:26/6:26
Day's Length: 12 hours
Average High/Low: 74/52
Average Temperature: 63
Record High: 96 – 1900
Record Low: 35 – 1928

The Daily Weather

Eighty-degree afternoons come five percent of September 26ths; 70s are observed 40 percent of the time, 60s forty-five percent, 50s ten percent. Nine days in ten are clear to mostly sunny, and rain falls just once or twice in a decade. Lows in the 30s, like highs in the 90s, are rare today.

Natural Calendar

The sugar beet, pear, cabbage and cauliflower harvests commence near this date in the Great Lakes region. Farmers have brought in a good percentage of the third cut of alfalfa, and fall apples and grapes are getting close to a fourth picked throughout the Lower Midwest. In Wisconsin, Massachusetts, New Jersey, Oregon and Washington State, the cranberry harvest begins as berries darken in the cooler weather. Along the Atlantic coast, blue crabs become more plentiful.

Daybook

1984: Buzzards circling North Glen. First fat Osage fruit on the road.

1985: About a third of the goldenrod faded. Three monarch butterflies seen.

1986: The white snakeroot, goldenrod and false boneset are dying quickly. One white autumn violet found blooming in the woods. Squirrels seem to be getting noisier. Woolly-bears and monarchs increasing on Wilberforce-Clifton Road. Another opossum killed last night along Grinnell. Lilac bush reported blooming near Hilt Road.

1987: About a third of the goldenrod has gone to seed at South Glen. It is peak color time for the ash and shagbark hickory, very early pivot for first tier of leaves. More raccoons, opossums killed along the roads. More woolly-bears are out, more monarchs seen. Some beggarticks fading.

1988: A large flock of geese in cornfield stubble along the way to Wilberforce.

1989: The ash at my school window is three-fourths gone, locusts half yellow.

1990: Cascades: Wingstem gone. Creeper is red everywhere now. Yellow Springs Creek is clear, small fish common. Pink and yellow dogwood leaves here and there, but the canopy is whole and still green. Zigzag goldenrod and asters are in late full bloom, some past their prime. Last of the jumpseeds jumping. Touch-me-nots have lost most of their leaves. All the white snakeroot has gone to seed. Crickets and cicadas strong.

1992: Craneflies, tiny, spinning in the sun. Last of the Japanese Beetles die off, only two sluggish ones found in the roses.

1993: Full-blooming *Helianthus giganteus* along the airport road in a small exotic habitat grown up on land once completely stripped by the road crews. Swamp buttercups full there too, and false boneset, and a last lobelia.

1999: Coming back from northern Ohio, I found the landscape completely changed from what it was just a few days ago. Now the ashes have reached early full color, gold and maroon. Locusts and black walnuts are suddenly bright yellow. Every few miles, a red or an orange maple. The tree line is no longer dusky and worn; it's coming alive with October color, has a bold, autumnal look. No more ambivalent early September. Soybeans all brown, some being harvested.

2001: First Osage fruit down at Susi's. First local corn fields seen being harvested this afternoon. A few ashes completely turned, some gold, some red.

2002: Kelleys Island: Fishing for four hours without a bite. High afternoon cirrus clouds, huge circle around the sun and three sundogs at one time. Then at 1:00 a.m., rain and hard wind from the northeast. Wind and rain for the rest of the day.

2003: More than a dozen monarch butterflies on the cutover wingstem in the Butterfly Preserve this afternoon. Honeybees in the small white asters.

2004: A cardinal sang at 6:10 a.m. sharp. No monarchs seen for about a week, in spite of sunny and warm days – perfect monarch weather. All along the road to Huber Heights this afternoon, the woods were in early leafturn, some ashes at their peak, box elders, silver olives and catalpas pale or yellowing, many cottonwoods down, some full gold, many maples bright orange: a major change from just a week ago when I went to Gethsemani. Throughout the day, hurricane Jeanne battered Florida.

2007: Starlings in the Stafford Street tree. In the alley, robin migration song: a small flock is passing through. The alley goldenrod is all rusted.

2008: The drive to Gethsemani in Kentucky under streaks of cirrus, lines of altostratus: Flashes of red sumac in the dry roadsides, and up into the hills, fluff of seed heads to the horseweed, late goldenrod, yellowing redbuds and honeysuckle, cottonwoods bare, bright orange maples, patches of purple New England asters, cluster of small white asters, empty tobacco fields with a few stalks left like standards from a battle, corn and soybeans brown, buzzards floating overhead, but not a single flock of starlings or grackles. West into Kentucky, the hills are dull with drought. Maybe half a dozen adolescent raccoons seen killed on the highway.

2009: One monarch seen. Discovered small green caterpillars with black heads eating the river birch leaves.

2010: Crows heard at 6:03 this morning.

2011: Gethsemani to Yellow Springs in the morning rain: the landscape turned so much since I drove along here three days ago, an ocher landscape now, golden green with mist and clouds, blurring, blending, mixes, intensifies the changes that happened almost overnight. North along the freeway, emerging into Sun and turquoise blue, white cirrus and choppy cumulus and dark purple stratus blowing in the southwest wind. At home, one monarch in the zinnias, all the New England asters in full bloom, zinnias and stonecrop and mums and boneset holding the garden together. Large patch of chicory noticed on the way to Beavercreek. No katydids heard on my walk tonight, but intense cricketsong.

2012: High, intermittent crickets at 6:00 this morning Driving towards Dayton, I found the highway tree line turning quickly, the ashes suddenly becoming purple, more maples joining, sumacs red and cattail foliage yellowed along the freeway, a tremendous change in just two or three days. At our pond, the green frog, Romuald, was sitting out on the rocks at noon. At Ellis Pond, the ashes have turned from dusky violet green to deep purple, the sweet gum is dark red, one scarlet oak is completely red, and a second is starting. All about me, everything is happening at once. And the pond geese, when I have come by the past few evenings, have been engaged in raucous conversation, squawking and honking and bleating. (And the shopping-center pond was full of geese this morning.)

2013: Ashes are turning throughout the region now, complemented by early maples. One hummingbird and a fritillary noticed today at home. False boneset completely gone to seed. At Ellis Pond, the ash groves have turned a deep green-purple, and half of one red maple has turned orange, one fringed on the top with color. No change in the oaks, the sycamores, the yellow poplars. Small white asters, a few orange jewelweed and a handful of swamp bidens are blooming, but all the other beggarticks and shore flowers are gone. One darner with powder-blue stripes on its wings flew along the bank of the pond. Later, weeding in the garden, I disturbed one black and brown woolly-bear caterpillar.

2014: Last night, mild, full insect chorus: tree frogs intermittent steady, static of the tree crickets steady, chirping field crickets, rasping katydids. Today, sun and warm: cabbage whites and painted ladies throughout the zinnias. In the pond, the arrowhead leaves are tattered from caterpillars and simply old, collapsing into the water. Scattered maples in town are turning red and orange. In the field around the Antioch Farm, many yellow sulphurs romping and mating.

2016: Only one or two silver-spotted skippers today, cabbage whites still common. No larger butterflies seen even though the New England asters are completely full. At the corner of High and West South College, the prairie dock has finished blooming, Large Osage fruits have shown up on sidewalks and in the streets now.

2017: Sun, heat: Two or three monarchs, two or three painted ladies, many cabbage whites, one or two silver-spotted skippers seen off and on through the day. In the afternoon, I heard robins, the first time since they left in July, and I saw a hummingbird in the shaded zinnias.

A message from Rick: "Was still dark at 5:30 a.m., morning of 9-26, when I stepped out back door and saw several glow worms still active around the pond. Unusual, I thought, as the temp showed 45. A few much warmer nights earlier, the 24th I think it was, I looked out to see a scattering of glow worms flashing away in the gravel area between house and garage (they must be everywhere, though easier to see amongst the gravel), walking among them like walking across a star strewn sky."

2019: Once again, a mild and sunny day, cradling clusters of painted lady butterflies, cabbage whites, monarchs, silver-spotted skippers, an occasional sulphur, one spicebush swallowtail. Now the tall goldenrod is darkening, and the knotweed flowers and the last phlox blossoms are suddenly gone. The New England asters and the zigzag goldenrod are still at the height of their color.

2020: A few geese calls overhead at dawn. In the garden, September slipping away without butterflies! Except that at noon, I walked out to find an ancient great spangled fritillary splayed resting on a pink zinnia. And once again, I surprise finches in the tithonias.

2021: Another cool and clear day, a deepening of the color of the purple asters, a glow to the full flowering castor beans, the failed zinnia crop poking up yellow and red here and there, the viburnum foliage all rusty orange, a monarch hanging around the garden throughout the day.

2022: Returning from Keuka Lake. Gusty, chilly wind and patches of heavy rain. Definitely early leafturn in the hills of western New York, the soybean fields darker gold to tan, the first corn harvesting seen. At home, 6:05 p.m., we were greeted by geese honking.

2023: Time count: a slight uptick in canna blossoms to 16, and the coloration of the garden seems to grow richer as the goldenrod and

New England asters complement the cannas and the scattered zinnias, the rush of small white asters, the scarlet-flowered castor beans, the pink hydrangea and the rosy-brown stonecrop. High overhead, now the wild lettuce flowers turn to the softest and brightest white down that is so light and ephemeral, dissolving when I try to save them for late winter planting. This afternoon, I scared away the heron that was stalking the koi. At the Glass Farm wetland habitat in the evening: the pond is overgrown with algae, the goldenrod starting to turn, the fields still strong but becoming a little dull.

In the course of each of the four seasons, inevitably, if the good weather continues for a period of time, rain, wind or snow follow. One must always think of the changes in heaven and earth. In the same way, one must be prepared for changes in the mind of a person...
Miyamoto Musashi

September 27th
The 270th Day of the Year

The spring comes like a tide running against a strong wind; it is ever beaten back, but ever gaining ground, with now and then a mad "push upon the land" as if to overcome its antagonist at one blow. The cold from the north encroaches upon us in about the same fashion. In September or early October it usually makes a big stride forward... but it is presently beaten back again, and the genial warmth repossess the land. Before long, however, the cold returns to the charge with augmented forces and gains much ground.

John Burroughs

Sunrise/set: 6:27/6:24
Day's Length: 11 hours 57 minutes
Average High/Low: 74/51
Average Temperature: 63
Record High: 89 – 1891/90 – 2019
Record Low: 33 – 1899

The Daily Weather

Today marks another pivot point for autumn: This is the first time since May 21st that there is a 25 percent chance of highs in the 50s. Temperatures warm to the 60s another 25 percent of the days, to the 70s thirty percent, and to the 80s twenty percent. Chances of rain increase over those for the 26th: Three days in ten are wet. Skies are totally overcast 15 percent of the time. There is a 20 percent chance of light frost this morning.

Natural Calendar

Water willows turn yellow in the river shallows as Early Fall deepens. In the sloughs, arrowhead is brittle. The wildflowers on stump habitats have disappeared. The earliest milkweed pods are opening. All the thistles have gone to seed. Wingstem has blackened with age or frost. Brome is white, burdock brown.

Japanese beetles can still be mating, but they are usually down to a fraction of their summer numbers. Chiggers and mosquitoes disappear from the garden if the weather has been cold.

Daybook

1987: About a fourth of the goldenrod is fading. Ashes: gentle peak of color. Maples turning more now. More raccoons and opossums killed along the roads. Beggarticks fading. Crickets strong day and night.

1988: Geese in the cutover cornfields around town.

1989: 6:20 a.m. Outside the back door, robin migrating song from all sides. To Caesar Creek, 60 degrees, clear, wind, barometer high at 30.40. Huge catfish gets away near far hole. The lake, two feet below its early- summer level, has made my cove just barely accessible. Learned from a husband and wife that the white bass would be hitting soon, following the shad up into the inlets. The bass came in last year the 3rd of October, the couple said. They gave me hooks, a yellow rubber worm, and live minnows.

Now the leaves are turning. The shift is underway. The gold is becoming more than just a suggestion; it is really there all across the shore. Goldenrod full to fading, asters strong, Queen Ann's lace, chicory and sundrops: scattered blooms here and there. The stump habitats on the water have disappeared now. Buckeyes dropping. Cicadas are quiet. Black walnut leaves, which I think held later than usual, are almost all gone now, fruit holding in clusters to the bare branches. Along the highway south, the artichokes have disappeared. One patch of milkweed has burst open on the Indian mound island.

1990: South Glen: Grackles up on the hills; flocks have been everywhere today, erratically zooming across the fields, back and forth, cackling and chirping, drowning out the crickets. Hickory nuts broken and scattered by the squirrels. Much of the goldenrod here is gone. Vervain is old and worn. Tree line still forest green, with only an occasional golden maple. One milkweed pod found open. Thistles all to seed. Mosquitoes still bite. One monarch butterfly. One autumn violet. Most Queen Anne's lace is brown. Virginia Creeper creates veins of red in the tree line.

1991: South Glen: Hickory becoming gold like the ashes. Poison ivy mostly violet or brown. Sumacs are deep red. Goldenrod mostly rusted. Wingstem blackened with age. Brome is white. Asters hold. One bellflower by the bridge. Zigzag goldenrod still all right. In town, the maple at High and Limestone is a fourth gold. Blue jays and crows loud this afternoon. A cabbage butterfly in the broccoli. Yellow jackets every few minute drinking at the birdbath. I saw a monarch chasing a locust leaf. Pokeweed stem, heavy red, fat, broken. The hollyhocks have all their winter foliage now, basal leaves that will hold until April and new growth.

1992: Gourds cut today, set on the picnic table to dry. The volunteer pumpkin was taken out of the garden last Sunday, put up on the porch for October.

1997: The last showy coneflower in the south garden is finally gone. Japanese beetles still here and mating, although their numbers are dwindling. Bed of mums planted along the west end of the pond. This morning at 6:15 I heard a titmouse, a cardinal, a wren, and a flock of crows - the crows circled the yard, coming in to look at me while I was standing on the back landing. Yesterday, cicadas were loud in the cool late afternoon. They were silent today.

1998: Crows at 6:00 a.m. Cardinal peeps three minutes later. Stonecrop is three-fourths gone in the east garden.

1999: Soft morning, so quiet before dawn, Venus rising behind Orion, one or two crickets, no wind. Crows at sunrise. Cardinal at 8:17 a.m. In the Little Miami River, the water willows are yellow now, the leafturn of the river bed. In the pond, the domestic willows follow suit, the arrowhead now becoming brittle and brown.

2000: Corn and bean fields all dry and brown, but few have been harvested. Definite red tone increasing along some tree lines, the late September shift of the ashes. Some goldenrod stands have turned, but there are patches of yellow sundrops in full bloom. Virgin's bower behind the grocery store has been done about a week now. Only two rudbeckias left at Susi's. At 6:45 p.m., the screech owl called three times.

2002: Kelleys Island, Lake Erie: Most leafturn has not begun. Some yellowing taking place on the ashes, some pink on the dogwoods. Only a few cottonwoods bare here. False boneset gone to seed, several heads picked for seed.

2004: The false boneset I picked two years ago on Kelleys Island has just finished blooming here in the north garden. The pink stonecrop is completely done, the red still holding. The sky, clear at 4:30 this morning, now is completely overcast, the outer edge of Hurricane Jeanne's southeastern spin reaching southwest Ohio. The road south to Washington Court House showed none of the leafturn I saw yesterday west of Yellow Springs. Harvest, however, is underway throughout the area, record crops of corn and soybeans coming in.

2008: Gethsemani: The courtyard wildflowers are gone this year, only fragments of purple loosestrife, one sundrop, one orange jewelweed, one chicory, not one of the false white snakeroot the official identification of which has bedeviled me for years. Black stalks of mullein and teasel. But the chestnuts are still there, some old and fallen, some green and ready. Yellow poplars all around are spotted with gold. Bluebirds in the garden walk, a pileated crying then moving west overhead, crows and jays all day. Out in the hills, hickory nuts down, pawpaw foliage golden, not a single fruit, tarnished thorny greenbrier, sassafras deep red, late ironweed, fields of new pencil flowers, *Stylosanthese biflora,* and a wild garden of mistflower, a small violet Joe Pye, *Eupatorium coelestinum.*

2009: Cardinal at 6:20 this morning. Full bloom of New England asters and Jerusalem artichokes and late volunteer coneflowers. Seven Shasta daisies are still in bloom. First small bowl of Heritage raspberries picked from the new plants for breakfast. Two monarchs and a hummingbird seen. Three violet clematis flowers open, false boneset about a third faded, almost no more heliopsis. One cutback ironweed has opened, adding new color to the northwest garden.

2010: Overcast and intermittent light rain this morning. Crows slept in until 6:15.

2011: Cool and partly cloudy today, only a few cabbage whites seen in the yard, and no hummingbirds. Tonight brought a return of several katydids to the neighborhood. And the cricket chorus was loud and varied, chirps of the field crickets, harsh grating of what I believe are tree crickets, and tremulous wavering of other crickets. Occasionally, the ghostly call of the whistling cricket.

2012: High static of tree crickets this soft, mild morning. Heard the frog croak once before daylight. A short cardinal chirp at 6:20 a.m., crows for just a few moments at 6:52. A huge orb-weaver, its web - attached to the roof to the west and to the honeysuckles to the east - shining from the early rain, lay above the stonecrop. The white mums and the yellow mums are completely open in the north garden. Six bouquets of zinnias and a few purple dahlias picked for the house and porch.

2013: Crows at 6:20 this morning, a robin peeping as I walked Bella around 9:00. Intense sun and mild today, but no large butterflies seen, only a painted lady (*Cynthia*) and several cabbage whites. A hummingbird visited the zinnias in the afternoon, and I glimpsed a large fritillary at Annie's. A short walk in Glen Helen along the Talus Trail: The canopy was completely green and intact. Short's aster (*Aster shortii*) was dominant at the entrance to the trail. Deeper in the woods, more of the same, plus zigzag goldenrod (*Solidago flexicaulis*) and blue-stemmed or wreath goldenrod (*Solidago caesia*). Green papery seedpods of the American bladdernut (*Staphylea trifolia*) found hanging on shrubs near the path.

2014: Painted ladies and cabbage whites continue common in the zinnias, weather warm and sunny. Astilbes planted with Tat, stonecrop and a small oakleaf hydrangea transplanted with my sister Tat. At Ellis Pond, the ashes are deep purple, dogwoods red-purple.

2015: I walked in the garden before leaving for Italy, the morning soft and clear: Two monarchs visiting, blending with the orange tithonias.

2016: One painted lady butterfly, half a dozen cabbage whites, scattered silver-spotted skippers on this bright, mild day. At the Covered Bridge: white snakeroot the strongest; almost all the wingstem has gone to brittle seed; most ironweed is puffy and soft; the cup plants are black with age. When the sun went down over the ridge, the woods became cold, and it closed in around me; across the river where the sun still made the trees and river bright, the world seemed alive and inviting and open. Showers of locust leaves across the roads as we drove home.

2017: Two painted ladies in the morning zinnias, more in the afternoon, one yellow sulphur before supper, and two monarchs in the cosmos field at the northwest end of town. I feel everything is about counting and measuring now.

2019: At least three painted ladies and three monarchs, one skipper, one small fritillary, many cabbage whites seen in the yard in a brief walkthrough. The canna lilies, the full stonecrop, the New England asters, the castor beans, tithonias and the zinnias keep the garden strong and bright. At Ellis Pond, the bidens are breaking down, but the blue-winged dragonflies are still here. This afternoon, a hummingbird visited the feeder and explored the flowers.

2020: The whole town shading into autumn day by day. The earliest tree on the block this year is TK's maple, turning and shedding at the corner of High and Limestone. One monarch came by this morning, to slim pickings in the flowers as powdery mildew and drought take their toll. I noticed that the virgin's bower has disappeared from its tangle in Janet's redbud tree and the honeysuckles. One silver-spotted skipper, a small checkerspot and three playful cabbage whites during the afternoon. On a late-afternoon drive south to The Narrows park, we entered a whole new season, full Early Fall, orange maples everywhere.

2021: This morning, at least three pale fold-wing skippers in the asters, one monarch visiting. From Madison, Wisconsin, 400 miles northwest of Yellow Springs, Tat reports early color in many maples. Stink bugs noticed at the back screen door yesterday and today And Jill said she had had stink bugs trying to get in her back door.

2022: On returning from New York, I noticed that the bracts of common hop fruit that seemed fresh just a week ago had turned brown while we were gone. The New England asters, however, have reached full flower, just as the tall goldenrod is beginning to rust. Two stink bugs at the back door yesterday. The last prairie dock flower fades on High Street. Two cabbage whites and many small bees in the flowers. A robin heard peeping in the honeysuckles. On a walk to the Glass Farm wetland, Jill and I saw webworm "nests" fallen to the ground, blackened and tattered. False boneset was decaying, but bright goldenrod still dominated the fields. A few field thistles held on. Geese flew over in the late afternoon. In the Caribbean, Hurricane Ian strikes western Cuba as a Category 3, heads to Florida.

2023: Time count: 17 canna blossoms. Two cabbage white butterflies visited the garden. In the aster beds, the climbing false buckwheat foliage pales, blossoms darkenng, in patches, adding complexity to the tangle of flowers. Short night walk: full-throated tree crickets, field crickets, tree frogs, screaming crickets, and finally, as we approached the school oak trees, the katydids chimed in.

The human body is not a closed or static object, but an open, unfinished entity utterly entwined with the soils, waters, and winds that move through it—a wild creature whose life is contingent upon the multiple other lives that surround it, and the shifting flows that surge through it.

David Abram

September 28th
The 271st Day of the Year

*Silver Maple just
blushes at the tips. Thousand
grackles chattering.*

John Blakelock

Sunrise/set: 6:28/6:23
Day's Length: 11 hours 55 minutes
Average High/Low: 73/51
Average Temperature: 62
Record High: 91 – 1905 and 2019
Record Low: 32 – 1909

The Daily Weather

This is usually one of the warmest, sunniest, and driest days of late September. Rain falls only 20 percent of the years, and the sun fails to shine just 15 percent of the years. Highs in the 80s come 25 percent of the time, 70s fifty percent, 60s twenty percent, 50s five percent. Frost occurs 15 percent of the mornings. Twenty percent of the nights remain in the mild 60s.

Natural Calendar

The landscape is collapsing through sunny days toward Middle Fall. At the old Mill habitat, a few bellflowers still bloom (had been broken off in the summer, grew back, blossomed now). Clearweed, zigzag goldenrod and pink smartweed are still unhurt. Chicory is still blue along the highways, climbing bindweed still blue in the alleys. A few jumpseeds are still jumping.

Only the cutover areas have wingstem, heal all, burdock, velvetleaf, jimsonweed, black-eyed Susans flowering. Most tall field goldenrod is dying from the ground up. Milkweed and thimbleplants are bursting. The New England asters, the stonecrop and Jerusalem artichokes are seeding. Ironweed and horseweed heads puff up. Queen Anne's lace grows tight and dark. Touch-me-nots have all faded, pods still popping.

Robins cluck migration signals in the honeysuckles. Crows caw before sunrise. Starlings flock around the soybean fields. Long flocks of grackles pass over the village. Terns and meadowlarks, yellow-rumped warblers and purple martins migrate through the township. The last cicadas sing through the warmer afternoons. Green frogs croak when showers threaten. Katydids call when the evenings are mild. Tree crickets chatter without pause. Field crickets sing one-note songs even in the cold.

Almost all trees have some color change now. Enough sweet gums, oaks, tulip trees, hickories, locusts and maples have joined together to bring the whole landscape close to the edge of Middle Fall. Pokeweed stems are red, blackberry branches purple. Enough leaves have come down to reveal most of the scarlet creepers. Some years, black walnut, buckeye, cottonwood, ironwood, box elder, poplar, wild cherry and pawpaw are bare.

Daybook

1982: South Glen: Canopy thinning. Fallen leaves begin to dominate the undergrowth. Nettles paling, are green-yellow-brown. Zigzag goldenrod identified. Clearweed, chicory, and pink smartweed still strong. Only the cutover areas have wingstem, heal all, burdock, black-eyed Susans flowering. Most tall goldenrod dying from the ground up. Insects seem frantic in the Early Fall flowers, more bees than in summer, the activity more intense. Milkweed pods are fully developed, most leaves gone from their stems. One scraggly tall bellflower seen. Touch-me-not pods still brittle, still popping. Maples becoming more prominently red and orange.

1983: Huge flock of blackbirds in the trees near Wilberforce. Buzzards still circle South Glen. More leaves starting to turn. Golden hue to the roadside scrub trees and bushes. A pivot time.

1985: Natural history fills now with dying leaves and the end of flower cycles. Tree after tree joins in the collapse of summer, some foliage turning color overnight. In the fields, aster, beggartick, and goldenrod blossoms start to disappear; their departure parallels the leaf fall, the end of the insect season, the end of the spider season, acceleration in bird migration, everything seeming to unravel (or develop) at once.

1988: Upper Clifton Gorge: Asters and goldenrod full bloom. White snakeroot late full, many fading. Most all the Virginia creeper is red. Musky smell of fallen leaves. Shagbark hickory half yellow. Other trees spotty, patchy, turning, ready for rapid transition. New England asters perfect full. Field thistles are almost completely gone. Blue-stemmed goldenrod identified.

1989: Long flock of blackbirds like in 1983, during the same pivot time for color. Huge rainbow in the cirrus clouds at noon. My ash tree's leaves have almost all fallen.

1990: Covered Bridge: Sycamore leaves lying on the path with their July bark, red Virginia creeper beside them. Orange poison ivy berries, bright in the fencerow at Grinnell. Walnuts and Osage fruits are down. Zigzag almost complete here. Cardinal sings at dusk.

1993: Trumpet creepers have been gone for several weeks now. The sunflowers have deteriorated, and the late white snakeroot. All the flowers delayed by the drought have finally finished their cycles. Soybeans are all brown along Grinnell Road. The corn harvest is underway along Wilberforce-Clifton. Barberries are red at the corner of High and Dayton Streets. Rose hips have turned alongside them.

1995: The cottonwoods are dusky but holding, and the ashes have just blushed a little. At Grinnell Pond, the white snakeroot is still in full bloom, the zigzag goldenrod is waning but strong. The large-flowered beggarticks haven't started to wilt yet. At home, the New England asters are at their best, but in the woods and along the street in front of the house, the smaller white varieties haven't even opened. In some ways, it's still the middle of September.

1997: Last night I set up the telescope; the sky was so clear. Jupiter was due south, its moons lined up in a row, Saturn bright, its rings clear. At 6:10 a.m., suddenly the birds sang for a while: the crows moved into the trees, and over on Limestone, a cardinal sang briefly. Above me in the bare pussy willow, a titmouse came and chirped. No doves calling. Bat seen at 6:45 p.m. At the supermarket, blueberries were gone. Peaches went last week.

1998: Cardinal heard at 7:55 a.m. Geese fly over at 8:54 a.m. Large beetles mating on Neysa's statue at the college.

2004: Leafturn continues to accelerate, making 2004 an early year.

2005: Now a few ashes are turning (although my ash at school is only a third yellow), more maples, more cottonwoods, more grape vines. At home, the virgin's bower is and the false/false boneset are finally done blooming. A few rose of Sharon hold. The pale violet Janice Brown day lily still blooms, and the New England asters are strong and vibrant, often full of white cabbage moths. The yellow tea rose has two blossoms, the new pink shrub rose as four. The elephant ears in the east garden have surged this past month, are now over six-feet tall, filling the entire dooryard. The late July planting of lettuce will be ready in a couple of weeks. The basil, planted in late June has been ready to harvest since the end of August. The green frog still croaks before thunderstorms. Dragonflies still hunt at the pond. Monarchs come by every day.

2007: The days continue clear and warm and bright. Two weeks ago, much of the landscape was still deep, late-summer green. Now, ashes are gold and dusky maroon, a few maples and dogwoods are red and orange, cottonwoods and catalpas and sweet gums and shagbark hickories are yellow, and grape vines and nettles are bleached with age. Locust leaves drizzle steadily to the undergrowth. The serviceberries are almost bare. The black walnut trees keep only their last fruit. Purple poison ivy and Virginia creeper outline the changes.

At home, the virgin's bower is done flowering. The false boneset and New England asters are in decline, but the cabbage butterflies still swarm around them. A few rose of Sharon and Japanese honeysuckle blossoms hold on. The last jumpseeds along the front sidewalk jump when my fingers stroke them. Craneflies swarm, a fraction of their winter size. Dragonflies still hunt our backyard pond. The koi still feed with gusto, their water almost as warm as it was in August. Monarchs and painted ladies and swallowtails come by every day. The chrysanthemums we bought on Saturday still hide their color.

A cardinal called out at 6:10 this morning, sang off an on for about an hour. Crows came and went. Robins started peeping their migration signals outside in the honeysuckles at 7:04. When I walked the alley after breakfast, I heard starlings whistling and chattering toward downtown. Sitting in greenhouse working at 8:15, I listened to the tapping of a yellow-bellied sapsucker on the siding of the house, an old friend returning from spring on the way back to Tennessee.

In the South Glen this afternoon, kingfishers were screaming up and down the river throughout my walk. Late goldenrod was still in bloom, along with white snakeroot and the small white asters and the violet heart-leafed asters. In the North Glen, the zigzag goldenrod, orange jewelweed and the blue-stemmed goldenrod still blossomed at the far side of their season.

I looked for buzzards circling above the woods. They used to come here by the hundreds, waiting on the high currents for October. I saw only one today. Driving south to Wilmington near dusk, the round moon coming up over the mottled fields, I noticed the milkweed pods were open, glittering, disheveled.

2008: Walt Tuleke, the Yellow Springs paw-paw man, says it was the best year for paw paws he has ever seen, the fruit ripening almost a month later than usual.

2009: Saw Walt today this year, too! Paw-paws had come in about three weeks ago, he said. Five monarch butterflies seen in the butterfly bushes today. Wonderful Sun and wind. Leaves and walnuts tumbling down. One hummingbird visited the feeder. The northeast maple is almost as bare as Don's walnut tree. Starlings off and on in the north honeysuckles.

2010: Rain and cool all day. A flock of starlings and blackbirds was crossing town as I left to drive to Springfield at 7:30 a.m. Not a single butterfly seen.

2011: Don's cherry tree is bare. Serviceberry trees are gold and shedding. Clucking and chortling of starlings somewhere in the back trees this afternoon. No monarchs or swallowtails for close to a week. Crickets still sing in the day and evening, but no katydids tonight.

2012: One throaty call from Romuald, the frog, close to 6:00 this morning, crows by 6:35. Serviceberry trees along Dayton Street are holding their leaves this year, and not even keeping up with the ash or maple coloring. Along the way to Beavercreek: many ash trees have reached full color, some of them shedding.

2014: Sunny, bright, warm: Painted ladies, silver-spotted skippers, even a couple of monarchs today. Many hostas and lilies transplanted in the east and north gardens. New England asters and false boneset still full bloom. At the meditation walk in the North Glen: White snakeroot almost three-fourths gone. Narrow-leafed zigzag goldenrod still full, Short's aster and small white asters common, one tall bellflower. Black walnut leaves, maple leaves drizzle down, the canopy thinning, the river low, the waterfall at the Cascades only a trickle. After the walk, Krista brought out a fresh pawpaw, sweet and aromatic, to share. In town, Don's serviceberry foliage is about half fallen. Katydids strong throughout a short walk with Tat in the evening.

2015: The sense of the passing days often confuses me, and I need more and more days in order to find out what they might mean. I must have forgotten the first time, I tell myself, or I must have missed something. I feel that if I simply repeat an act or an observation or a day, I will finally see something different or see what I thought I saw once before, or what I should have or might have seen, and that I will probe the truth a little further, learn other secrets, find what I must have been looking for.

But repetition calls my bluff. My perspective changes every time I begin again. The more days I have, the less I know. Each day is its own master, and my awareness of its nature fluctuates with the intricate interplay of light and shape, sound and texture and emotion. My mind, setting its attention to a particular memory or scent or interaction, is carried by associations to create a new landscape. A slight shift of the season or marker or mood produces an entirely different set of connections, with kaleidoscopic results, patterns with truly uncountable combinations and colors, reforming, adjusting, reshaping at the slightest movement or perspective.

And so I drift downstream through Early Autumn, unrolling the map of the days in a way that reveals their arbitrary bonds and ephemeral, instantaneous seasons. My hunger for repetition, says the river of time, is the deceptive hunger for permanence. All the images are fleeting, it says, and the ride is the only thing.

2016: The days gradually cooling. Now soft rain. Hackberry leaves have littered the north lawn, and the trees of heaven have started to turn at the tips.

2017: A cool wave settles in overnight without clouds or rain. Two painted ladies, several cabbage whites in the morning, the same in the afternoon. The sidewalk is speckled with small maple seeds, and they crunch and pop when I walk on them. Hackberry leaves trickle into the yard, and errant butterflies. Hummingbirds at the zinnias before sundown.

2018: After chilly days of rain and clouds, morning fog and then a day of full sun. A few moments in the north gardens: Four monarchs, two monarch caterpillars, one sulphur and, on a yellow dahlia, a honeybee harassing a small native bee, similar to a mason bee, finally succeeding in driving it away. Milkweed beetles, which emerged in great numbers about a month ago, are starting to spread throughout the milkweed.

2019: Heat continues. Patchwork of bird calls this morning, some crows, some geese. The first milkweed pod has opened on North High Street. Zinnias, tithonias, castor beans, canna lilies, New England asters, a few dahlias and the drifts of sedum (its flowers turned from pink to a rich red) hold the garden back in Late Summer and the start of Early Fall.

2020: Barometer on a steady decline, a deep and wide valley appearing on my graph, the approach of Middle Fall. Hazy sun and mild morning, crows before dawn, robins clucking in the honeysuckles. Working outside, I was hearing a whooshing sound, like leaves falling, like rain falling on the leaves (but there was no rain), like a vast flock of grackles and starlings off in the distance. Sparrows chirping around me in the yard, feeding heavily. And then it started to rain.

2021: Only two. cabbage whites seen today, despite sunny and mild weather. More blue jays heard in the neighborhood. Bird feeders cleaned out after a month quarantine for a mysterious virus. All down High and Limestone Streets, black walnuts are falling more intensely, are all over the road and sidewalk.

2022: Full flower of New England asters and small white asters. Roadsides show tall pale violet asters. Throughout town, the small and large-flowered coneflowers have completed their seasons. More shades of gold and ochre to the village foliage.

2023: Full moon day, rain, chilly 60s: Before dawn, tree crickets and field crickets still strong. At first light, the blue jays were calling. By sunrise: crows, a few robins, the rattle of a downy woodpecker. Jill's lawn is covered with silver maple leaves. No starlings or grackles heard this autumn. Time count: 16. canna lily blossoms.

On Jeanie's Dying

*Autumn lies
to say presence is passing.
Matter deceives,
like all of the cycles:
Even the tides,
the days and the nights,
the summers and winters,
the yins and the yangs.
Do not believe
their message of passage.
Presence is sticky.
All is a haunting.
Everything stays.*

September 29th
The 272nd Day of the Year

Autumn deepens
just so, the color of
the chrysanthemums.

Taira no Sadafun (10th Century Japan)
Translated by Liza Dalby

Sunrise/set: 6:29/6:21
Day's Length: 11 hours 52 minutes
Average High/Low: 73/51
Average Temperature: 62
Record High: 94 – 1953
Record Low: 34 – 1951

The Daily Weather

Only five percent chance of an 80-degree high today, but a 60 percent chance of 70s. Cold days in the 50s come 20 percent of the time, and 60s occur 15 percent of the years. Chances of rain are 30 percent; skies are overcast 25 percent of the days. Nights in the 40s and 50s are the rule, with frost on the lawn one dawn in twenty.

Natural Calendar

New England asters and false boneset are still bright as goldenrod becomes tufted and gray to the sound of starlings in the trees. Spicebush is yellowing as the ashes enter their full color season. Box elders are shedding. The toothed leaves of beggarticks darken purple overnight. Daddy longlegs disappear from the undergrowth. Bird migrations reach their peak throughout Ohio.

Daybook

1984: To the Ohio River: Trees stable throughout the trip, some fading along the shoreline. Colors of the foliage depended on the species, not on the distance south. Major changes only in the low sumacs (bright red now), the ashes (turning dusky violet), and the hickories (yellowing). Goldenrod is in full bloom, along with the white snakeroot, asters, and Queen Anne's lace. Some tobacco was hanging in barns, some being harvested, some still in the fields.

1988: The drought earlier this year seems to have given energy to the goldenrod and asters. They seem brighter, more abundant to me than in previous years. The woods are still rich with golds and blues, the integrity of the flowers distracting from the slowly disintegrating canopy. Green acorns all over the paths at the Grinnell Swamp upper habitat.

1989: Starlings chattering in the afternoon trees at Wilberforce.

1992: Full breakdown of the landscape just before Middle Fall. At the Mill, all the wingstem is gone, many goldenrod rusted, a few asters to seed. Wood nettle leaves are curling, a new stage of decline. Still a few bellflowers (they must have been broken off in the summer, grew back, bloomed now). Still a few jumpseeds. Thin-leafed helianthus done along Springfield Airport Road. Touch-me-nots at Grinnell have all faded. No ironweed noticed. Cicadas are silent now. As the temperature dropped into the 30s tonight, the crickets grew quiet. No katydids.

1993: Frost coming tonight. Monarchs still visited the late phlox and the zinnias in the cold afternoon sun.

1997: Cardinals singing off and on throughout the morning. After last night's wind, the pond and back yard are full of yellow locust leaves. Japanese beetles still eat the sundrops and roses.

1999: This morning, I looked out of the greenhouse window just as a squirrel leapt up into the air over the pond, and one of the large koi splashed. Was the squirrel just getting a drink, and the fish scared it?

2000: Steady drizzle of deep yellow locust leaves. Full turning of the ash. Last jumpseeds jump in front of the house. Some of the

New England asters are done. A deep gilding taking place throughout the canopy. Large flock of grackles, thousands, heading north toward Springfield at 6:30 a.m.

2001: Cardinal at 6:10 a.m., sang off an on for an hour. Crows came and went. Robins peeping their migration song outside in the honeysuckles now at 7:04. The goldenrod is aging in the north garden, the last of the flower seasons turning.

2003: Portland, Oregon: The leaf-turn seems about the same in Portland as it is in Yellow Springs. Only light shading of maples here and there.

2004: Antioch School students banded numerous monarchs in Chillicothe – no shortage of those butterflies reported there.

2007: Gethsemani: This past weekend, I drove into Kentucky through the full range of Early Fall, its different subseasons depending on how the soybeans or corn or goldenrod or tobacco, harvest complete or pending, blended with the tree line.

The specific time of year also hinged on the number of fragile ashes along the roadsides, or the advance of the violet Virginia creeper, or the number of box elders, catalpas, tulip trees, sycamores, crab apples, sweet gums, cottonwoods, locusts, hackberries, redbuds or early maples and pears and oaks in any given location, late September revealing itself only partially as a function of the slant of the earth, each species of tree following its own calendar.

I uncovered micro-seasons of place from mile to mile that showed me topographies of rainfall in the dun or the green of the roadside grass or the sharp rust of vegetation killed by drought, the variety of habitat within a range of 200 miles, observed only from the road, suggesting the wild complexity of just a few hours in one autumn day.

My moods rose and fell while each yard, field and woodlot opened temporal and spatial cross section after cross section, created a process of definition and redefinition in which the borders of this particular day continually shifted and were transformed, as though the inevitability of winter were irrelevant, as though it were a kind of game in which natural history became simply a matter of belief and disposition.

As far as the ashes – they have made part of the trip the peak of Early Fall, the near side of the best. Their leaf fall will begin next week, will be over for them by the 10th.

At Gethsemani, the landscape was almost completely in Late Summer. Even the wingstem was soft and bright. Some decay in the false boneset, the white snakeroot and winged snakeroot and tickseed sunflowers, but the impression was more of the end of August than the beginning of October. And everything definitely behind the 18th of 2006 when I was here. Butterflies everywhere throughout my walk to the mountain. One tiger swallowtail, several blacks, some painted ladies, a hackberry and an assortment of others I couldn't identify.

2008: Cicadas sang in the warm, sunny afternoon. Katydids were calling when I walked Bella at 6:30 this evening. A red squirrel, the first I've ever seen here, explored the shed today.

2009: Cardinal sang in the cloudy morning, 6:24, the latest so far this year. Crows followed. This afternoon, Jeanie found a giant wheel bug, *Arilus cristatus*, on the north screen. Soybean fields are rusty brown along the road to Xenia. Early leafturn throughout the area. Sudden decline of the Jerusalem artichokes after just a couple of days at their best. White fall crocus has toppled over.

2010: Clear and cool this morning, crows at 6:20. By midday, the butterflies were back on the butterfly bushes, two or three monarchs and a handful of silver-spotted skippers. Late in the afternoon, two more monarchs seen, this time on the New England asters, and even one male tiger swallowtail on the zinnias.

2011: Strong crickets this evening, but no katydids. Temperature near 60 after a day in the low 70s.

2012: A soft, blue day, sun and cool, yesterday's fog did not return, only high altostratus filtering the sun as we sat at the school and listened to eulogies of Jeanie and memories, and I cried and cried.

2013: At the Cascades: The canopy gilded and thinning, showers of mottled maple leaves. Blue stemmed goldenrod and Short's asters the only flowers in bloom. Intermittent thumps of black walnuts dropping to the ground. The sound of the waterfall enhanced by the opening of the high trees and the undergrowth. Crows and a pileated woodpecker and steady cricket trills.

2014: Crows at 6:22 this morning. Worked in the garden with Tat transplanting day lilies. At least two monarchs seen, and numerous painted ladies, only a few cabbage whites. Showers of locust leaves through the afternoon.

2015: Campello Alto, Italy: Rosemary in bloom beside a deep patch of yellow autumn crocuses and then violet crocuses in abundance along the old railroad tracks; also chicory, many hawkweeds in bloom, blue vervain-like plants, white campion (*Silene latifolia*), an abundance of Jerusalem artichokes. Fully formed acorns on small-leafed oaks. One field of sunflowers still in full flower in the Umbrian hills above Montefalco. Tobacco yellow-green, and being cut in one large plot. The grape harvest here has begun: tractors pulling carts full of grapes on the highways. The landscape, not quite as ochre as in Ohio, is still dusky Late Summer. Spoleto at Ivano and Neysa's: pomegranates not quite ripe, maybe twice the size of golf balls. Ivano's parents brought us freshly pressed, *Succo mosto,* pre-fermented grape juice, thick, sweet, rich.

2017: Another cool day, morning low of 44 degrees. When I went out to the garden before work at 9:45, two painted ladies were sampling the zinnias. At Ellis Pond, the large ash grove still kept maybe a fourth of its leaves, but the ashes that had been dark purple a week or so ago were bare. Sun and mild throughout the day, crickets and katydids exuberant in the clear evening, gibbous moon clear and high in the southeast.

2018: Not a cloud today, chilly, fire in the stove, monarchs and cabbage whites in the tithonias and New England asters. One polygonia butterfly in the dooryard and a small checkerspot in the zinnias. Not a single painted lady butterfly seen this summer and fall. The woods full of asters and goldenrod, paced at home by the New England asters. In the milkweed, the red and black milkweed beetles gradually grow larger, reach maturity, leave their clusters to explore the whole milkweed plot. No hummingbird seen today.

2019: Hot and sun. Three painted ladies at one time in the zinnias. Only a monarch once in a while. I didn't see the hummingbird today. Soybean fields mostly dry and brown in the local countryside. Crickets still vociferous at night, katydids not as common in the neighborhood.

2020: With new moon on the 17th and lunar perigee on the 18th, the strongest high-pressure system of the summer moved in abruptly, reaching 30.50 on the barometer, bringing a cool and sunny week.

My graph of barometric pressure showed the peak on September 20 and then a quick decline on the 21st. then a gradual slope from the 22nd through the 25th, the barometric needle barely moving from day to day, the record of that period appearing as a plateau across time. And the weather remained sunny and dry throughout all of that, highs in the middle to upper 70s, lows in the 40s and 50s, perfect Early Fall weather, perfect butterfly weather (if there had been butterflies).

Then on the 26th, the atmospheric tableland suddenly collapsed into a gorge, the barometer dropping from 30.10 to 29.75, the humidity rising, clouds moving in. The morning of the 27th was gentle, fine for working outside. I cut a little wood, weeded the north garden.

Then came a hard rain at three in the afternoon. The barometer bottomed out at 29.70 and then started to rise, leaving the first major chasm of autumn on my graph.

This morning is bright, misty, chilly, fresh after yesterday's storm. Black walnut leaves and locust leaves all over the streets and sidewalks, the ochre landscape deepening with moisture. More maples, it seems, have turned orange. Adverse to heights, I reflect on the visual record of the recent fall from summer, the stability of the brief leveling, and then the violent plunge, allow myself to go back to relive the gentle descent of the dissipating high-pressure system. I rest on the quiet floor of the prelude to fall then topple over the edge into October.

This afternoon, dark clouds, three vultures way high over the village, circling. At Ellis Pond, the ash grove has turned dusky purple, and the algae that lay across the water throughout the past month has almost disappeared, countered by the rain and chill. Tonight as I walk Ranger along Stafford Street: drizzle and wind. Prelude: the full moon is coming on October 1.

2021: Bird seed in the feeders finally after a month hiatus. No butterflies in the morning. One maple on Dayton Street fully turned, the exception. Chickadees and titmice found the seed right away, were active through the afternoon. Geese again at about 6:00 this evening as Jill and I walked the Catholic graveyard.

2022: Hurricane Ian has devastated western Florida, Sanibel Island cut off from the mainland with its causeway washed out. Here, my barometer reads 30.55, the highest so far since spring.

2023: Light rain. Tree crickets, field cricket chirps, low trills of tree frogs. A lone cardinal calls steadily at first light.

All are but parts of one stupendous whole,
Whose body nature is, and God the soul.

Alexander Pope

September 30th
The 273rd Day of the Year

All nature is so full, that that district produces the greatest variety which is the most examined.

Gilbert White

Sunrise/set: 6:30/6:20
Day's Length: 11 hours 50 minutes
Average High/Low: 72/50
Average Temperature: 61
Record High: 94 – 1897 and 2019
Record Low: 28 – 1888

The Daily Weather

A surge of warm air overtakes the Lower Midwest 50 percent of the time, and highs rise above 80 half of the afternoons on this date - just like they did back during the first two weeks of the month. Chances of highs in the 70s are 25 percent, for 60s 15 percent, for 50s ten percent. Clouds and rain occur four years in a decade. For the first time this season, lows drop below 60 a full 90 percent of the nights, but frost occurs only one morning in fifteen years on this date.

Natural Calendar

Milkweed pods have started to split, marking the end of September. Honey locusts are half yellow. Buckeye trees are in the middle of full leafdrop some years; other years their foliage is gone. Hickories are gold like the ashes. The first mulberry, sycamore, and cottonwood leaves have come down in the wind.

When the milkweed pods come open, then frost season is on the way, and Canadian geese, great-crested flycatchers, blue-gray gnatcatchers, ruby-throated hummingbirds, Eastern wood peewees and bank swallows move down their flyways toward the Gulf of Mexico. Crows are the only birds to call before dawn. Monarch butterflies become more numerous, still visit the late phlox and the zinnias in the afternoon sun. Bees compete for the remaining nectar. Winter's craneflies swarm, a fraction of their December size.

Barberries and rose hips are red. Late Summer's clearweed has green seeds. Older wingstem and ironweed are done blossoming. Wild lettuce leaves are stained with decay. Queen Anne's lace and bright blue chicory die back suddenly. The first goldenrod is brown. White vervain is gray, streaked with maroon, tattered, laced from insects. Beggarticks are ready to stick to your clothing. Roadside sunflowers enter their final week.

Daybook

1984: Beggarticks, tattered, going to seed in the north garden.

1985: Sweet gum trees completely yellow on the campus at Wilberforce. At South Glen, the smaller box elders and saplings are losing their leaves much earlier than the larger, contributing to the rapid thinning of the woods.

1986: Cardinal sings at 6:00 a.m. One cottonwood on Corry Street is almost bare. Two chubs caught around 8:00 this morning. No carp have struck for about three weeks.

1987: At Wilberforce, the colors are changing quickly now. Ashes are turning maroon and yellow, and all the locusts are bright gold. Strong windstorm this afternoon; coming home, I saw hundreds of buzzards circling above the woods, riding on the wild air currents.

1988: Beggarticks start to fade. Cardinals sing much less frequently this week. Crickets still chirping in the evening.

1989: A last cicada sang once, a few seconds only, in the heat of the afternoon. A cardinal followed, then was silent. Craneflies swarming in the back yard, but they are only a fraction of their winter size. Is this their first day out? Starlings loud at the dairy at 6:30 p.m. Katydids and crickets loud as ever tonight.

1990: Geese fly over 6:45 p.m. Locusts and box elders fall quickly in the yard. At my parents' home on Frederick Circle in Madison, Wisconsin, the leaves are at early turn, maybe the beginning of Middle Fall, about two weeks ahead of Yellow Springs.

1996: Sitting in the west room working. At 8:15 a.m., I listen to the tapping of a yellow bellied sapsucker on the north siding of the house, an old friend returning from spring on the way south again.

1997: The pickerel plant in the garden pond has suddenly died back now. No frog heard for the past few days. Cicadas and birds are quiet today. No monarchs seen for a while.

1998: Rapid decline of New England asters. Squirrels have been chattering through the days. Tansy finally starts dying back, had been bright through August and September. Goldenrod accelerates its rusting process. Downey woodpecker calling.

2001: Screech owl south of Limestone Street at 4:45 this morning. Then a robin migration call at 6:10, then crows and cardinals almost together at 6:12. Now, 6:25, the morning is quiet again.

2003: Return to Yellow Springs from Portland, Oregon (and the birth of Jeni's Jack Patrick on the 29th). Coming in over Cincinnati, only a vague and mottled autumn blush to the trees below. Driving home I saw goldenrod was about a third done for the year. New England asters and Jerusalem artichokes were still prominent.

2005: These days, I hear starlings chattering and whistling in the trees every morning. I watch the drying of goldenrod until it blends with the dead Bermuda grass, foxtail, smooth brome, orchard grass. The black walnut and cottonwood trees along my block are bare.

Near the river, I find one blue lobelia, one tall bellflower, some red clover, scattered white snakeroot. In my journal, I write down the yellowing of wild grape leaves, yellow milkweed, yellow elms, yellow shagbark hickory, yellow spicebush, a locust yellow around its red thorns, nettles bleached with age, the last huge silver spider webs hanging in the black wingstem shining in the sunrise, timothy all fallen from its stalk, the calls of October crows.

Red and blue dragonflies are still out by the swamp. Crickets are jumping in the warm grass, but I don't see daddy longlegs hunting, Leaves cover the path, sycamore, sassafras, dogwood, ash. My mulberry tree has one bright yellow leaf. I try to avoid running over woolly bear caterpillars as they hurry across the road in front of me. Small flocks of robins are migrating through the neighborhood. Below my honeysuckle hedge, I discover the first junco here for winter.

2007: I am going through my annual autumn spiritual renewal now that equinox has passed. I go through a similar season, my annual spring spiritual renewal, before spring equinox. Well, I can't really say that these periods are renewals so much as periodic, cyclical, physiological seasons during which I am much more likely to go to church, read more nonfiction, pray more, reflect more, examine my conscience more. I am more sentimental during these times, more emotional.

2008: Don's cherry tree is bare. Full color in the trees on the way to Wilmington, ashes all full throughout the countryside. False boneset is now gray, and goldenrod rusting most areas. At Wilberforce, my ginkgo is yellowing early. Mateo's first Jerusalem artichoke is open. Autumn crocus still purple in the alley. The viburnum at the north side of the house is a deep red-orange. The alley apple tree keeps a couple dozen apples.

2009: Cardinal at 6:24 again this morning. Soybean fields all brown and brittle. Major early leafturn along the road to Xenia.

2010: Sunny and cool, moon overhead at dawn, no butterflies until early afternoon, then only cabbage butterflies and skippers. The finches come and go at their feeders, but I haven't seen any bright plumage in weeks; the males must turn in early September. And no hummingbirds have come by for several days.

2011: Temperatures forecast to fall into the middle 30s tomorrow night. Crows at 6:20 this morning, a full quarter of an hour later than a few weeks ago. Inventory at the end of September: New England asters and small white asters full, Peggy's virgin's bower completely gone but others in town still in bloom, false boneset fading quickly, mums and zinnias and dahlias and a few phlox still bright, knockout roses still completely full of blossoms, some of the spiderwort plants are flowering, some of the deadnettle, all of the basil and alyssum.

Most of the crabapple leaves are down, as are the black walnut and the box elder leaves. Ashes are peaking in different places. Redbuds are yellowing, Lil's burning bush is red all across the top. Peggy's Limelight hydrangea blooms are darkening. Many of our late hostas are still full of violet blossoms.

Jumpseeds are gone at Moya's. We have a few that are still soft and not ready to jump. Last night's rain and wind brought down black walnuts all over the sidewalk and in the alley. A few cricket windows in the morning and afternoon. A few cabbage whites in the garden despite temperatures in the 50s. As a cold wave moved through this evening, only a few crickets heard, one or two field crickets and a few Carolina ground crickets. The honeysuckles at the front of the house were silent for the first time since the end of July.

2012: A cool, sunny day, and at noon, the back trees (box elders and locusts and one of the white mulberries shedding) were filled with grackles and starlings, clucking and whining and whistling.

2013: Clouds and mist, mild and soft: crows very late at 6:40. A large, green praying mantis on the north window screen this morning. No orb-weavers, no hummingbirds for at least two days now. At Ellis Pond, very little change in the trees. The ashes are still dark chocolate green, as is the sweet gum. One red maple has turned all orange, but the sugar maples and oaks hold at late-summer color. Along the banks of the pond, the leaves of the standard beggarticks are now a dusky purple, and all but one of the swamp beggarticks are done blooming. The *aster pilosus* or Heath Aster was in fresh full bloom. Only one cabbage white seen today. Ed reports seeing two toads today.

2014: Taking Tat to the airport: Orange sunrise, rays shooting up into the east from behind golden clouds. A great flock of grackles/blackbirds heading southwest, and a murmuration of starlings crossing the freeway north. Full dusky color along the highways. At home several ash trees and cottonwoods full, the autumn allium all to seed, most of the tall goldenrod and the yellow coneflowers noticed gone except for a few scattered small-flowered varieties. Only the Jerusalem artichokes are vigorous, shining and tall. The zinnias are less bright, shaggier. The New England asters are still at their peak, and Jeanie's two yellow roses are still full, as are all the pink Knockout roses. A hummingbird seen late in the afternoon, checking out the zinnias.

2018: Sun and warm, crows faithful about 7:00 a.m., saw a few butterflies: cabbage whites, a polygonia, monarchs, small checkerspots. The drive to Columbus showed brown corn and soybean fields, an ochering of the land, several maples outstanding with early color.

2019: High in the 90s again today, sporadic cardinal song at 6:20 and squirrel chattering, tree cricket buzz, crows and blue jays calling, cries of a red-shouldered hawk. The female hummingbird was working the canna lilies this morning, painted ladies, one Eastern black swallowtail and a few monarchs seen in the zinnias and tithonias. At Ellis Pond, a large flock of starlings was chortling in the high elms and sycamores.

In Montana, a record snowfall of three feet in some places, record low temperatures. In Yellow Springs, the average temperature for this September is 73.8, eight degrees above average, and rainfall has been less than an inch, 2.50 inches below normal. Of course, there has been no frost. Monthly average temperatures in the range of 72 degrees were recorded a number of times in the past century, but this is the warmest on record.

2020: Autumn having arrived, Venus high in the east before sunrise, clear skies and temperature in the 40s, trees going mad with color. So easy to forget last year's record high! The September average for this year almost two degrees above normal, but well below that of the last couple of years. Rainfall definitely down two and a half inches below the average of about three and a half inches.

2021: Another perfect day in the 70s with sun, not a cloud. But only a few cabbage whites in the garden. Monthly temperature of 68.9, a couple of degrees above average, rainfall good at about three inches.

2022: Temperature average for the month: 67.7.

2023: Temperature average for the month: 68.6, almost a degree above the recent average, three degrees above the average of the 1980s. Precipitation was just a little over an inch, about two inches below normal. The garden status: Full bloom of small-flowered asters, New England asters, tall goldenrod, stonecrop, red-flowered castor beans, pink blossoms on the Endless Summer hydrangea, zinnias, and time count for canna lilies is 16. The Carolina viburnum is full violet, the river birch is shedding, honeysuckles with red berries, hackberry trees ochre. Two cabbage white butterflies were in randori this morning, and bees continue to visit the asters. The cup plants complement the taller castor beans and the statuesque wild lettuce. Under last night's full moon, the crickets and katydids were in full voice. In all, a fine close to the Early Fall garden.

Ruminations for the Dayton Daily News

In his natural history of Ohio, *Idle Weeds,* David Rains Wallace writes: "If time is a story, the present is merely a hiatus between the significant events that were and will be.

"If time is an ocean, however, the present is not less important than other moments, which stretch away on all sides, any more than a single water molecule in an ocean is less important than the others."

I like to believe this impression of time, especially as autumn deepens. The changes in the leaves and flowers, the increasing insect calls and the weakening of birdsong leave no doubt that winter lies ahead and there is no going back.

Wallace's vision removes the borders and relative importance of events and allows my mind to go beyond what seems closed and terminal. The image of time as an ocean of objects and acts liberates me from a story that has a beginning, a middle and an end. Chapters of such a traditional narrative fall out of sequence, the plot line is cut, and life's linear prose becomes an elusive stream of consciousness.

If the month ahead belongs to a great tide, it erases the contours of youth and age, good and bad, loss and gain. My personae, the people who I think I am, are washed away. My shape is free, and I drift with flocking starlings and fields of tufted goldenrod and rasping katydids into an October Sea.

The world globes itself in a drop of dew. The microscope cannot find the animalcule which is less perfect for being little. Eyes, ears, taste, smell, motion, resistance, appetite, and organs of reproduction that take hold on eternity, -- all find room to consist in the small creature. So do we put our life into every act. The true doctrine of omnipresence is that God reappears with all his parts in every moss and cobweb. The value of the universe contrives to throw itself into every point.

Ralph Waldo Emerson

Bill Felker's three collections, *Home is the Prime Meridian: Essays in Search of Time and Place and Spirit* and *Deep Time Is in the Garden: New Essays in Search of Time and Place and Spirit,* and *The Virgin Point: Meditations in Nature,* as well as the entire twelve volumes of *A Daybook for the Year in Yellow Springs,* are available on line. For more information or to order autographed copies, visit www.poorwillsalmanack.com.